COMPLETE EDITION

JAZZ GUITAR

Beginning • Intermediate • Mastering

JODY FISHER

CONTENTS

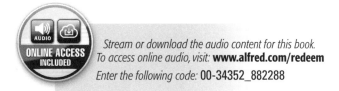

Stream or download the audio content for this book.
*To access online audio, visit: **www.alfred.com/redeem***
Enter the following code: 00-34352_882288

Alfred Music
P.O. Box 10003
Van Nuys, CA 91410-0003
alfred.com

Copyright © MMX by Alfred Music
All rights reserved. Printed in USA.

ISBN-10: 0-7390-6637-4 (Book & Online Audio)
ISBN-13: 978-0-7390-6637-9 (Book & Online Audio)

Cover photography by Jeff Oshiro
Chord and scale illustrations by David Jacobs
Audio tracks recorded and engineered
by Steve Robertson at Standing Room Only Studios,
Fontana, CA

Alfred Cares. Contents printed on environmentally responsible paper.

BEGINNING JAZZ GUITAR

TABLE OF CONTENTS

(continued on next page)

ABOUT THE AUTHOR

Jody Fisher has worked professionally in virtually all styles of music during his career, from straight ahead and contemporary jazz to rock 'n' roll, country, pop and show groups. He taught Guitar and Jazz Studies at the University of Redlands in Southern California and at the Idyllwild School of Music and the Arts (ISOMATA). An active performer in the Southern California area, he still maintains a private teaching practice and serves on the faculty of the University of La Verne. Jody is also the author of many other publications from Alfred Music.

PHOTO • LARRY LYTLE

00

Track 01

Companion online audio is included with this book to make learning easier and more enjoyable. The symbol shown on the left appears next to every example in the book that features an MP3 track. Use the MP3s to ensure you're capturing the feel of the examples and interpreting the rhythms correctly. The track number below the symbol corresponds directly to the example you want to hear (example numbers are above the icon). All the track numbers are unique to each "book" within this volume, meaning every book has its own Track 1, Track 2, and so on. (For example, *Beginning Jazz Guitar* starts with Track 1, as does *Intermediate jazz Guitar, Mastering Jazz Guitar: Chord/Melody* and *Mastering Jazz Guitar: Improvisation*.) Track 1 for each book will help you tune your guitar.

See page 1 for instructions on how to access the online audio.

INTRODUCTION

Welcome to *The Complete Jazz Guitar Method,* a comprehensive series of books designed specifically for the modern jazz guitarist. *The Complete Jazz Guitar Method Complete Edition* consists of four separate volumes now available in this one edition. Each of the four volumes (*Beginning Jazz Guitar, Intermediate Jazz Guitar, Mastering Jazz Guitar: Chord/Melody* and *Mastering Jazz Guitar: Improvisation*) is an important step along the way to jazz mastery.

Over the years, only the most dedicated students have succeeded in mastering this very expressive musical art form. In spite of the mountains of instructional books, recordings, and videos that are available, most students remain in the dark about some very basic concepts regarding jazz and jazz guitar. I believe this is because very few teachers and authors provide an overall picture of what a person needs to learn. Students learn some scales, a few licks, an arpeggio or two, a few chords, and end up wondering how it all fits together.

My approach in this book is to begin with very basic information, and then proceed logically, covering the harmonic, melodic and technical concepts that are needed to see the complete picture. The study of jazz is a lifetime pursuit, but it doesn't have to take a lifetime to learn the basics and start playing.

This book is for the self-taught student as well as those studying with a teacher. The book can also be used as a reference source. If you are just beginning your jazz education, you should definitely start with the first section of this book and proceed from lesson to lesson and section to section. If you have been studying for awhile you might want to skip around, although you should make sure you don't miss any important information along the way.

This book is different in another way. In the past, you needed separate books for studying improvisation, chord melody and a host of other topics. While this book does not claim to say it all, it does combine most of the important topics. In the first two sections (*Beginning* and *Intermediate*), each chapter is divided into lessons, and each lesson is divided into two separate sections. The "A" sections deal with harmonic and chordal topics and the "B" sections cover information about single line improvisation. Every page, and every topic, can—and should—be supplemented with further information, whether from other books or teachers.

If you are primarily interested in chords and harmony, feel free to proceed through only the "A" sections. If improvisation is your main interest, just study the "B" sections. Since most sections correspond to each other, studying both sections in each lesson will be the most valuable course for many students.

The "Coda" section at the end of *Beginning Jazz Guitar* contains information that you will find helpful in the areas of technique, practicing, and various other jazz related concepts. You should thumb through this section frequently as you will no doubt find tips and advice concerning the areas of study you are working on.

However you decide to use these books, it is my sincerest wish that you will learn and love jazz and contribute to its life and breath.

CHAPTER 1

Getting Started

This is not a book for complete beginners. This chapter is a review of the concepts you will need to use this series. You can refer to *Beginning Blues Guitar* by David Hamburger or *Beginning Rock Guitar* by Paul Howard, both available at your local music store, if you need further clarification of these concepts.

OPEN POSITION CHORDS

You need to know the basic open-position chords as well as the standard barre chord fingerings. Changing from one chord to another should not be a problem. If you don't know these chords, learn them well before proceeding.

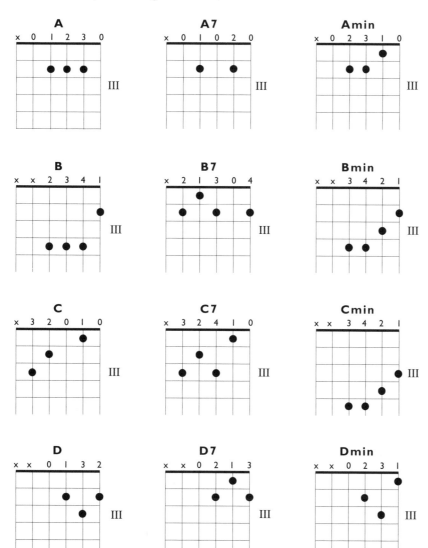

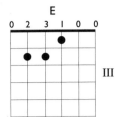

E

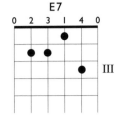

E7

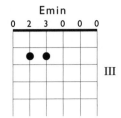

Emin

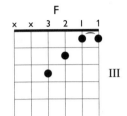

F

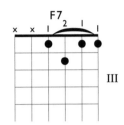

F7

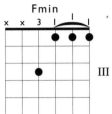

Fmin

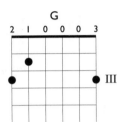

G

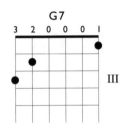

G7

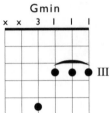

Gmin

BARRE CHORDS

With the root on the sixth string.

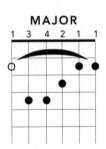

MAJOR

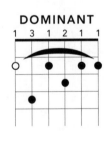

DOMINANT

MINOR

With the root on the fifth string.

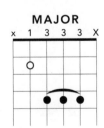

MAJOR

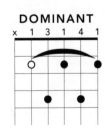

DOMINANT

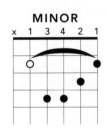

MINOR

READING MUSIC AND TABLATURE

STANDARD MUSIC NOTATION

Reading standard music notation is a necessary skill for anyone interested in learning to play jazz. Once you get the idea, you'll find that it's really easy, and then a whole world of instructional books and great music will open up for you. There are two basic elements to standard notation: pitch and rhythm. Every note has a particular note name (pitch) and particular duration (rhythm). The line or space on a note falls on tells you the pitch.

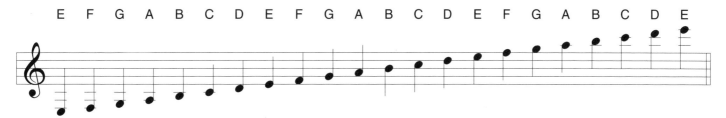

Every piece has numbers at the beginning, called the time signature, that tell us how to count the time. The top number represents the number of beats or counts per measure. The bottom number represents the type of note receiving one count. The most common time signature, $\frac{4}{4}$, is shown below. In $\frac{4}{4}$ time, there are four beats per measure, and the quarter note (♩) receives one beat.

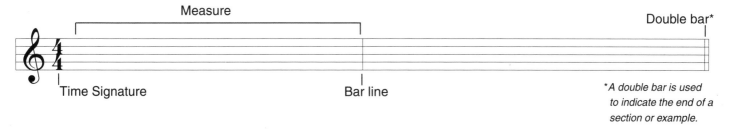

*A double bar is used to indicate the end of a section or example.

The appearance of the note—the type of note head or stem that it has—tells you the rhythm. Rests tell you when and how long not to play, which is also an important aspect of rhythm. Here are the note values:

TABLATURE

Tablature is a system of notation that graphically represents the strings and frets of the guitar fingerboard. Each note is indicated by placing a number, which shows the fret to play, on the appropriate string.

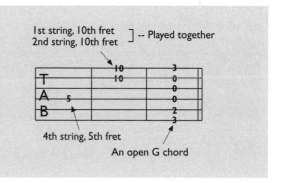

BLUES PROGRESSIONS AND STRUMMING

You need to be familiar with these basic *progressions*. *Progression* refers to the movement of one chord to another. In jazz, a progression is often referred to as *the changes*.

You will need to know some basic strumming patterns as well. The patterns themselves are not that important. The idea is that you should have the coordination to strum a pattern while changing chords. Read the section on "Basic Strumming Technique" on page 88 for some tips.

STANDARD BLUES PROGRESSION

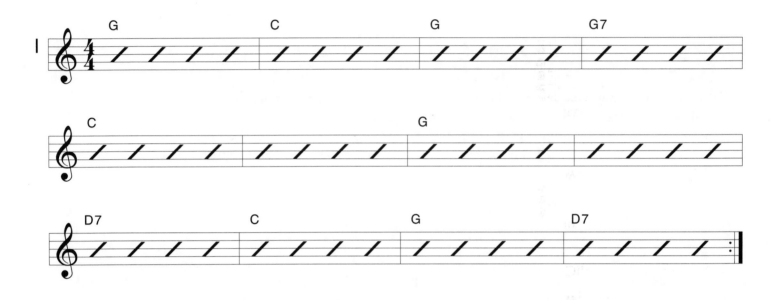

MINOR BLUES PROGRESSION

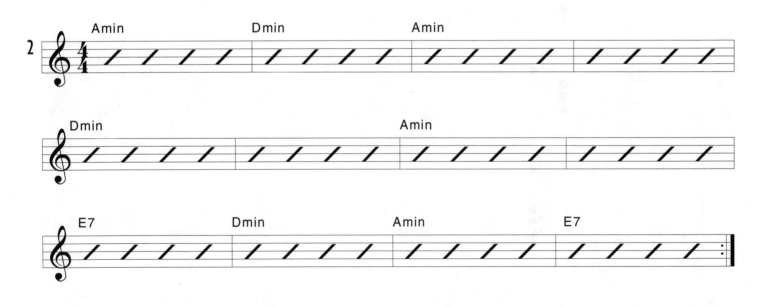

:‖ = *Repeat* sign. Jump back to the beginning, or to the previous beginning repeat sign ‖:, and play the section again.

PENTATONIC SCALE FINGERINGS

It is helpful to have some experience improvising in a very basic blues or rock context. You should be familiar with the following minor and major pentatonic scale fingerings.

C MINOR PENTATONIC

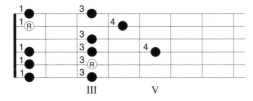

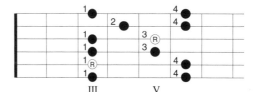

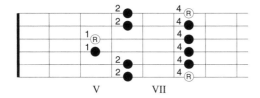

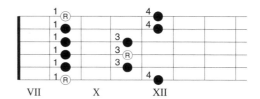

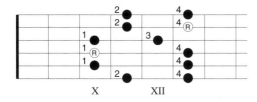

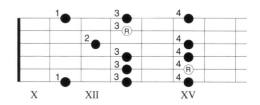

C MAJOR PENTATONIC

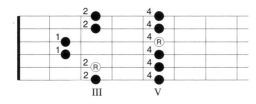

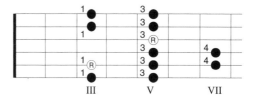

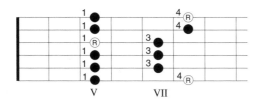

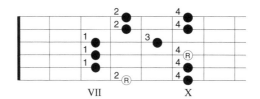

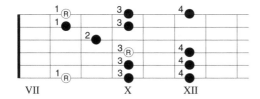

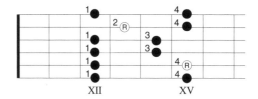

CHAPTER 2

Lesson 1A: Basic Theory

THE CHROMATIC SCALE

In our western music system we have twelve tones that are repeated over and over spanning many octaves. We call this set of tones the chromatic scale. All of the notes in the chromatic scale are one half step (one fret on the guitar) away from each other. Two half steps would equal a whole step (two frets on the guitar).

Here is a chromatic scale covering one octave (starting and ending on the same tone):

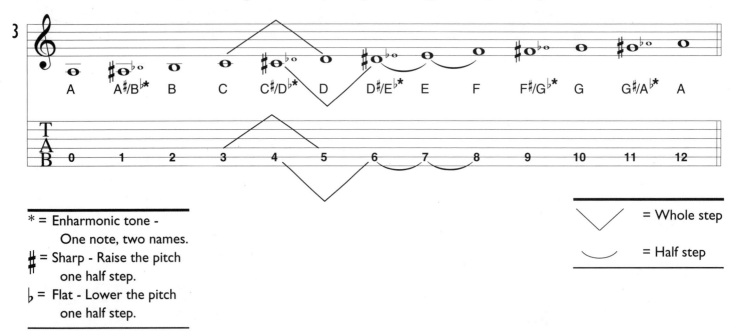

* = Enharmonic tone -
    One note, two names.

♯ = Sharp - Raise the pitch
    one half step.

♭ = Flat - Lower the pitch
    one half step.

= Whole step

= Half step

THE MAJOR SCALE

In our culture, most of our musical resources are derived from the major scale. A major scale can begin on any one of the twelve tones found in the chromatic scale. The whole step/half step formula for a major scale is:

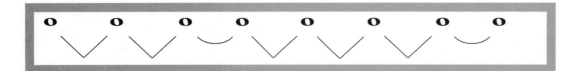

To build a C Major scale, start with the note C. Now we move one whole step up to find the next note, which is D. Another whole step will bring us to the note E. One half step away from E is F. (Take a look at Example 3 and you will notice that there are no sharp or flat notes between E and F or B and C.) Continuing, a whole step up from F is G, another whole step up brings us to A, and yet another brings us to B. Our last move will be a half step up from B to C. We have just constructed a C Major scale.

C Major Scale

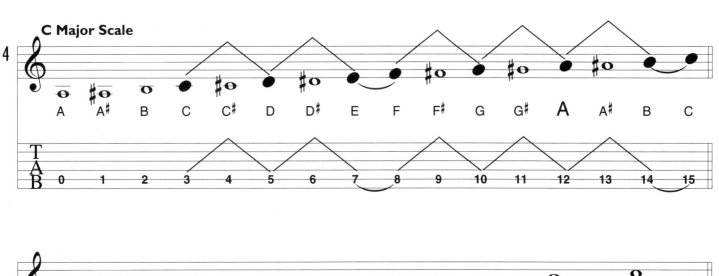

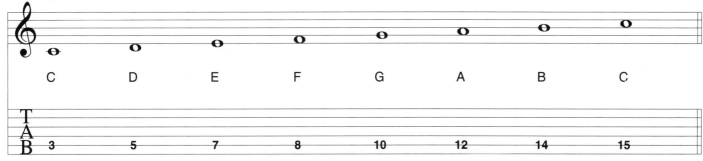

E♭ Major Scale

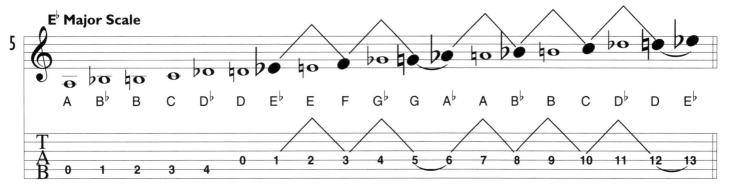

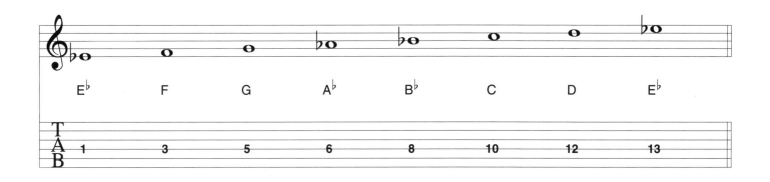

What you need to do now is construct all twelve major scales on paper, away from your guitar. Construct them in the following order*: C, F, B♭, E♭, A♭, D♭, G♭, B, E, A, D and G. Check your results against the example below and start memorizing them by recitation away from your instrument. The importance of knowing this cannot be over stressed. Nearly every theoretical concept will be based on this information, and the better you know these scales, the easier your musical studies will be.

Here are the major scales in music and TAB.

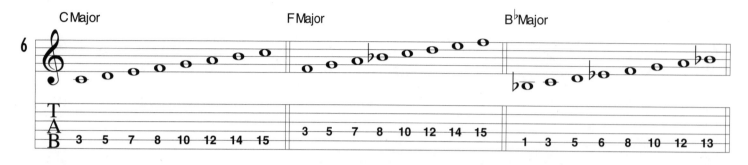

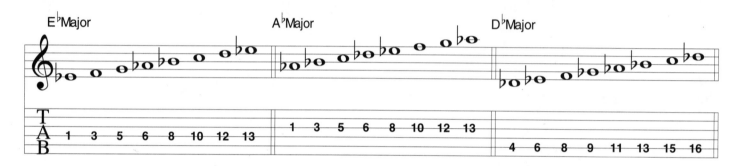

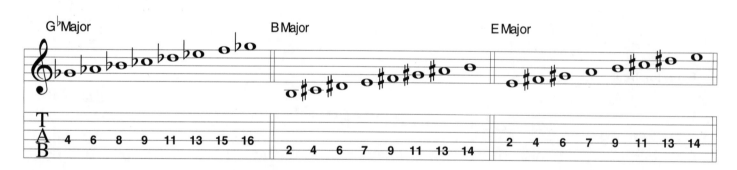

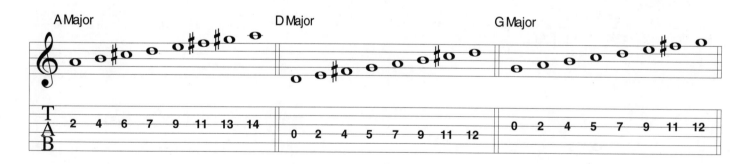

Here are the scales again in a handy reference list. Memorize, memorize, memorize!!

C	**Major:**	**C D E F G A B C**
F	**Major:**	**F G A B♭ C D E F**
B♭	**Major:**	**B♭ C D E♭ F G A B♭**
E♭	**Major:**	**E♭ F G A♭ B♭ C D E♭**
A♭	**Major:**	**A♭ B♭ C D♭ E♭ F G A♭**
D♭	**Major:**	**D♭ E♭ F G♭ A♭ B♭ C D♭**
G♭	**Major:**	**G♭ A♭ B♭ C♭ D♭ E♭ F G♭**
B	**Major:**	**B C♯ D♯ E F♯ G♯ A♯ B**
E	**Major:**	**E F♯ G♯ A B C♯ D♯ E**
A	**Major:**	**A B C♯ D E F♯ G♯ A**
D	**Major:**	**D E F♯ G A B C♯ D**
G	**Major:**	**G A B C D E F♯ G**

*Note: When arranged in this order, the number of flats in each flat scale increases by one, and the number of sharps in each sharp scale decreases by one. This is a helpful memory tool. Notice that each scale starts four steps above the last (from C to F is four whole steps: C, D, E, F). This is called a "cycle of 4ths," and many of the concepts in this book are presented in this order. See page 17 for more information about the cycle of 4ths.

KEY SIGNATURES

The area between the clef and the time signature at the beginning of a tune is called the key signature. The sharps or flats found in the key signature are derived from the major scale that is the basis for the tune. The number of sharps or flats, or their absence, therefore, will tell you the key of the tune. Each key designation corresponds to one of the major scales. In other words, if you see three sharps in the key signature, you know the tune is in the key of A, because the A Major scale has three sharps. Four flats mean the tune is in A♭. The absence of sharps or flats means the tune is in the key of C, because there are no sharps or flats in the C major scale.

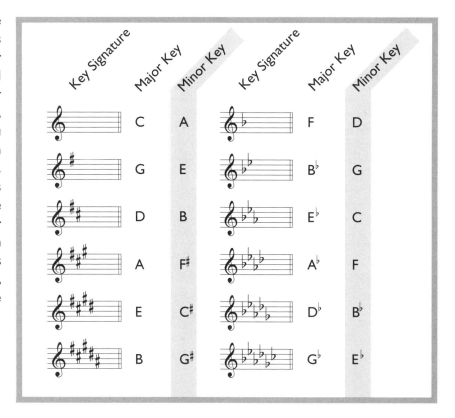

INTERVALS

The distance between two notes identifies their musical relationship. An interval name describes this distance. It is important to be able to recognize intervals by both sight and sound, and know where they lie on the fingerboard. When determining an interval's name, be sure to include both notes in your count through the musical alphabet, starting with the bottom note and counting upward. For instance, the distance from C to F would be counted like this: C-1, D-2, E-3, F-4. So, the interval from C to F is a 4th.

Along with the numerical name of each interval there is a qualifying name (Major, minor, Perfect, etc.) As you continue with your studies, you will see that this is very important information to have about an interval. The following is a list of intervals you need to be familiar with.

Perfect =	This word has been used for centuries to describe the most pure sounding intervals: octaves, 4ths and 5ths.
Major =	The larger form of an interval that is not "perfect."
Minor =	The smaller form of an interval that is not "perfect."
Diminished =	The name for a "perfect" interval that has been made smaller.

THE CYCLE OF 4THS (OR 5THS)

Chances are you have seen this diagram in other books and have wondered how it could have anything to do with playing music. Actually, it has a lot to do with learning about and analyzing chord progressions. Think of it as a learning aid. How you use it has to do with what it is you are studying. For now, it is only necessary to understand its basic layout.

In many styles of music, like rock, pop, country and jazz, chords tend to move in patterns. One of the most common patterns in these styles is the movement of a 4th. The cycle (or *circle*) of 4ths shows this movement. The twelve roots (of chords or keys) are shown around the cycle. If you follow them counterclockwise each root is a 4th higher than the one before it—hence the name *cycle of 4ths*. If you follow them clockwise each root is a 5th higher than the one before—hence the name *cycle of 5ths*. Most jazz studies are taught using the cycle of 4ths. This book will do the same. It would be a good idea to memorize the order of 4ths as it will be referred to often.

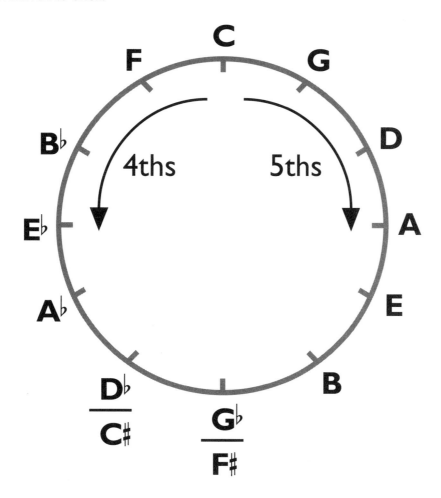

READING ROMAN NUMERALS

We use Roman numerals for fret numbers in scale and chord diagrams, and to label harmonies. Here is a chart showing Roman numerals, in upper and lower case, and their Arabic equivalents:

I, i	1	IV, iv	4	VII, vii	7	X, x	10	XIII, xiii	13	XVI, xvi	16
II, ii	2	V, v	5	VIII, viii	8	XI, xi	11	XIV, xiv	14	XVII, xvii	17
III, iii	3	VI, vi	6	IX, xi	9	XII, xii	12	XV, xv	15		

Lesson 1B: Major Scale Fingerings

In this book you will be learning six different fingerings for the major scale. Three of these fingerings will have their roots on the sixth string and three will have their roots on the fifth string. We will identify these fingerings by what string the lowest root is found on and with which finger that root is played. The first fingering below will be labeled 6/1 because the lowest root is found on the sixth string and fingered with the first finger. The second fingering will be called 5/1 because the lowest root is found on the fifth string and fingered with the first finger. These two examples are shown in the key of C Major. Memorize these and practice them over the entire fingerboard. Check out the section on page 91 about memorizing scales two strings at a time. Next practice them with the melodic patterns in Examples 8 and 9.

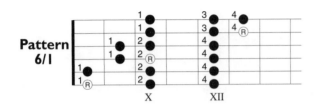

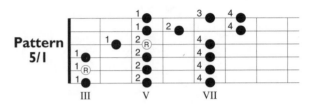

Examples 8 and 9 show how to start melodic patterns that can be continued through the rest of the scale fingerings as given above. Just keep repeating the same melodic shape until you reach the highest note in the fingering. Then, be sure to turn it around and play it backwards. Notice that Example 9 is in $\frac{12}{8}$ time. The best way to count $\frac{12}{8}$ is as follows: 1-and-ah 2-and-ah 3-and ah 4-and ah. It should feel like four beats per measure, with each beat divided into by three. See page 93 for more information about melodic patterns.

Lesson 2A: Triad Theory & Root Position Fingerings

MAJOR TRIAD THEORY

Triads are three-note chords. It is essential for a guitarist to have a complete understanding of these basic chords before studying their larger extensions. Most larger chords are built from triads.

Chords are derived from scales. Look at the C Major scale in Example 10. Notice that each note is given a number indicating its position in the scale. That number is referred to as the *degree*. For instance, E is the third degree.

Triads are built from the root, 3rd and 5th degrees of the major scale (R, 3, 5). These notes can be altered in such a way as to give us four different types of triads: *major*, *minor*, *diminished* and *augmented*.

The major triad is built from the unaltered root, 3rd and 5th degrees of the major scale (R, 3, 5). In C, when we take the root (C), the 3rd (E), and the 5th (G), we have a C Major triad: C E G.

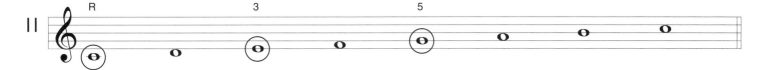

MAJOR TRIAD INVERSIONS

When the notes are sounded from bottom to top in root, 3rd, 5th order, it is referred to as being in *root position*. When the notes are sounded in 3rd, 5th, root order, the term *first inversion* is used. The order 5th, root, 3rd is called *second inversion*. No matter how you play it, however, it is still a C Major triad.

12

    Root Position   First Inversion   Second Inversion

A

MINOR, DIMINISHED AND AUGMENTED TRIADS AND THEIR INVERSIONS

The minor triad is built from the root, flatted (or lowered) 3rd (written ♭3, said *flat three*) and 5th degrees of the major scale. Once again, in C, we begin with the root (C), the ♭3rd (E♭), and the 5th (G), to make our minor triad: C E♭ G.

The same inversion system used for the major triad also applies to the minor triad.

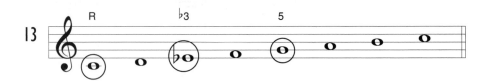

The diminished triad consists of the root, ♭3 and flatted (or lowered) 5th degrees (written ♭5, said *flat five*) of the major scale. In C, combine the root (C), the ♭3rd (E♭), and the ♭5th, (G♭), and you have a C diminished triad: C E♭ G♭.

The same inversion system applies to diminished triads.

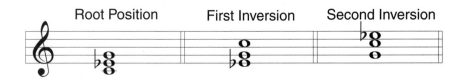

The augmented triad consists of the root, 3rd and sharped (or raised) 5th (written ♯5, said *sharp five*) degrees of the major scale. In C, take the root (C), the 3rd (E), and the ♯5, (G♯) to construct the C augmented triad: C E G♯.

The same inversion system applies to augmented triads.

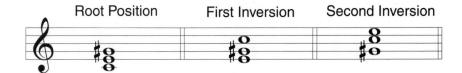

That's the story on triads. It really isn't very complicated, but it is very important that you have a working knowledge of them. It's be a good idea to write out all the triads in all the keys, and in all inversions, away from your guitar. You will start to see why it is so necessary to have all the major scales memorized.

THE FOUR BASIC STRING SETS

It's time to place all of these triads on the fingerboard. What we are going to do first is divide the guitar into four string sets. For instance, considered together, the sixth, fifth and fourth strings are a string set.

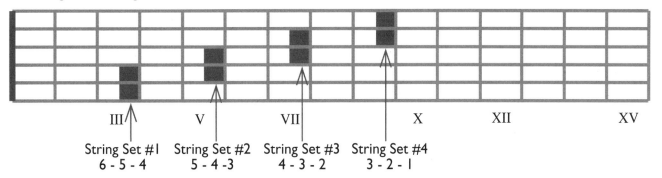

III   V   VII   X   XII   XV

String Set #1   String Set #2   String Set #3   String Set #4
   6 - 5 - 4   5 - 4 -3   4 - 3 - 2   3 - 2 - 1

The mission is this: over the next three lessons, build major, minor, diminished and augmented triads in all keys, all inversions, on all string sets, and become familiar with their shapes on the fingerboard.

ROOT POSITION TRIAD FINGERINGS

Let's start in the key of C. On the **first string set** we'll find a root position major triad here:

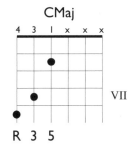

Now, turn this major triad into a minor triad:

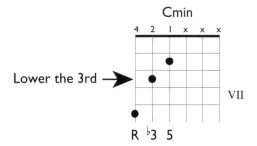

The diminished triad looks like this:

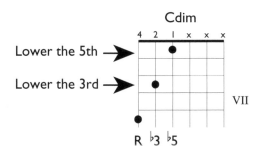

Here is the augmented triad shape:

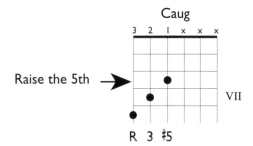

The next step is to find the remaining root position triads on this string set in the keys of F, B♭, E♭, A♭, D♭, G♭, B, E, A, D and G.

On the **first string set**, the triads look like this.

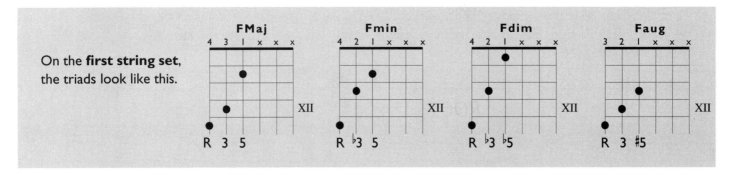

So you see, it's really just a matter of recognizing the shapes and sliding them around the fingerboard, like barre chords.

On the **second string set**, the root position triad shapes look like this:

Now locate these shapes in the other eleven keys.

Here are the root position triad shapes on the **third string set**:

Start sliding around to all the other keys. Always be conscious of where the scale degrees lie and the names of the notes themselves.

These are the root position triad shapes on the **fourth string set**:

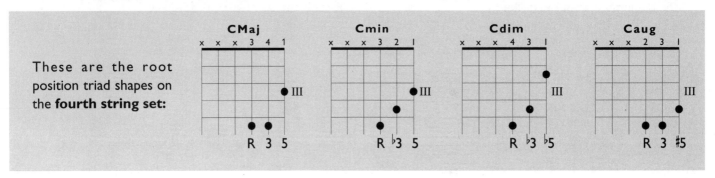

Once again, find them in all the keys!

Now let's try putting some of these triads to work in a more musical setting. Learn and practice the following *etude* (study) until all the moves are second nature. Try to memorize the sounds of all four types of triads as you enjoy playing this. Experiment with different *feels* (rhythms) and *tempos* (speeds).

ETUDE #1: ROOT POSITION TRIADS

Track
2

Lesson 2B: Two More Major Scale Fingerings

Here are two more major scale fingerings to practice. We will call the first fingering 6/2 because its lowest root is found on the sixth string and is played with the second finger. The second fingering shown will be called 5/2. Its root is on the fifth string and, once again, it will lie under your second finger. These patterns are shown in the key of C Major.

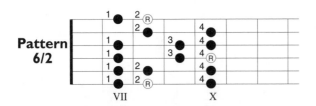

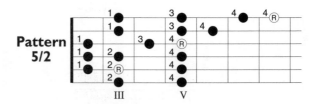

Try these new fingerings in the following melodic patterns. The first melodic pattern incorporates the use of *eighth-note triplets*. As you know, eighth notes (♪) receive one half of a beat in $\frac{4}{4}$ time. In other words, you can play two eighth notes in the time it takes to play one beat. In the case of triplets, however, you can play three notes in one beat. The easiest way to feel eighth note triplets is to count as follows: 1-trip-let—2-trip-let—3-triplet—4-trip-let, with the number landing on each down beat in the measure. This sounds just like $\frac{12}{8}$ time (see Example 9, page 18). Check out this example:

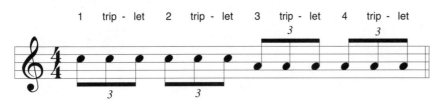

Use pattern 6/2. Follow the pattern up through the entire fingering given above and back down.

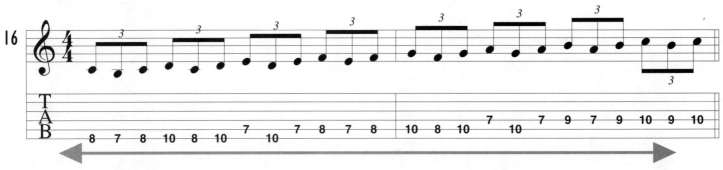

Use pattern 5/2. Follow the pattern up the entire fingering and back down.

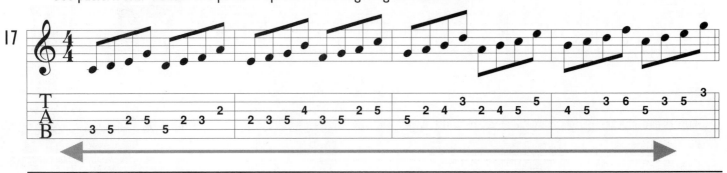

Lesson 3A: First-Inversion Triads on Four Strings

Let's take a look at the triad fingerings in the first inversion. Our approach will be the same, but of course the notes in the triads will be sounded (from bottom to top) in 3rd, 5th, root order.

Here is what they look like on the **first string set** in the key of C Major.

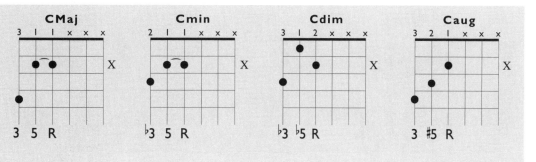

First inversion triads on the **second string set**:

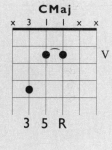 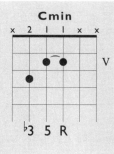 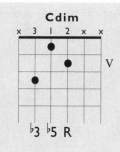 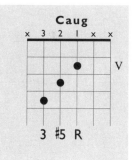

First inversion triads on the **third string set**:

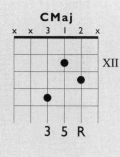 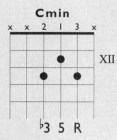 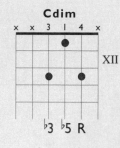 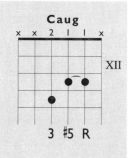

First inversion triads on the **fourth string set**:

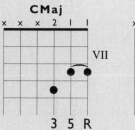 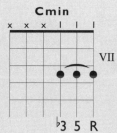 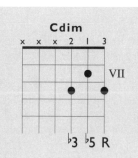 

Run these shapes through all twelve keys. Be aware of what scale degrees and note names you are playing.

After you are comfortable with the first-inversion triad shapes try your hand at this new etude. Once again try to recognize the differences between the four different types of triads. Experiment with different feels and tempos.

ETUDE #2: FIRST-INVERSION TRIADS

Track 3

Lesson 3B: Two More Major Scale Fingerings

Learn and practice these last two fingerings for the major scale. The first one is called 6/4 because the lowest root is on the sixth string and played with your fourth finger. The second one is named 5/4. Its lowest root lies on the fifth string and, once again, is played with your fourth finger.

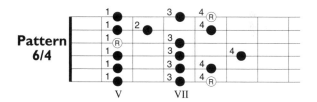

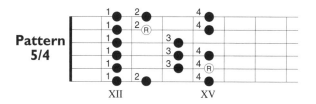

After you have worked with these melodic patterns play all the major scale fingerings with every melodic pattern you have learned. Play them forwards and backwards in all octaves of the fingerings you know.

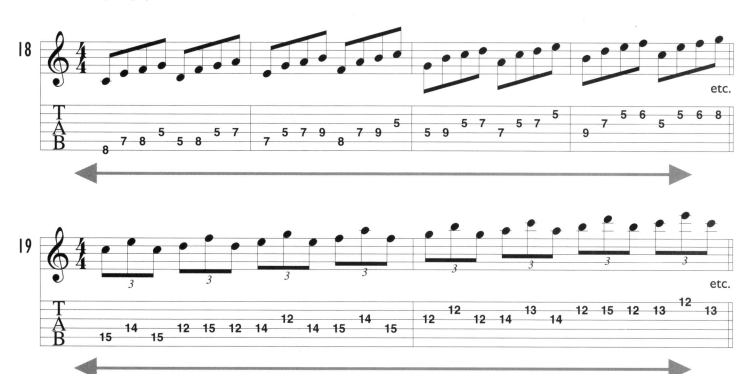

Lesson 4A: Second-Inversion Triads on the Four String Sets

Now we are ready to study the second-inversion triads. Once again we will locate them on the four string sets and then practice them in all twelve keys.

On the **first string set:**

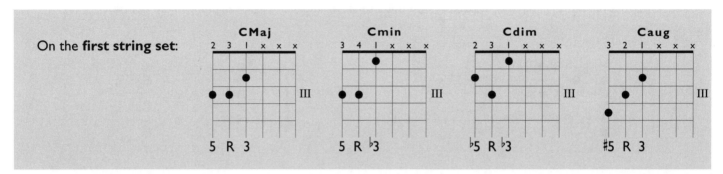

On the **second string set:**

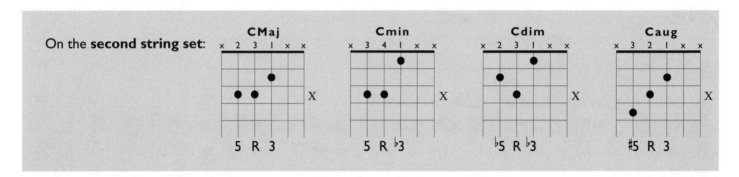

On the **third string set:**

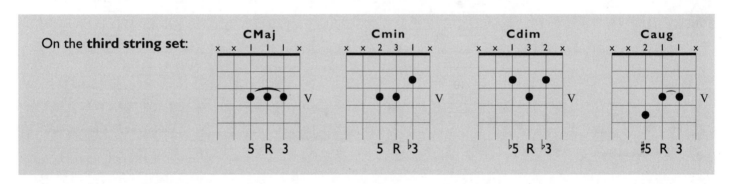

On the **fourth string set:**

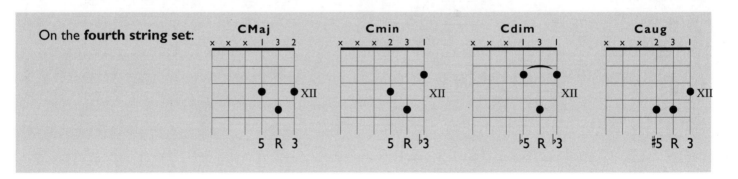

Enjoy putting these second-inversion triads to use while studying Etude #3.

ETUDE #3: SECOND-INVERSION TRIADS

Track 4

Lesson 4B: Major Scale Etude

Here is an etude that will help you see some of the melodic possibilities contained in the major scale. This one will use fingerings 6/1, 6/2 and 6/4 in the key of C Major. It will show how all the fingerings relate to each other. Soon you'll be shown specific connecting exercises, but for now, simply learn and enjoy this tune! The chords that go with this etude may not be familiar to you yet, but they are included here so that your teacher, or a friend, can accompany you.

ETUDE #4: THE MAJOR SCALE

Track 5

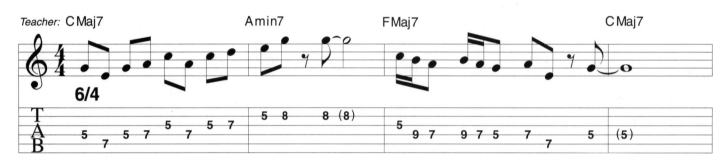

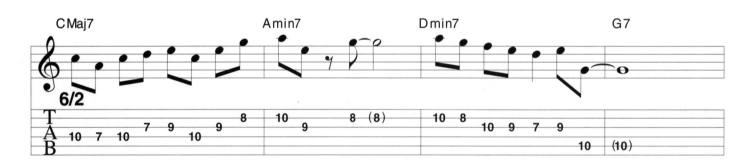

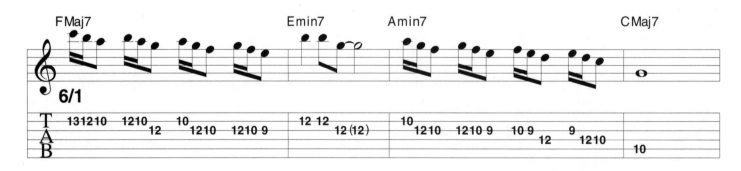

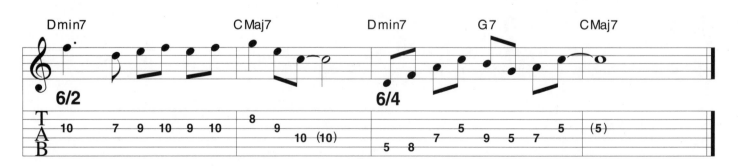

CHAPTER 3

Lesson 1A: Constructing Larger Chords

Building larger chords is no different than building triads—there are just a few more notes involved. Like triads, we use formulas. If we want to construct a CMaj7 chord, we need to know the formula for major 7th chords. In the lessons that follow, you will learn exactly what the various formulas are. It will be easy since they are not that complex and you will be digesting this information a little at a time.

HOW LARGER CHORD FORMULAS WORK

Most chords are built on top of triads, so constructing larger chords is simply a matter of adding additional scale tones to the original triad. See Example 20.

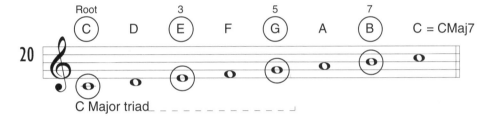

The formula for Maj7 chords is: Root-3-5-7. This means that we combine the root, 3rd, 5th and 7th degrees of the major scale to build the chord. Notice that what we have actually done is add the 7th degree to a major triad.

EXTENSIONS

Many chords use notes that actually lie beyond a one octave major scale. Since an octave contains only eight notes, these would include chords that have 9ths, 11ths and 13ths. These are called *extensions*. Where do these notes come from? We get the extended notes (beyond the octave) by continuing the major scale up through a second octave. Look at Example 21 and observe how the notes are numbered.

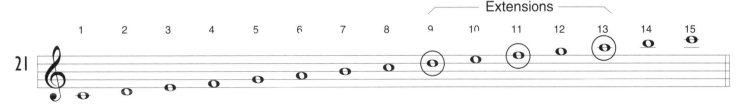

Here is an example of how this works using a Cmin11 chord. The formula is: Root-♭3-5-♭7-9-11. Chords are usually named for the highest extension present. So, even though the ♭7 and 9 are part of the chord, it is still called min11.

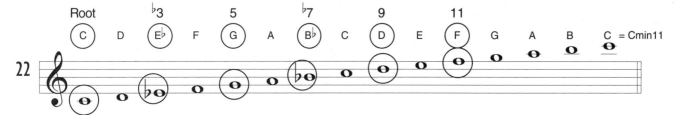

INVERTING LARGER CHORDS

Larger chords can be inverted like triads, too. The only difference is that since they have four notes, they invert three times instead of only two. Example 23 shows the CMaj7 chord in root position and in all three inversions.

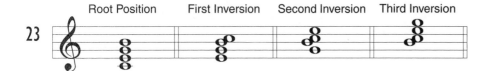

VOICINGS

Other arrangements of the notes, *or voicings*, can also be used. In this case, each note in a chord is referred to as a *voice*. Here are two examples of voicings for the CMaj7 chord.

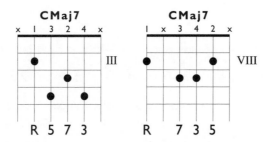

The guitar presents fingering problems that don't exist on the keyboard, our chordal cousin. It will sometimes be necessary to eliminate certain tones from the chord you are building. These will be explained as each type of chord is discussed in future lessons. Don't let this limitation bother you. There are more great sounding chords to play than you could ever possibly learn.

Another consideration is how to execute these larger chords with the right hand. Most chords in this book can be played with a pick, while some work better when fingerpicked. Refer to pages 88 and 89 for more information on this subject.

Lesson 1B: Major Scale Etude

Here is a second major scale etude. This one utilizes fingerings 5/1, 5/2 and 5/4 in the key of F Major. Working slowly and carefully will guarantee you success and add to your enjoyment. Check the fingering often.

ETUDE #5: THE MAJOR SCALE

Track 6

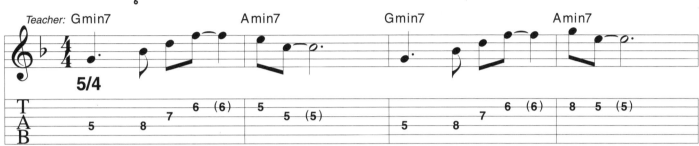

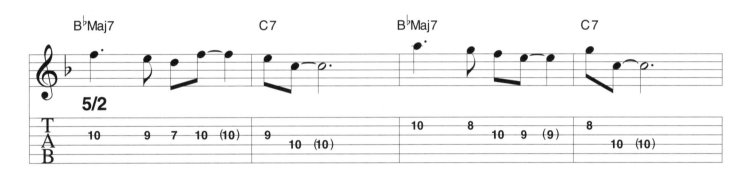

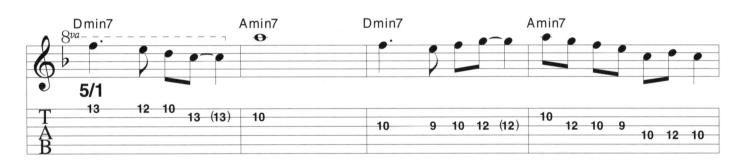

8va = Play one octave higher than written.

Lesson 2A: 6th Chords

MAJOR 6TH CHORDS

Major 6th chords (6) are common in jazz because they are a good substitute for major chords. The formula for Maj6 chords is as follows: Root-3-5-6. In the key of F, this would be spelled F, A, C and D. In the key of C it would be C, E, G and A. Practice spelling major sixth chords for the other ten keys.

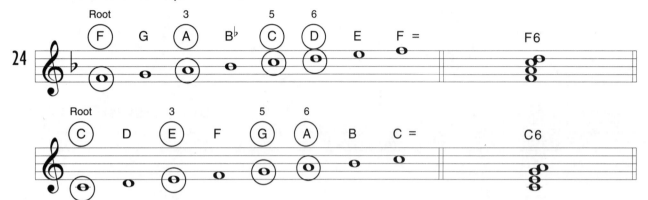

Here are four examples of Maj6 voicings. Notice that some of these voicings require you to dampen an inside string. If a string is marked with an "x" in the fingering, it should not be sounded. For instance, in the first voicing below, you can use 4 to dampen the fifth string. The only other solution is to fingerpick instead of strum. There are dozens and dozens of possible voicings. A good chord book can be a handy reference to have, but do try to come up with some voicings of your own. This will reinforce your knowledge of chord theory.

C6: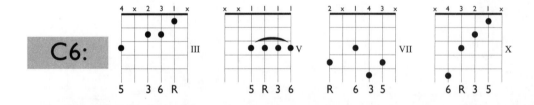

MINOR 6TH CHORDS

In jazz, minor 6th chords (min6) are common replacements for minor chords. After you learn some of these voicings, play any song you know and try using them in place of the minor chords you would ordinarily use. The 6th adds a beautiful element to the minor quality.

The formula for min6 chords is: Root-♭3-5-6. In the key of G Major, this would be G, B♭, D and E. In D Major it would be D, F, A and B. Practice spelling the min6 chords in the remaining keys. Here are some sample voicings:

Cmin6: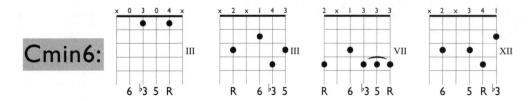

In each chord lesson, you will find chord progressions to practice using the new voicings, along with chords from previous lessons. It might be a good idea to read the section on learning difficult chords on page 90. You may also find the section on making chord changes helpful as well. Enjoy!

ETUDE #6: 6TH CHORDS

Track 7

Lesson 2B: Connecting Major Scales

Getting around the guitar fingerboard smoothly is an art. So far, you have learned six different fingerings for the major scale, with each one staying in one area of the fingerboard. Here are some ways to connect these major scale fingerings that will help you move fluently around the neck. Practice these and try to make up your own connections. Practice very slowly until these fingerings are seamless.

Connecting 6/4 and 6/2

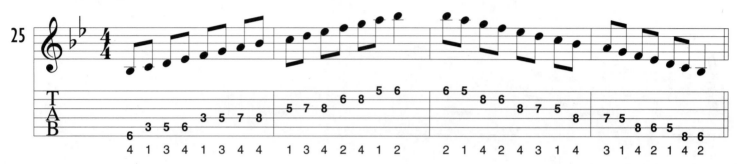

Connecting 6/2 and 6/1

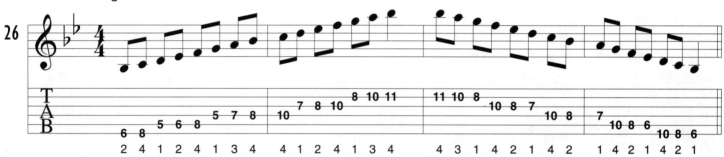

Connecting 6/1 and 5/4

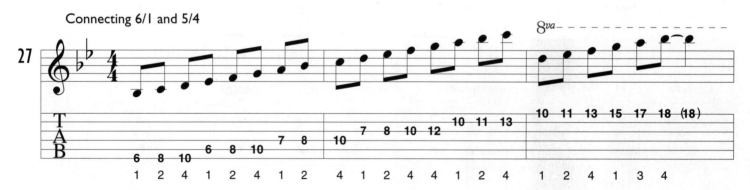

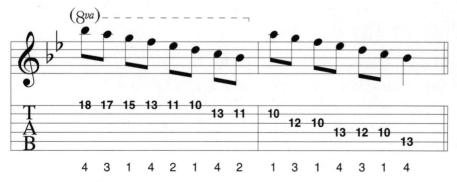

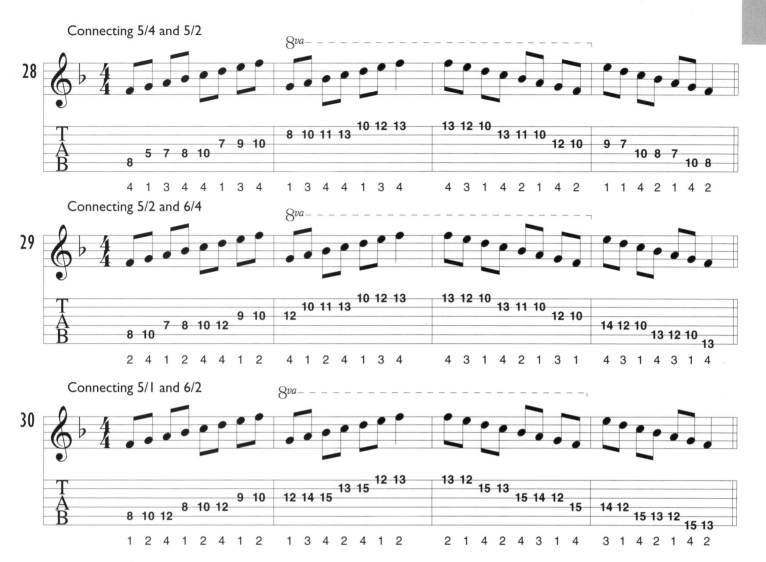

*Jazz/rock fusion giant **Al DiMeola** developed his astonishing technique by spending several hours a day practicing scales with a metronome. In 1974, when he was only 19 years old, he joined Chick Corea's band Return To Forever, and has since made over 20 solo recordings.*

Lesson 3A: 7th Chords

MAJOR 7TH CHORDS

Major 7th chords (Maj7) are commonly used in place of plain major chords. The formula for a Maj7 chord is Root-3-5-7. In the key of F this would be F-A-C-E. In the key of B♭ it's B♭-D-F-A. Practice spelling Maj7 chords for the other ten keys.

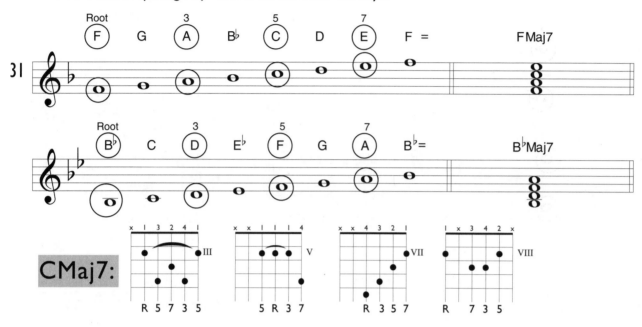

MINOR 7TH CHORDS

Minor 7th chords (min7) are common replacements for plain minor chords. The formula for a min7 chord is Root-♭3-5-♭7. In the key of G this would be G-B♭-D-F. In the key of D it's D-F-A-C. Natural signs ♮ will be used in these examples to show when sharped notes are naturaled for note a ♭3 or ♭7. Practice spelling the min7 chords in the other ten keys.

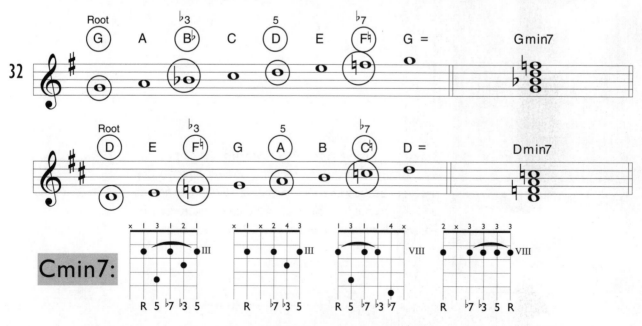

DOMINANT 7TH CHORDS

Dominant 7th chords (7), sometimes simply refered to as "dominant," play a very important role in chord progressions. You will be learning about this in great detail in the intermediate book of this series. For now, it is enough to know that the formula for a 7 chord is Root-3-5-$\flat$7. It has a natural 3, like a major chord, and a $\flat$7 like a min7 chord. In the key of E it is spelled E-G#-B-D. In the key of A it's A-C#-E-G. As you have done with the other chords, practice spelling these in all keys.

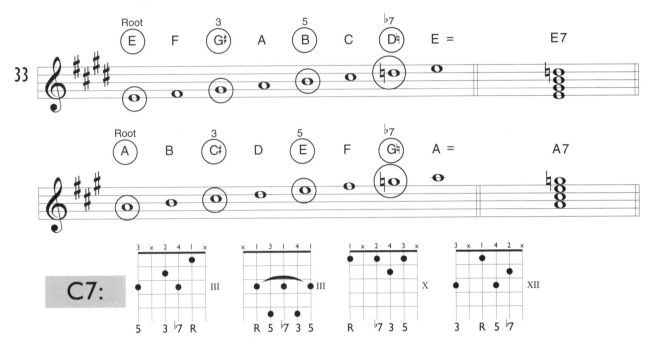

C7:

Frank Gambale (b. 1958), an Australian jazz fusion guitarist, is renowned for his use of the sweep picking and economy picking

ETUDE #7: 7TH CHORDS

Track 8

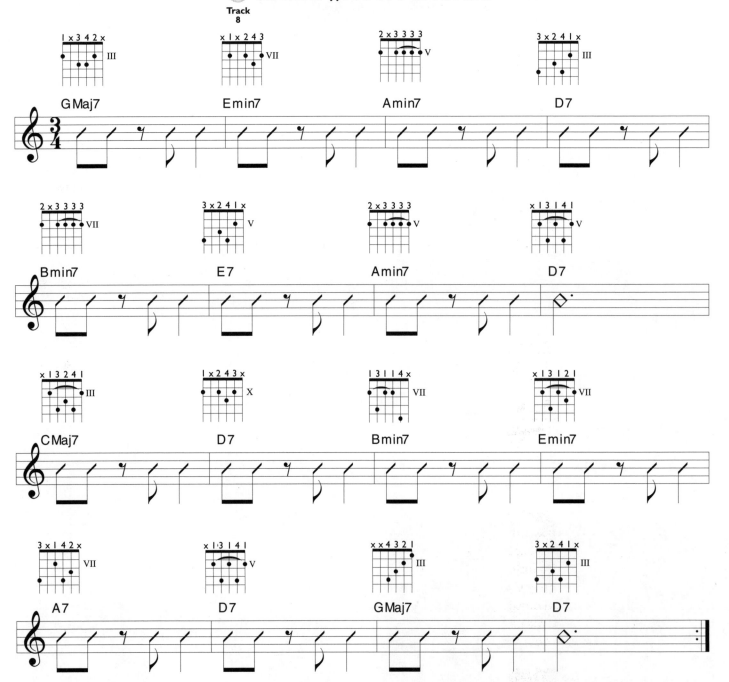

Lesson 3B: Three-Octave Scales

The six major scale fingerings you have learned span two octaves. They are useful for playing in one position at a time. In the next two lessons, you will be shown four three-octave major scale fingerings. These will eventually help you play horizontally, (on the fingerboard, that is—not while laying down), which is a very natural approach for all stringed instruments. When you start improvising with the major scale (in just a few lessons) you will find that your ideas are very different when you approach the scales in this manner. You may find, depending on the length of your fingerboard, that your instrument will not accommodate a three-octave scale in some keys. Simply practice these fingerings only in keys in where the full three octaves can be played.

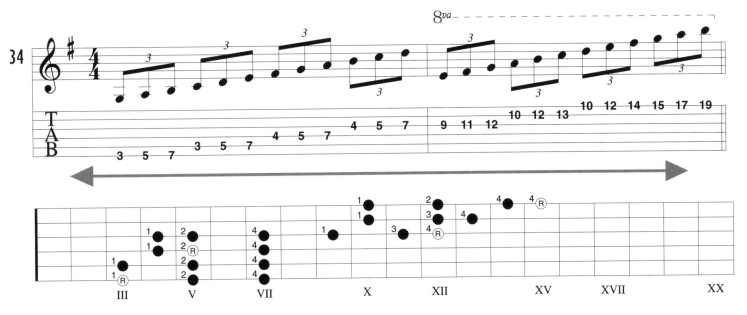

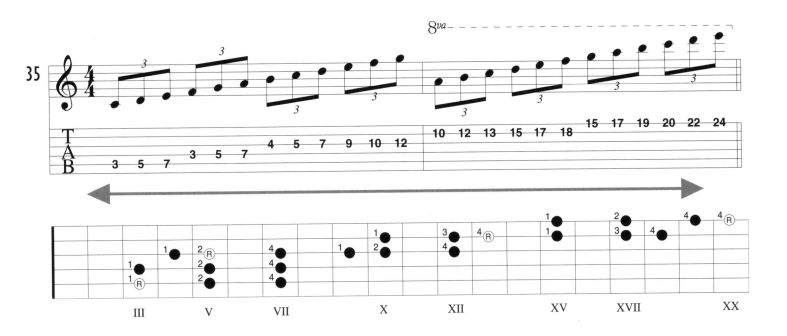

Lesson 4A: 9th Chords

EXTENSIONS & CHORD FAMILIES

Chords that include 9ths, 11ths or 13ths are usually referred to as extended chords. Extended chords are generally used to enhance smaller chords, such as triads and 7th chords. This kind of thinking can make a chord progression more interesting and sound more musically sophisticated—it simply gives you more to listen to.

One very important feature of jazz harmony is that chords can be freely substituted for other chords within their "family." We can think of there being three basic "families:" major, minor and dominant. In other words, if the written chord progression contains a CMaj7 chord, you may replace it with a C6, CMaj9, CMaj13, or any other chord in the C Major family. A Cmin7 could be replaced with a Cmin6, Cmin11, Cmin13 or any other C minor chord. With dominant chords the same idea holds true. A C7 could be replaced with C9, C11 or C13. Many students are surprised that this is possible. Yes, it will change the sound of the tune; and yes, that is perfectly alright. The chords you choose when playing a song help to define your own individual sound and style.

After some of these voicings become easy for you, try using them in songs you already know. Experiment freely, but let good taste dictate your choices.

MAJOR 9TH CHORDS

The formula for a major 9th chord (Maj9) is: Root-3-5-7-9. In the key of C, that's C-E-G-B-D. In F it's F-A-C-E-G.

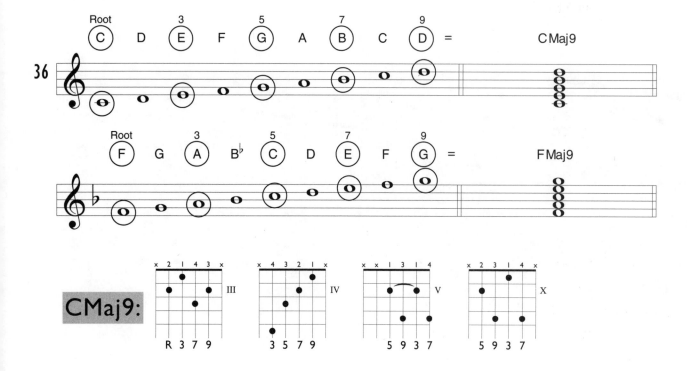

MINOR 9TH CHORDS

The formula for a minor 9th chord (min9) is: Root-♭3-5-♭7-9. In the key of G it's G-B♭-D-F-A. In D it's D-F-A-C-E.

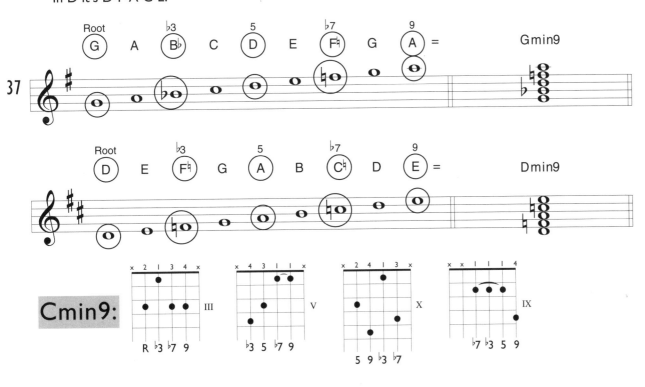

DOMINANT 9TH CHORDS

The formula for a dominant 9th chord (9) is Root-3-5-♭7-9. In the key of E♭ that's E♭-G-B♭-D♭-F. In B♭ it's B♭-D-F-A♭-C.

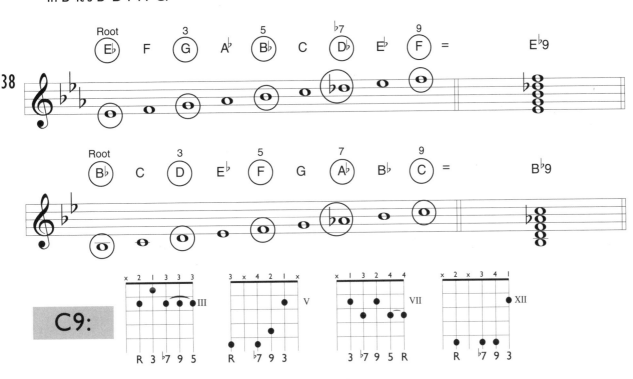

ETUDE #8: 9TH CHORDS

Track 9

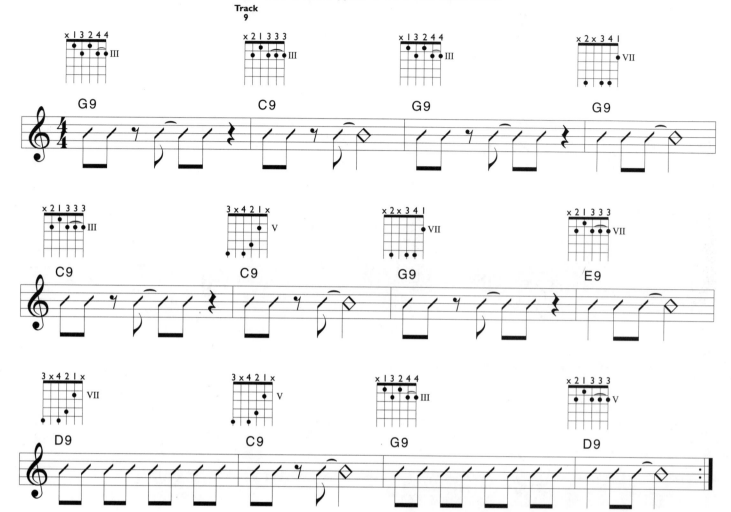

John McLaughlin (b. 1942.), also known as Mahavishnu John McLaughlin, is an influential English jazz fusion guitarist and composer. Best known for his 1970s electric band, The Mahavishnu Orchestra, his guitar playing includes a range of styles and genres, including jazz, Indian classical music, fusion, and Western Classical music

PHOTO • SARAMA MINOLI

ETUDE #9: MORE 9TH CHORDS

Track
10

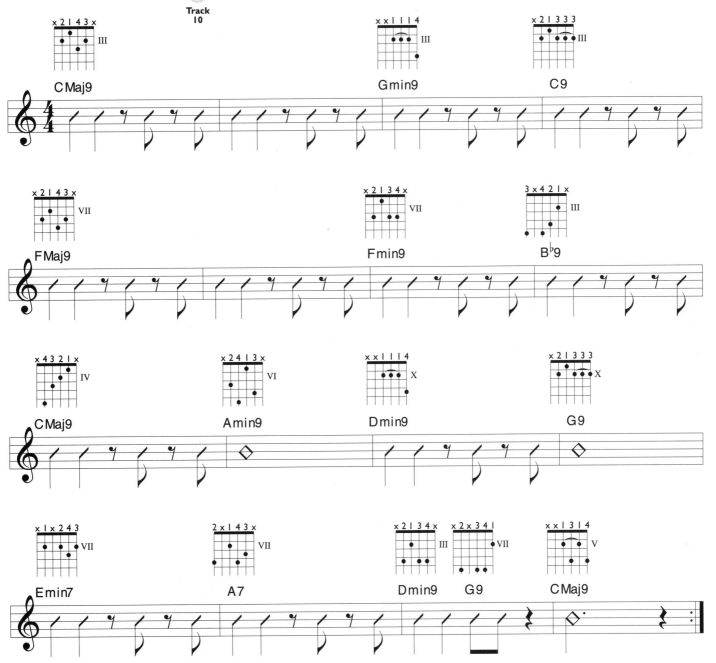

Lesson 4B: More Three-Octave Scales

Here are two more ways to play a three-octave scale. Once again, be sure to practice these in as many octaves as your instrument will allow.

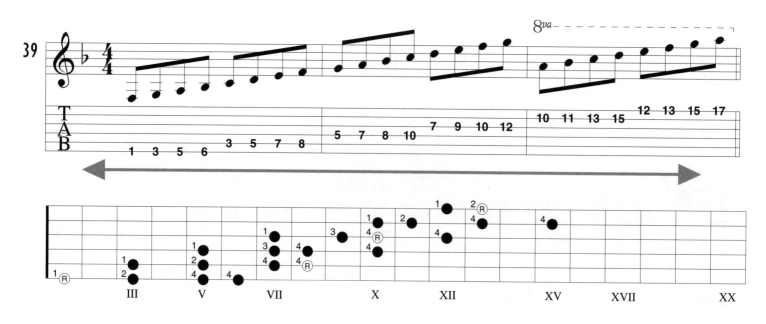

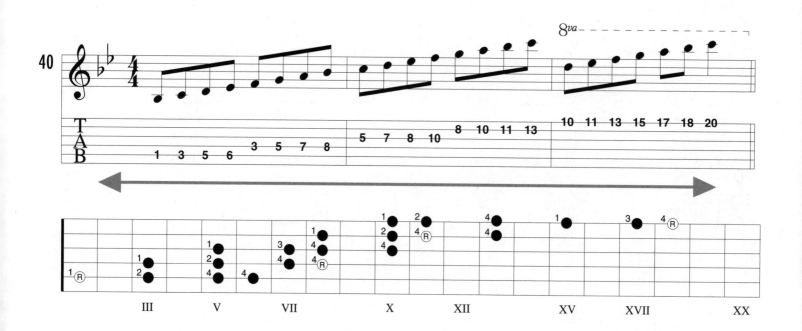

Lesson 5A: Other Chords You Need to Know

The previous lessons have introduced you to many new chord shapes and sounds. This is just the beginning. Serious jazz players spend their lives looking for great new chords to play.

Remember, in jazz we often enhance the chords we play by adding different extensions. You now have some experience working with 6ths, 7ths, and 9ths. You can extend any chord with 11ths and 13ths in exactly the same way. After you learn some of these, try substituting them for other chords. It takes a little while to develop an ear for some of these sounds, but give it time and you will grow into them.

In order to construct some of these bigger chords, we sometimes have to eliminate some notes. Roots, 5ths and 9ths can be dropped in various combinations. Why can we do this? The combination of remaining voices can actually imply the missing sounds. As with all rules, there are exceptions, but it is generally not a good idea to drop 3rds and 7ths because these are the tones that define major, minor and dominant chords.

In the following chord types, do not drop:

Major 3, 7
Minor .... ♭3, ♭7
Dom .... 3, ♭7

MINOR 11TH CHORDS

The formula for a minor 11th chord (min11) is Root-♭3-5-♭7-9-11. In the key of F that's F-A♭-C-E♭-G-B♭. In A it's A-C-E-G-B-D.

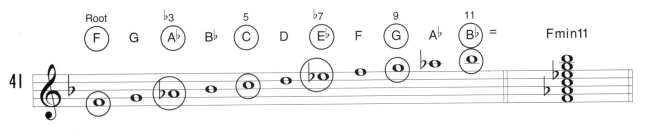

Cmin11:

DOMINANT 11TH CHORDS

The formula for a dominant 11th chord (11) is Root-3-5-♭7-9-11. In B♭ that's B♭-D-F-A♭-C-E♭.

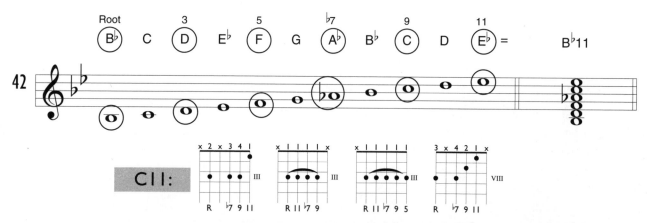

MAJOR 13TH CHORDS

The formula for a major 13th chord (Maj13) is Root-3-5-7-9-13. In C that's C-E-G-B-D-A. Usually, there is no 11th in this chord because it would clash with the 3rd.

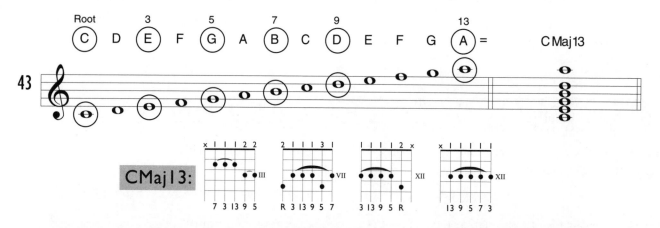

MINOR 13TH CHORDS

The formula for a minor 13th chord (min13) is Root-♭3-5-♭7-9-13. In the key of A♭ that's A♭-C♭-E♭-G♭-B♭-F.

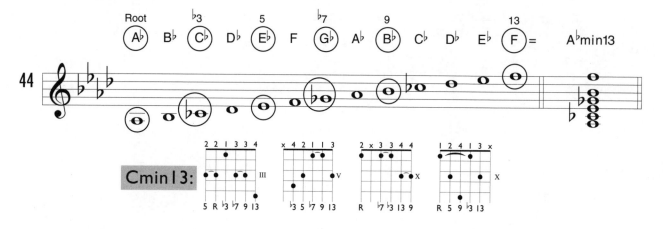

DOMINANT 13TH CHORDS

The formula for a dominant 13th chord (13) is Root-3-5-♭7-9-13. In D that's D-F♯-A-C-E-B.

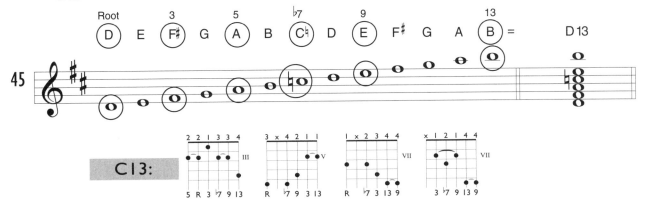

C13:

MAJOR ADD9 CHORDS

A major add9 chord (add9 or Maj add9) produces a nice substitute for a plain major chord. It is simply a major triad with a 9th added: Root-3-5-9. In E♭ that's E♭-G-B♭-F.

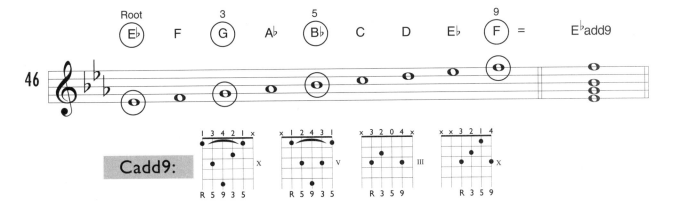

Cadd9:

MINOR ADD9 CHORDS

Minor add9 chords (min add9) can replace plain minor chords. The formula is Root-♭3-5-9. In E that's E-G-B-F♯.

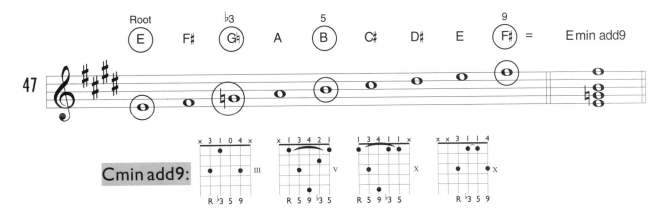

Cmin add9:

MIN7♭5 (HALF-DIMINISHED) CHORDS

Minor 7 ♭5 chords (min7♭5) are also commonly called half-diminished chords (ø7), and they are constructed by adding a ♭7 to the diminished triad. The formula is Root-♭3-♭5-♭7. In C that's C-E♭-G♭-B♭.

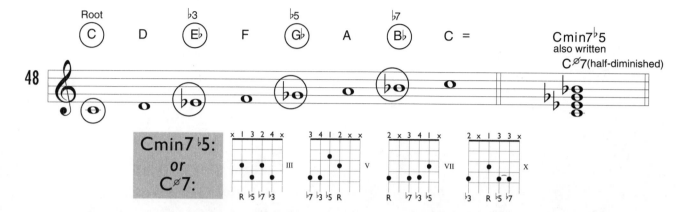

DIMINISHED 7TH CHORDS

Diminished 7th chords (dim7 or °7) are also built from diminished triads. Root-♭3-♭5-♭♭7. The double-flat ♭♭ indicates that the 7th should be lowered two half steps (a whole step). In the key of G it's spelled G-B♭-D♭-F♭.

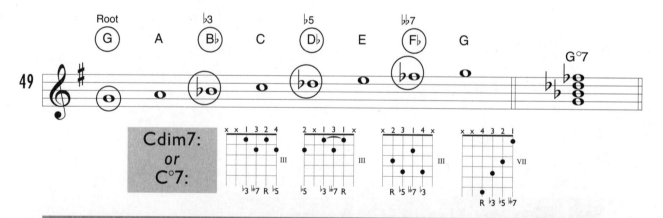

DOMINANT 7TH SUSPENDED CHORDS

The formula for a dominant 7th suspended chord (7sus4, sometimes referred to as a "sus" chord) is Root-4-5-♭7. In F that's F-B♭-C-E♭.

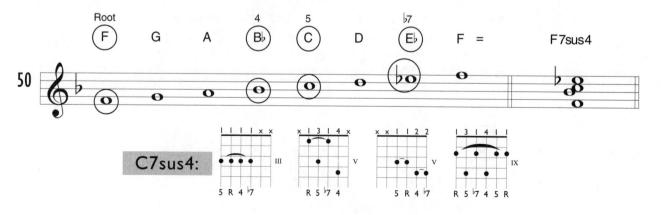

MINOR(MAJ7) CHORDS

Minor(maj7) chords [min(Maj7)] are minor triads with a natural 7th. They are found in minor chord progressions. The formula for a min(Maj7) chord is Root-♭3-5-7. In the key of A that's A-C-E-G♯.

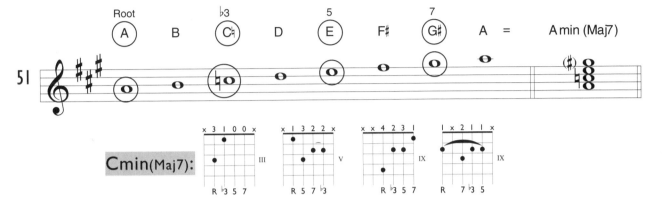

Cmin(Maj7):

DOMINANT 7TH AUGMENTED CHORDS

Dominant 7th Augmented chords (7aug) chords are built by adding a ♭7 to the augmented triad: Root-3-♯5-♭7. In B that's B-D♯-F×-A. [× = double sharp. Raise the note two half steps (one whole step).]

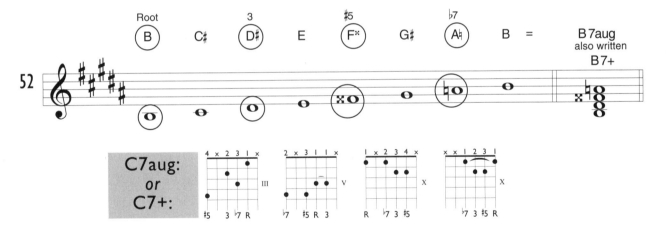

C7aug: or C7+:

I realize this is a lot of information. After you have mastered the chords from the previous lessons, start adding them to your playing. It takes a long time to absorb this material and it takes experience to use it tastefully. Occasionally, turn to this lesson and pick up a new chord. Have patience, but if you want more voicings right away, I suggest you obtain a copy of Alfred's Guitar Chord Encyclopedia.

ETUDE #10: MORE CHORDS

Track 11

Lesson 5B: Two Tunes Using the Major Scale

Here are two tunes for you to enjoy that utilize several different fingerings for the major scale. *Noah's Groove* is based loosely around a minor blues progression, and should be played at a medium tempo (not too fast). *Blues for Maggie* is an example of what we call a "straight-ahead" blues.

NOAH'S GROOVE

Track 12

Medium Groove

BLUES FOR MAGGIE

Track 13

Shuffle*

* **Shuffle** = The rhythm should "swing." This implies a triple "feel" in the accompaniment.

Herb Ellis (b. 1921) came to prominence performing with the Oscar Peterson Trio from 1953 to 1958, alongside pianist Peterson and bassist Ray Brown.

CHAPTER 4

Lesson 1A: The Harmonized Major Scale

When we harmonize a major scale in a traditional manner, we stack 3rds on top of each scale degree. If we stack them three notes high, we get triads. If we stack them four notes high, we get 7th chords. Even though 7th chords will be used in these examples, the same logic would apply to chords that include higher extensions.

Every scale has seven chords that are natural to its corresponding key. We can measure the intervals in each individual root-position chord stack from the root to each note to learn the chord's type. After you harmonize each major scale, you will notice that the harmonic pattern is the same for every key. In other words, the first and fourth chords (I and IV) are always Maj7 chords. (We use upper case Roman numerals to indicate harmonies based on major triads, and lower case Roman numerals to indicate harmonies based on minor or diminished triads.) The second, third and sixth chords (ii, iii and vi) are always min7 chords. The fifth chord (V7) is always a dominant 7th, and the seventh chord (vii) is always min7♭5 (half-diminished).

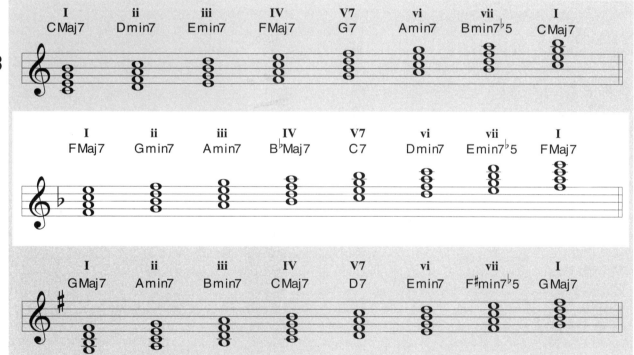

Remember, we can think of each note in a chord as being a voice. Notice that as we move from chord to chord through the chord scale, each voice moves in a scale-wise motion (from root to root, 3rd to 3rd, etc). Each chord is given a corresponding Roman numeral. Major and dominant chords will always use upper case numerals (I and IV for major, V7 for dominant). Minor and diminished chords will always use the lower case—ii, iii and vi for minor, vii for diminished or min7♭5 (half-diminished).

Exercise Harmonize all twelve major scales on paper, in cycle of 4ths order. After you have done this, practice reciting the chord names in every key. Simply say the notes in each scale with the chord names attached. For instance, for the key of D you would recite: DMaj7, Emin7, F♯min7, GMaj7, A7, Bmin7 and C♯min7♭5. To a large extent, your success in future lessons will depend on how well you know this material.

Lesson 1B: Improvising with the Major Scale

WHAT IT'S ALL ABOUT

Improvisation is the art of composing a new melody spontaneously. It is the central skill people think of when they think of jazz. Can you just play anything you want? Not exactly. Your improvised melody must fit the chord changes of the song you are improvising on. So the study of improvisation is largely the study of compatibility of notes and chords.

In this study you are collecting data. You will learn about the different *devices* you need to improvise freely. Scales and melodic patterns are two devices with which you already have some experience. You will be using them in this chapter as you start improvising. Your lifetime as an improviser will be spent learning and perfecting the use of other devices such as licks, arpeggios and neighbor tones, among countless others. You will eventually develop a mental catalog of devices that you can call on to come up with interesting improvised solos.

Improvising is a bit more than just learning which scales go well with which chords. Mood, feel, tone and spontaneous flashes of inspiration play a big part. While the goal of improvisation is to play new and inspired ideas all the time, the reality is that a large part of improvising is actually the creative reorganization of information you already know. The more devices you know, the more comfortable you are in all keys, and the better you know your fingerboard, the more control you will have of your improvised solos.

How do you get started? After you have read and understood the next section about diatonic thinking, look at the several chord progressions that follow. First practice the chord changes so that you can play them fluently and are familiar with the sound of the progression. Next, record the chord progression over and over. While listening to the playback, play the appropriate major scale up and back a few times. Just listen to the way the notes behave over the background chords. After a few minutes, try making up short melodies with the scale. Keep your ideas simple and try to use little pieces of some of the melodic patterns you have learned. Don't worry if your solos aren't quite smokin' yet. The objects of this lesson are to get used to the sound of the major scale and to have fun—that's all. If you have some experience improvising with pentatonic scales in a rock or blues context, you may find that it takes a little longer to learn how to manipulate the sounds in the major scale. Just have patience and practice regularly. Be sure to read the following sections in the CODA chapter at the back of this book: "How Jazz Works," "Using Melodic Patterns" and "Limiting Rhythmic Options."

Your study of the major scale will start with improvising over diatonic progressions. These are progressions that consist of the chords natural to the key. This book will deal with *progressional* improvising. This simply means that a single scale will work well (sound good) over an entire chord progression.

DIATONIC THINKING

As you learned in Lesson 1A of this chapter, when we harmonize the major scale in 3rds, we produce seven different chords. These chords are the primary chords in the key of the scale. In progressional improvisation we think diatonically. This means we may use the major scale over any of the chords that are constructed from it. For instance, look at this progression:

CMaj7-Amin7-FMaj7-G7

You could improvise over this with the C Major scale because all of these chords are natural to the key of C. Here are some more examples demonstrating this concept:

Chord Progression	Major Scale	Diatonic Harmony
GMaj7-Emin7-CMaj7-D7	G Major Scale	I-vi-IV-V7
D-G-A-G	D Major Scale	I-IV-V-IV
Amin7-Dmin7-Gmin7-C7	F Major Scale	iii-vi-ii-V7
Cmin7-Dmin7-Cmin7-Dmin7	B♭ Major Scale	ii-iii-ii-iii

Play along with the audio that accompanies this book, or record the following progressions, and improvise utilizing diatonic thinking. Use a C Major scale because CMaj7 is I and Dmin7 is ii in the key of C.

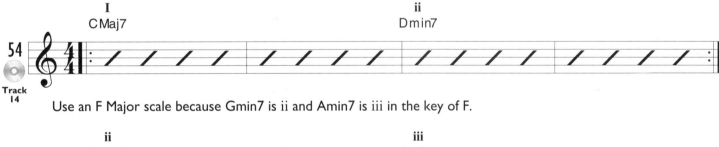

Use an F Major scale because Gmin7 is ii and Amin7 is iii in the key of F.

Use a B♭ Major scale because B♭Maj7 is I, Gmin7 is vi, Cmin7 is ii and F7 is V7 in the key of B♭.

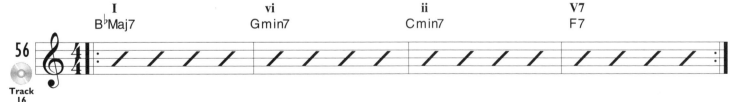

Use a G Major scale because GMaj7 is I, Amin7 is ii, Bmin7 is iii and CMaj7 is IV in the key of G.

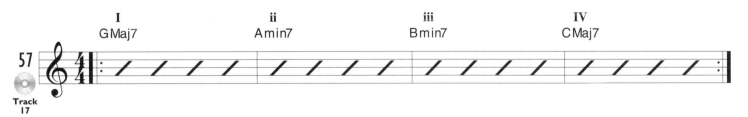

Use an F Major scale because FMaj7 is I and B♭Maj7 is IV in the key of F.

| **I**
FMaj7 | | | **IV**
B♭Maj7 | |

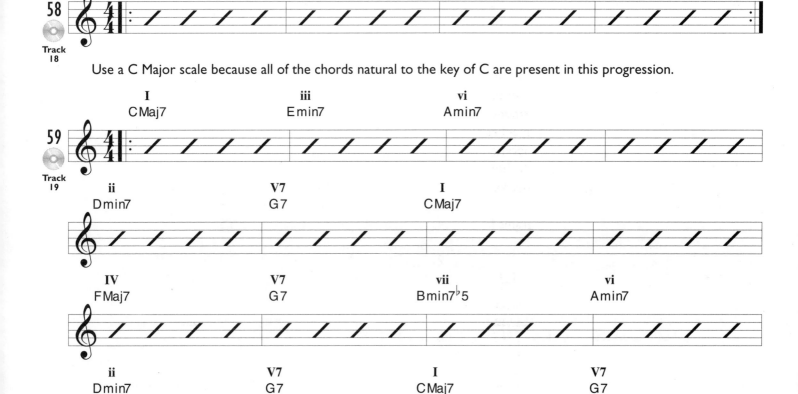

Track 18

Use a C Major scale because all of the chords natural to the key of C are present in this progression.

Track 19

I CMaj7	**iii** Emin7	**vi** Amin7	
ii Dmin7	**V7** G7	**I** CMaj7	
IV FMaj7	**V7** G7	**vii** Bmin7♭5	**vi** Amin7
ii Dmin7	**V7** G7	**I** CMaj7	**V7** G7

You can even use this approach when a tune moves briefly into another key. Just change scales to fit the new key. First, use a C Major scale because Dmin7 is ii, G7 is V7, CMaj7 is I and Amin7 is vi in the key of C. Then switch to an F Major scale because Gmin7 is ii, C7 is V7 and FMaj7 is I in the key of F. Finally, switch back to the C scale to finish the progression.

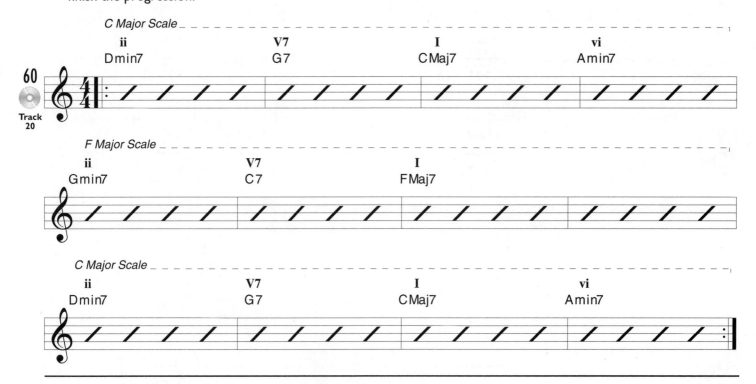

C Major Scale
| **ii**
Dmin7 | **V7**
G7 | **I**
CMaj7 | **vi**
Amin7 |

Track 20

F Major Scale
| **ii**
Gmin7 | **V7**
C7 | **I**
FMaj7 | |

C Major Scale
| **ii**
Dmin7 | **V7**
G7 | **I**
CMaj7 | **vi**
Amin7 |

Lesson 2A: Major Chord Scales

To put your knowledge of the harmonized major scale to work, you must know where all the chords lie on the fingerboard—and the more voicings you know, the better. Learning *chord scales* will increase your knowledge of diatonic harmony while adding many new chord voicings to your repertoire.

A chord scale is simply the chords in a key played scale-wise (I-ii-ii-IV-V-vi-vii). Constructing chord scales up and down the fingerboard is one sure-fire way to make certain you are comfortable with diatonic harmony in any key. The chord scales that follow are shown on various string sets and chosen for either their usefulness or interest level. This is an area of study you should spend time experimenting with. It is one of the best ways to expand your chord vocabulary. Practice each chord scale until each voice in every chord is clear and balanced. Then, play it in several other keys.

Play through each row of chord diagrams from left to right.

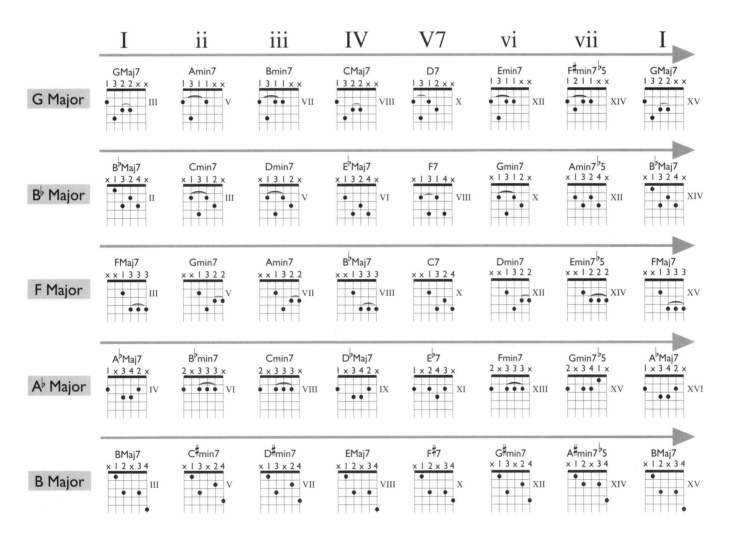

Lesson 2B: Two Tunes
Based on the Major Scale

Here are two short tunes for you to work on. Here is the best procedure for learning a new song:

1. Learn the chord progression in two areas of the fingerboard (memorize both if possible).
2. Learn the melody. If you can, try to learn it an octave higher than written as well (memorize if possible).
3. Playing along with the audio that is available for this book or a recording you make of the chord progressions, practice improvising over the chord changes using the appropriate major scale. At first use only whole notes, then half notes, quarter notes and finally eighth notes. Then play as freely as you want. Listen carefully. At this point, the content of your solo is not as important as just getting used to the sounds. Try to use all the major scale fingerings you know. Use the G Major scale in *Ruby, My Dearfly*, and a C Major scale in *Fly Like a Beagle*.

RUBY, MY DEERFLY

Track 21

Swing

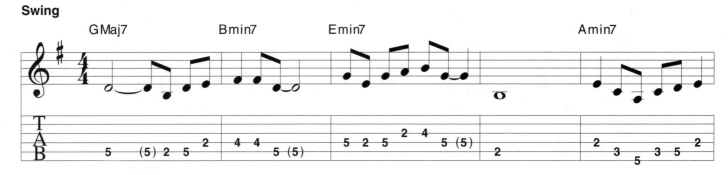

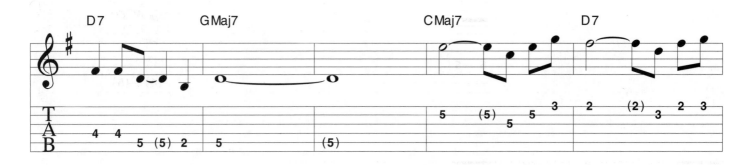

Leave out at the end.

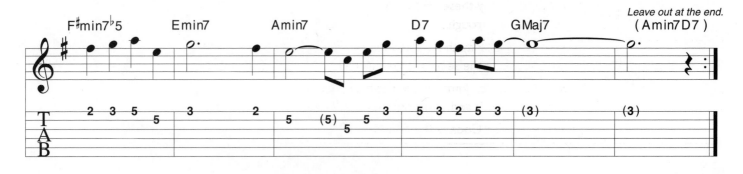

FLY LIKE A BEAGLE

Track 22

		= *First Ending.* Play these measures the first time through.
		= *Second Ending.* Play these measures instead of the first ending the second time through.
D.C. al Coda		= *Da Capo al Coda.* Jump to the beginning (*Capo* in Italian is "Head") and play until the *Coda* sign.
⊕		= *Coda sign.* The Coda is the conclusion.

Lesson 3A: More Major Chord Scales

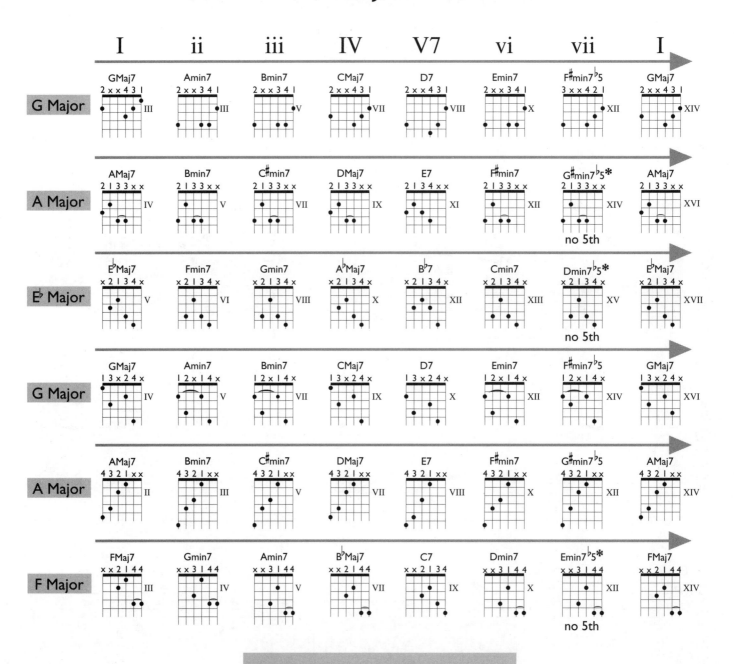

	I	ii	iii	IV	V7	vi	vii	I

* Note: Chords ii through vii will have the same spelling as the I chord when the scale is harmonized along a single string set. So, if the I chord is spelled with no 5th (R-3-7-3), the vii chord will have no ♭5 (R-♭3-♭7-♭3). This is an exceptional case, since we would usually want the ♭5 present to define the min7♭5 harmony.

Lesson 3B: Two More Tunes
Based on the Major Scale

Try these tunes on for size. Follow the procedure for learning a new tune outlined on page 60. Learn the melody in two octaves, learn two sets of chord voicings and be able to solo using the major scale. Use the E♭ Major scale for *Noisy Nights* and the F Major scale for *The Creature*. Have fun!

NOISY NIGHTS

Track 23

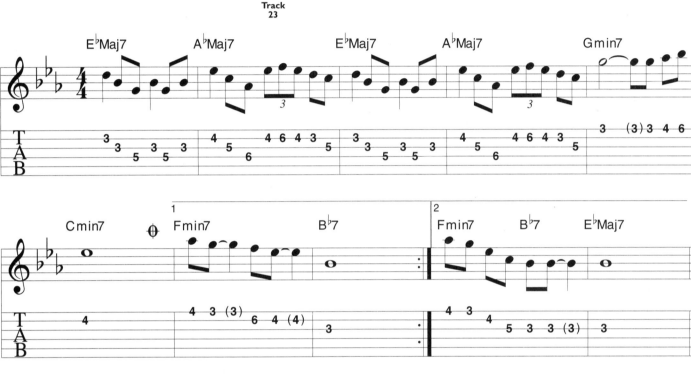

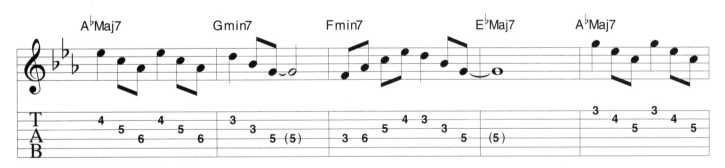

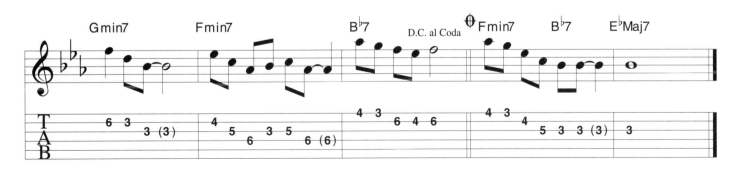

THE CREATURE

Lesson 4A: More Major Chord Scales

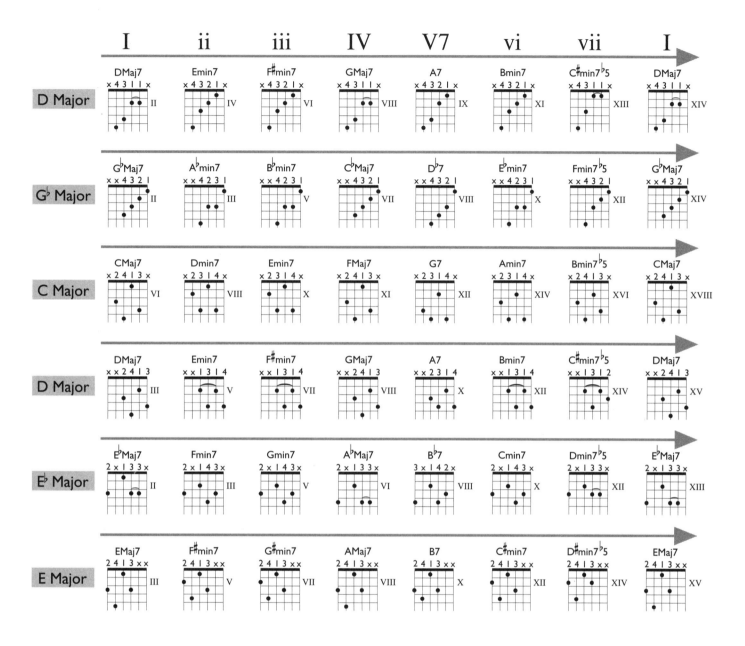

Lesson 4B: Two More Tunes Based on the Major Scale

Try these songs on for size. Use the procedure for learning a new song outlined on page 60. Improvise over *Julie in Wonderland* using the C Major scale, and use the D Major scale for *Samba de Shauna*.

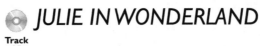

JULIE IN WONDERLAND

Track 25

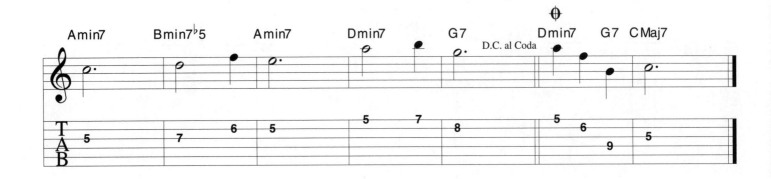

SAMBA DE SHAUNA

Track 26

CHAPTER 5

Lesson 1A: Roman Numerals and Transposition

There are two main reasons for the use of Roman numerals.

1. Communication. If someone is trying to explain a chord progression to you, it is easier to see the nature of the progression if they say, "ii-V-I in C, then iii-vi-ii-V-I in F, then ii-V-I in B♭" than if they rattled off a whole list of chord names. As you will see, many types of songs follow rather predictable patterns, and these patterns are usually described in Roman numerals.

2. Transposition. Transpose means to change the key. If you know your scales and the diatonic chords for those scales, transposing is no big deal. Learn all of your songs in Roman numerals. Then you will have learned the material in a "universal key." You can then simply "plug into" the actual key you want. Working on this now will save you much work (and possible embarrassment) later. Check out these examples and notice how the chords are different, but the progression stays the same:

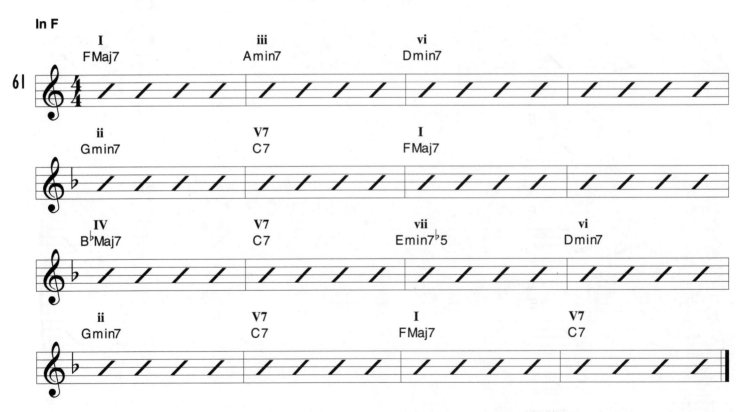

On the next page our progression appears in the keys of C and A♭ respectively.

In C

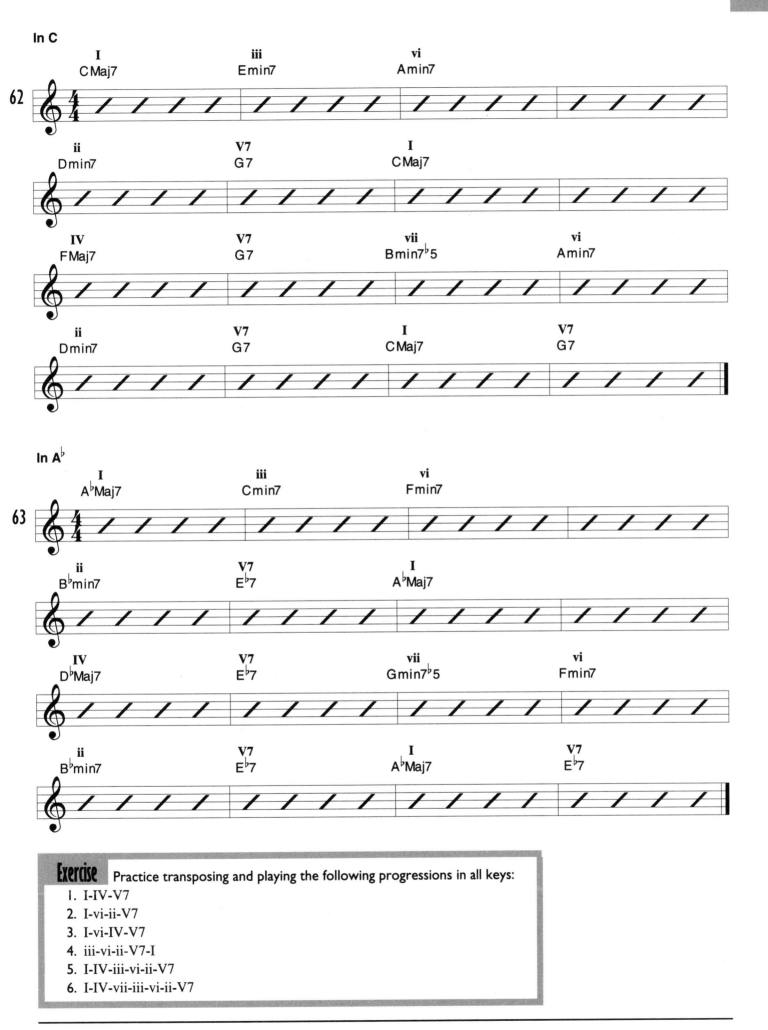

| I | iii | vi |
| CMaj7 | Emin7 | Amin7 |

62

| ii | V7 | I |
| Dmin7 | G7 | CMaj7 |

| IV | V7 | vii | vi |
| FMaj7 | G7 | Bmin7♭5 | Amin7 |

| ii | V7 | I | V7 |
| Dmin7 | G7 | CMaj7 | G7 |

In A♭

| I | iii | vi |
| A♭Maj7 | Cmin7 | Fmin7 |

63

| ii | V7 | I |
| B♭min7 | E♭7 | A♭Maj7 |

| IV | V7 | vii | vi |
| D♭Maj7 | E♭7 | Gmin7♭5 | Fmin7 |

| ii | V7 | I | V7 |
| B♭min7 | E♭7 | A♭Maj7 | E♭7 |

Exercise Practice transposing and playing the following progressions in all keys:

1. I-IV-V7
2. I-vi-ii-V7
3. I-vi-IV-V7
4. iii-vi-ii-V7-I
5. I-IV-iii-vi-ii-V7
6. I-IV-vii-iii-vi-ii-V7

Chapter 5—Lesson 1A: Roman Numerals and Transposition   **69**

Lesson 1B: Modes of the Major Scale—The Basics

Creating modes from scales is a way of generating new scales for improvising over various chords. To create a set of modes, you simply play the scale from a note other than the root and continue ascending for an octave.

Here is a C Major scale, which, by the way, is also known as the Ionian mode. If we played the notes in this scale from the note D, and continued until D appeared again, we would have created the D Dorian mode.

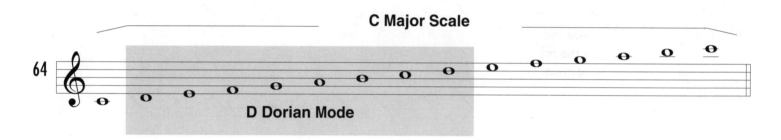

Each mode of the major scale corresponds to the diatonic chord that shares the same root. The C Ionian mode is used to improvise over CMaj7, the I chord. The D Dorian mode would be used over Dmin7, the ii chord. Here are the rest of the modes that we can generate from the C Major scale and their corresponding diatonic chords.

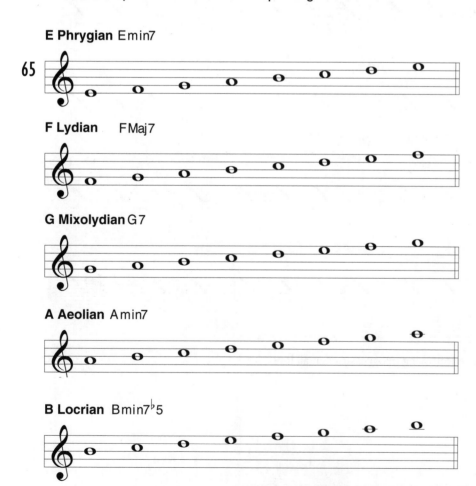

This works for all major scales and their diatonic chords. Here they are in G.

So far, the progressions in this book have been diatonic. As you play more advanced music you will find this situation to be less and less common. The modes of the major scale will help you improvise over chords in more complicated progressions that include some chords that may not be diatonic (natural to the key).

Exercise

We'll put these into practice soon, so you should to write out the modes for all the major scales and memorize their names.

G Ionian G Maj7

66

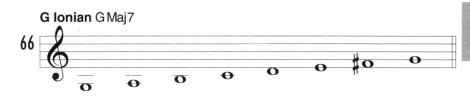

A Dorian A min7

B Phrygian B min7

C Lydian C Maj7

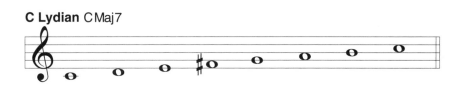

D Mixolydian D7

E Aeolian E min7

F♯ Locrian F♯min7♭5

Lesson 2A: More About Roman Numerals and Transposition

Life is easy when the chord progression you are transposing is completely diatonic, as in the previous examples. This will not be the usual case. Take a look at this progression:

$$\frac{4}{4}\ \text{CMaj7} \mid \text{E7} \mid \text{A7} \mid \text{Dmin7} \mid \text{E7} \mid \text{Amin7} \mid \text{D7} \mid \text{Dmin7}\ \text{G7}\parallel$$

CMaj7, Dmin7, Amin7 and G7 are all natural to the key of C, but E7, A7 and D7 are not. The chords that are natural to the key are indicated with Roman numerals, as usual. If the root of the chord belongs in the key, but the chord type is different than usual (for instance, it should be min7, but now it's 7), it is necessary to indicate the new chord type. It may also be necessary to change from lower case to upper case Roman numerals, or vice versa. For instance, in C: Emin7=iii, E7=III7. Or, Dmin7=ii, D7=II7). You may use sharp # and flat ♭ signs to show a non-diatonic root. For instance, in the key of C iii is Emin7, so E♭min7 would be ♭iii.

$$\frac{4}{4}\ \begin{array}{llllllll}\text{I} & \text{III7} & \text{VI7} & \text{ii} & \text{III7} & \text{vi} & \text{II7} & \text{ii} & \text{V7} \\ \text{CMaj7} & \text{E7} & \text{A7} & \text{Dmin7} & \text{E7} & \text{Amin7} & \text{D7} & \text{Dmin7} & \text{G7}\end{array}\parallel$$

You will often find songs having too many chords that fall outside of the key to use this system. When this occurs, check to see if a series of chords can be thought of as belonging to another key. You are then thinking of Roman numerals that are traveling through different keys. Check this out:

C: I   ii   V7   I   F: ii   V7   I
CMaj7 Dmin7 G7 CMaj7 | Gmin7 C7 FMaj7 |

C: I   ii   V7   I   VII7   E♭: ii   V7   C: ii   V7
CMaj7 Dmin7 G7 CMaj7 B7 | Fmin7 B♭7 | Dmin7 G7 ||

In this example we are using *parent key* thinking along with our usual thinking. The term *parent key* or *key center* refers to the major scale from which the chords were derived. Therefore, in the first two measures we are thinking of our parent key as C Major, so the progression is I-ii-V7-I. In measures three and four we would think of our parent key as F Major, so the progression is ii-V7-I. Measures five and six return us to the parent key of C. Our progression is now I-ii-V7-I-VII7. Notice that B7 is marked with an upper case Roman numeral, to show that it is not the usual B chord for the key of C, which would be Bmin7♭5 (vii). Next we used a combination of qualifiers and the new thinking in parent keys. Measure seven is ii-V7 in the parent key of E♭, and measure eight returns us to the key of C, where our progression is ii-V7.

A little hands-on experience will show you how automatic this kind of thinking can become. Don't put this off—you need to learn how to do this. You'll pick this up very rapidly if over the next few days you transpose four or five tunes into six different keys.

Lesson 2B: Modes of the Major Scale— Parallel-Approach Fingerings

There are numerous ways to think about and use the modes of the major scale. Many players like to think of them as separate scales apart from the major scale itself. The essence of this approach is to learn separate fingerings for each mode, rather than relating each mode back to its parent major scale. This is known as the "parallel-approach," and is a quite effective way of thinking. This book will also cover the "derivative approach," but you should realize that there are actually five separate approaches one could use. (These are covered in my *Guitar Mode Encyclopedia* published by the National Guitar Workshop and Alfred Music Publishing).

Here are two fingerings for each mode of the major scale. There are many more fingerings you could learn and this could take you months, or even years. In time it would be a very good idea for you to work up some more fingerings in various areas of the fingerboard.

D DORIAN

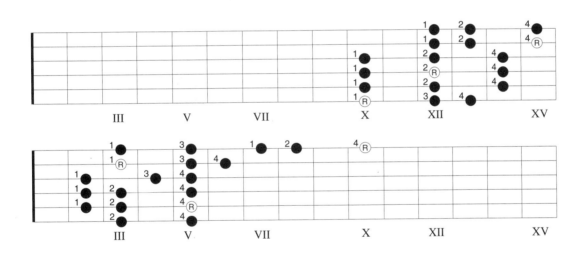

E PHRYGIAN

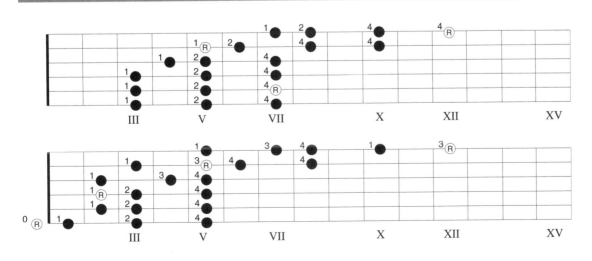

F LYDIAN

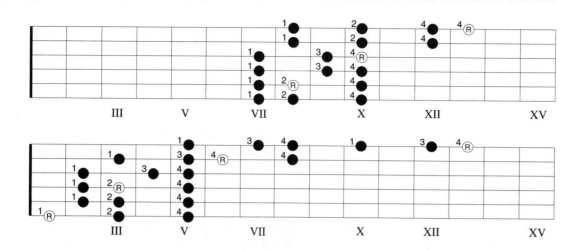

G MIXOLYDIAN

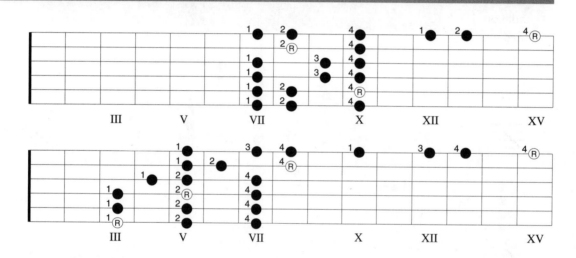

A AEOLIAN

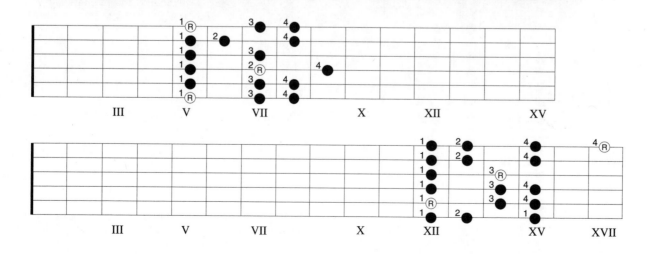

B LOCRIAN

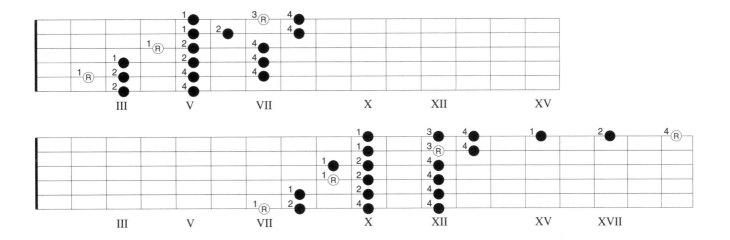

PRACTICE PROGRESSIONS

At first, it may be a good idea to repeat each measure of these chord progressions many times. This will help you get a handle on the fingerings for every mode, and enable you to move them around easily. You can record them to play over, or use the audio that is available with this book.

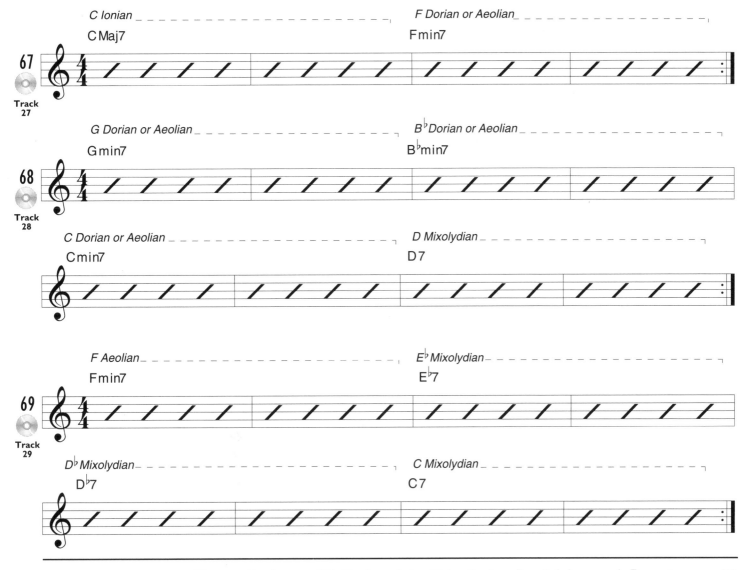

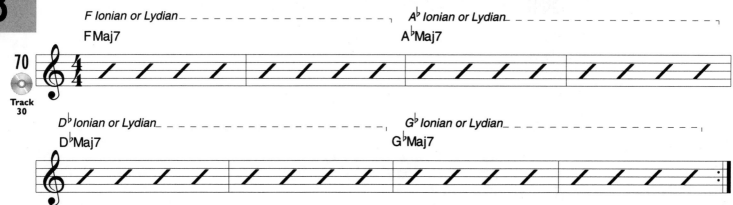

70
Track 30

F Ionian or Lydian _
FMaj7

A♭ Ionian or Lydian _
A♭Maj7

D♭ Ionian or Lydian _
D♭Maj7

G♭ Ionian or Lydian _
G♭Maj7

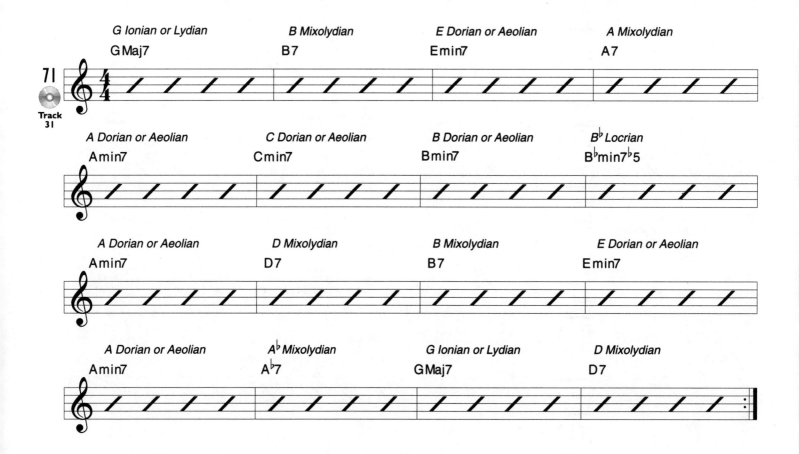

71
Track 31

| *G Ionian or Lydian* | *B Mixolydian* | *E Dorian or Aeolian* | *A Mixolydian* |
| GMaj7 | B7 | Emin7 | A7 |

| *A Dorian or Aeolian* | *C Dorian or Aeolian* | *B Dorian or Aeolian* | *B♭ Locrian* |
| Amin7 | Cmin7 | Bmin7 | B♭min7♭5 |

| *A Dorian or Aeolian* | *D Mixolydian* | *B Mixolydian* | *E Dorian or Aeolian* |
| Amin7 | D7 | B7 | Emin7 |

| *A Dorian or Aeolian* | *A♭ Mixolydian* | *G Ionian or Lydian* | *D Mixolydian* |
| Amin7 | A♭7 | GMaj7 | D7 |

Lesson 3A: Vertical Chord Scales

In all of the previous chord scales you have learned, the chords progressed up the fingerboard on a single string set, from lower to higher positions. This was valuable because it allowed you to see how each voice in each chord ascended scale-wise. It is also a good idea to learn chord scales in a vertical direction, across the string sets. This way you will learn all the diatonic chords in closer proximity. The examples on this page will use two adjacent string sets, as will Lesson 4A. Lesson 5A will use three string sets. Be sure to transpose all examples to every possible key.

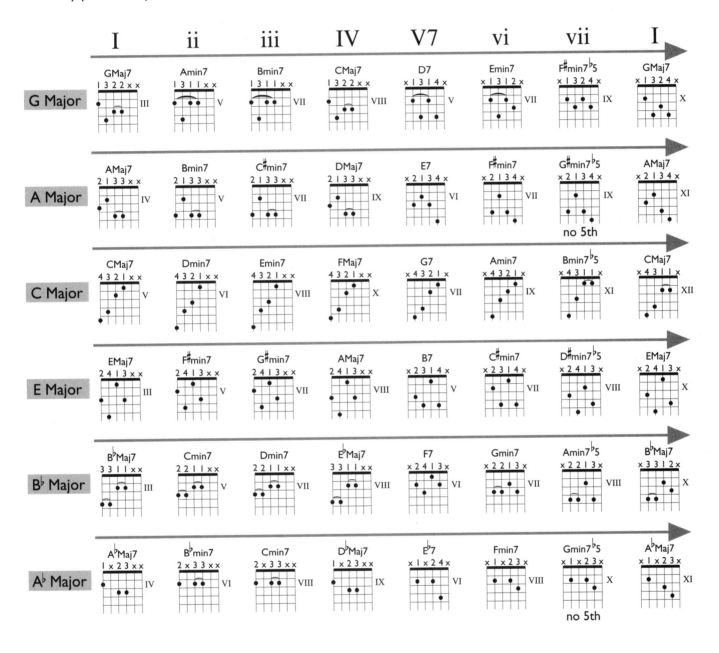

Lesson 3B: Modes of the Major Scale— Derivative Approach

In the previous two "B" lessons we started looking at the modes of the major scale. Lesson 1B focused on the basics of generating these modes. Lesson 2B talked about viewing these modes as separate scales with their own fingerings. One question most students have at this point is "Even though I understand the concept of creating modes, and have learned a few fingerings, aren't these just major scales that I'm playing?" The answer is yes! It's just that using different approaches to viewing the modes can actually create different sounds.

In the derivative approach, the player looks at a chord and decides to use a major scale from which it was produced. In some ways, this approach can be a faster way to learn the modes, although time should be spent thinking in terms of the parallel approach as well. In the derivative approach, when you see a Dmin7 chord, you might think: Dmin7 is the ii chord in the C Major scale, so if you use the C Major scale, but emphasize the D as the root, you are actually in the D Dorian mode. Dmin7 is the iii chord in the B♭ Major scale, so playing a B♭ Major scale, but stressing B♭ as the root, puts you in the D Phrygian mode. Or, Dmin7 is the vi chord in the F Major scale, so playing the F Major scale, emphasizing the D as the root, puts you in D Aeolian. Since you already know plenty of major scale fingerings, the derivative approach is a way to start using modes right away.

Since harmonizing any major scale always produces two Maj7 chords (I and IV), three min7 chords (ii, iii and vi), one dominant 7th chord (V7) and one min7♭5 chord (vii), it is safe to say:

1. Every Maj7 chord has two major scale choices to use for improvising.
2. Every min7 chord has three major scale choices to use for improvising.
3. Every dominant 7th chord has one major scale choice.
4. Every min7♭5 chord has one major scale choice.

Study this chart:

Chord	Scale Choice	Modal Sound
GMaj7	G Major (GMaj7 is the I chord)	G Ionian
	D Major (GMaj7 is the IV chord)	G Lydian
Fmin7	E♭ Major (Fmin7 is the ii chord)	F Dorian
	D♭ Major (Fmin7 is the iii chord)	F Phrygian
	A♭ Major (Fmin7 is the vi chord)	F Aeolian
A7	D Major (A7 is the V7 chord)	A Mixolydian
Dmin7♭5	E♭ Major (Dmin7♭5 is the vii chord)	D Locrian

Use the following progressions to gain an understanding of the derivative approach to the modes. Listen carefully to the difference in sound each mode produces over the same chord. You will probably enjoy some sounds right away. Others, you may have to grow into. Try not to make too much of a value judgment about the sounds various modes produce. Simply categorize. Context is everything. Knowing what sounds are available and where to find them is the whole point of this study. This will lead to a greater command over the overall effect of your improvised solos and your instrument in general.

Lesson 4A: More Vertical Chord Scales

Here is another set of vertical chord scales, this time on the middle and top string sets. Transpose these to several other keys.

	I	ii	iii	IV	V7	vi	vii	I
C Major	CMaj7 x 1 3 2 4 x III	Dmin7 x 1 3 1 2 x V	Emin7 x 1 3 1 2 x VII	FMaj7 x 1 3 2 4 x VIII	G7 x x 1 3 2 4 V	Amin7 x x 1 3 2 2 VII	Bmin7♭5 x x 1 3 3 3 IX	CMaj7 x x 1 3 3 3 X
E♭ Major	E♭Maj7 x 2 1 3 4 x V	Fmin7 x 2 1 3 4 x VI	Gmin7 x 2 1 3 4 x VIII	A♭Maj7 x 2 1 3 4 x X	B♭7 x x 2 1 3 4 VII	Cmin7 x x 3 1 4 4 VIII	Dmin7♭5 x x 3 1 4 4 X no 5th	E♭Maj7 x x 2 1 4 4 XII
D Major	DMaj7 x 4 3 1 1 x II	Emin7 x 4 3 2 1 x III	F#min7 x 4 3 2 1 x V	GMaj7 x 4 3 1 1 x VII	A7 x x 4 3 2 1 IV	Bmin7 x x 4 2 3 1 VI	C#min7♭5 x x 4 3 2 1 VIII	DMaj7 x x 4 3 2 1 X
F Major	FMaj7 x 2 2 1 4 x II	Gmin7 x 2 2 1 4 x III	Amin7 x 2 2 1 4 x V	B♭Maj7 x 2 2 1 4 x VII	C7 x x 1 1 1 2 V	Dmin7 x x 2 2 1 3 VI	Emin7♭5 x x 1 2 1 4 VIII	FMaj7 x x 1 1 1 4 X
G Major	GMaj7 2 x 1 3 3 x V	Amin7 2 x 1 4 3 x VII	Bmin7 2 x 1 4 3 x IX	CMaj7 2 x 1 3 3 x X	D7 x 3 x 1 4 2 VII	Emin7 x 2 x 1 4 3 IX	F#min7♭5 x 2 x 1 4 3 XI	GMaj7 x 2 x 1 4 3 XII
B♭ Major	B♭Maj7 x 2 4 1 3 x IV	Cmin7 x 2 3 1 4 x V	Dmin7 x 2 3 1 4 x VII	E♭Maj7 x 2 4 1 3 x IX	F7 x x 2 3 1 4 VI	Gmin7 x x 1 3 1 4 VIII	Amin7♭5 x x 1 3 1 2 X	B♭Maj7 x x 2 4 1 3 XI

Lesson 4B: Two Modal Tunes

During the 1960s many jazz artists started playing what is now termed "modal" music. Saxophonist John Coltrane, trumpeter Miles Davis and guitarist Gabor Szabo were at the forefront of this movement. Up until that time most jazz songs were characterized as having many chord changes traveling through many keys. Most jazz is still like this, but the modal movement added a new element to the style.

Modal tunes are usually based around very few chord changes, so improvisation is based on just a few scales. The melody is usually written in a single mode. Learning the following two tunes will help you get the feel for this style. After learning the melody and the chord changes, use the companion audio (or record the changes) and practice your modal improvisation.

NOSH 4 JOSH

Track 35

Use G Dorian (or think F Major scale) over Gmin7
Use A♭ Dorian (or think G♭ Major scale) over A♭min7

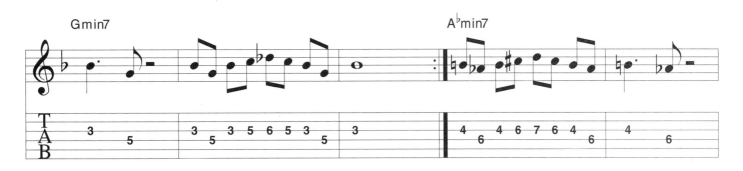

CHOCOLATE TUNA ENCHILADAS

Track 36

Use F Lydian (or think C Major scale) over FMaj7
Use A♭ Lydian (or think E♭ Major scale) over A♭Maj7
Use A Dorian (or think G Major scale) over Amin7

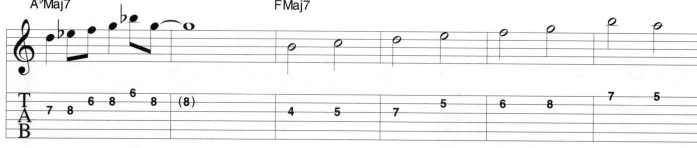

Lesson 5A: More Vertical Chord Scales

Here is the third set of vertical chord scales. By now you should have a firm grasp of this material. Try coming up with your own versions. There is not one "right way" to do this, and you will probably find ways that seem easier or more efficient to you. Experiment all you like, just make sure you always transpose your findings to several other keys.

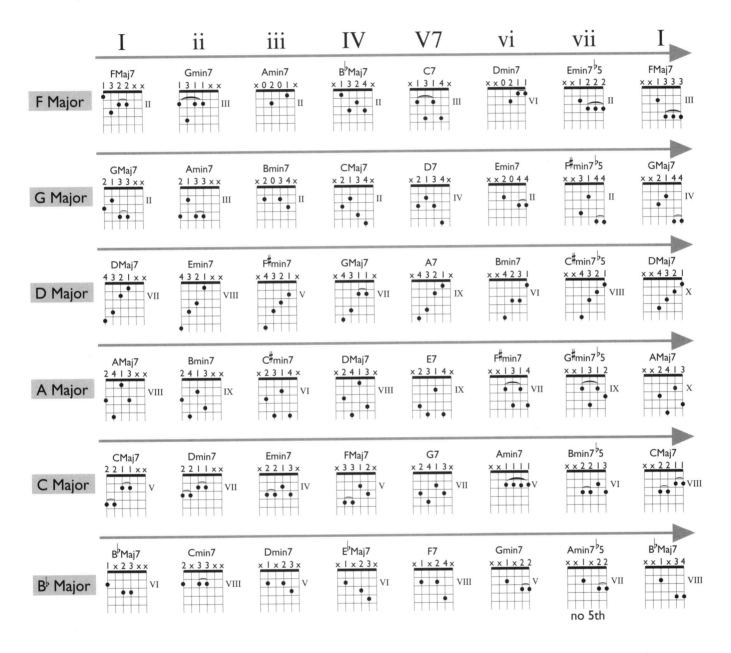

Lesson 5B: Two Modal/Diatonic Tunes

The tunes in this lesson contain situations where both diatonic thinking and modal thinking are necessary. When you have a tune that consists mainly of diatonic chords, use the major scale of the I chord. Then, when you get to a chord that is not natural to the key, switch to the modal approach.

MODELICIOUS

Track 37

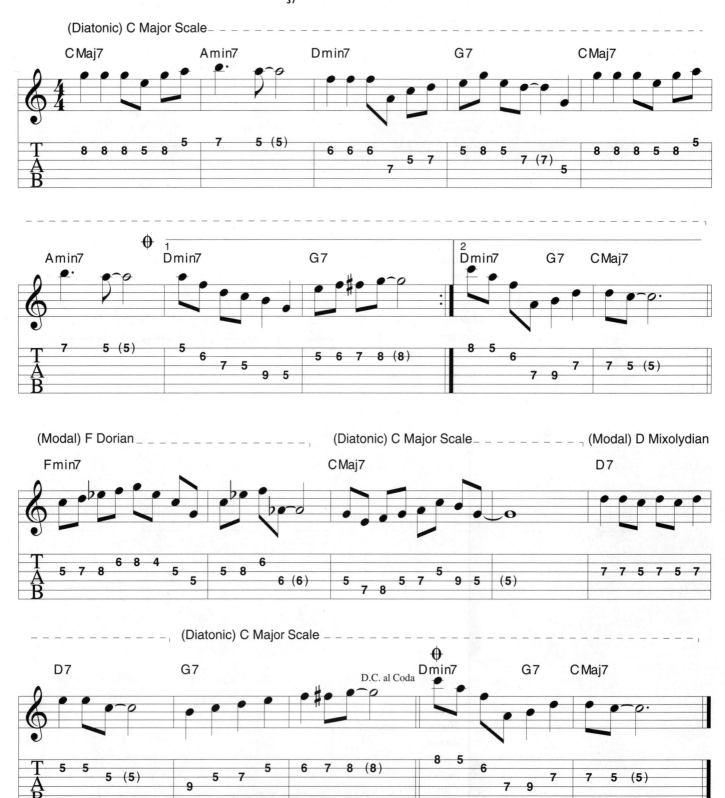

BLUE TOFU

Track 38

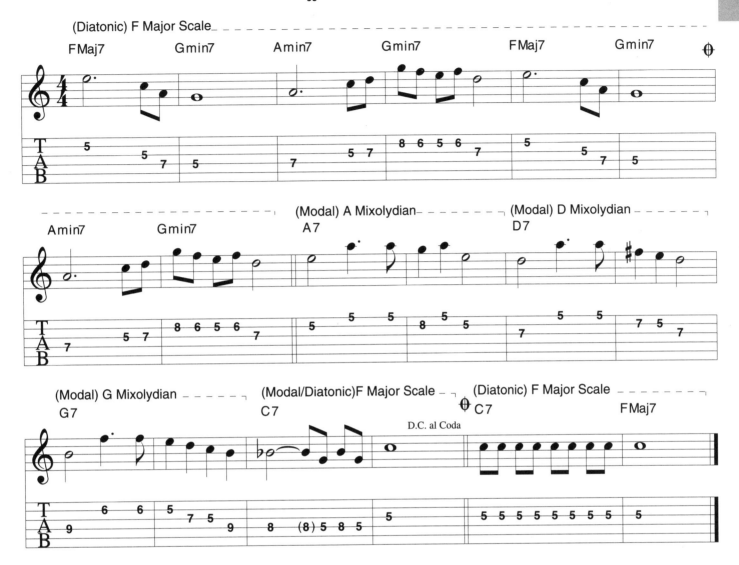

Gábor Szabó (1936–1982), the
Hungarian jazz guitarist, was
famous for mixing jazz, pop-rock
and his native Hungarian music. He
performed with artists such as Ron
Carter, Paul Desmond, Lena Horne
and Bobby Womack.

PHOTO • COURTESY INSTITUTE OF JAZZ STUDIES

How Jazz Works

Once you fully understand the basic format of jazz, it will never be confusing. A jazz arrangement generally follows this order:

1. One or more of the lead instruments in a group play the actual melody of the song (the *head*) while the rest of the band accompanies.
2. After the melody is played once or twice through, each band member takes turns improvising a completely new melody based on the chord changes (or "changes") of the original melody.
3. After all the musicians solo, the original melody is once again played and the song is ended.

There are many variations of this, but you get the general idea.

A good jazz guitarist must be able to:

1. Play a song's melody in two or three octaves.

2. Play the chord changes in several areas of the fingerboard.

3. Improvise freely through the chord changes.

You never really "finish" studying jazz. There is always more to know, and really, this process and a sense of musical growth is what should bring most of the enjoyment. The important thing is to take your time and enjoy the journey.

Technique

BASIC LEFT AND RIGHT HAND TECHNIQUE

What is good technique? If you ask ten guitar teachers, you will probably receive ten different answers! Teachers teach what works for them. While nobody can claim to have the only "right way," the basic idea is to train our hands to work so well that we can concentrate on musical content. You need to spend time working on technique in practice so that you don't have to think about it during performance. It can take many years to get to that point.

The funny thing is, good technical habits don't necessarily feel good or natural at first. Only after time do things start to feel comfortable. Don't let this be a stumbling block. The same is true for practicing certain techniques. Spend some weeks or months working with a new technique before deciding if it is useful to you.

Keep this in mind while reading on the top of page 87. It is a list of what I find to be the most important aspects of good left hand technique.

1. Position your thumb behind the neck in "hitch-hiking" position pointing away from you (not around the neck). The idea here is to keep the back of the hand and the forearm in a straight line. There should be little or no bend in the wrist.

2. Keep your palm off the neck. This will help keep your wrist straight.

3. Use correct fingerings. Good fingering is not necessarily based on immediate comfort but rather what will make your entry into and exit from a particular note or chord easier and more nimble. I believe the fingerings given in this book will help in this area, although it is certainly possible to find good variations.

4. Place your fingers directly behind the frets instead of in the middle. This will produce the best sound and you won't have to press as hard. Intonation (playing in tune) will be better too.

5. Release excess tension and let the elbow hang loosely by your side.

6. Keep your fingers hovering as close to the strings as possible when they are not being used. Economy of motion is very important for fluency.

There are many ways of picking with the right hand. For now you should concentrate on *alternate picking*, which is simply alternating down-strokes and up-strokes. The motion should come from the forefinger and thumb along with the wrist. Small movements will allow you to play more rapidly. Practice on open strings, as well as with the scales you are learning. Be sure your up-strokes and down-strokes have the same volume and tone. Working on this will ensure a smooth and lyrical sound. This takes time to develop, so have patience and work on it often. You will find that your technical ability is not static—it is either improving or deteriorating. Maintenance is very important.

POSTURE

In spite of what most of us have seen in concert and on television, good posture while playing the guitar is important. Slouching, reclining or wearing the instrument around your knees greatly diminishes your ability to play quickly and accurately. True, there are many great players with less than perfect posture but some of these players are good in spite of their posture—not because of it. Maybe they would improve dramatically if they changed the way they sit, stand or hold the guitar.

Always use a strap. If you are using your hands to hold onto the instrument, you will lose some playing ability. Let the strap do the holding. Adjust your strap so the guitar is positioned at the same level whether you are sitting or standing. This way, your technique will be consistent.

Try to practice in the same chair every day. Sitting on the bed one day, on the floor the next day and on a stool yet another day will lead to inconsistent progress.

Sit up straight and hold the body of the guitar against your body. Don't lay the instrument on your lap. Relax both arms from the shoulder all the way down to your fingertips. Don't push the neck out in front of you. Pull the neck in so that when you look down slightly to your left, the fingerboard is right under your nose.

If you are sitting, it is OK to cross your legs, or keep both feet flat on the floor. If your guitar sits on top of your right thigh, learn to tap your left foot, or vice versa.

All of these things really make a difference in letting you play to your fullest potential.

BASIC STRUMMING TECHNIQUE

The key to playing a solid groove is in the right hand strumming technique. The idea is to set and maintain a tempo and a beat that does not fluctuate during the song.

Step 1. Imagine or try to hear the song in your mind's ear before you start to play. This will keep you from beginning the song too fast or too slowly, which is a common problem for inexperienced players.
Step 2. Tap your foot to capture what you hear in your mind.
Step 3. After you are sure of the tempo, start playing, keeping a firm hold on whatever pulse you have established.

Hold the pick firmly between your thumb and forefinger, let the other fingers float over the top of the guitar, and let the motion come from the wrist—not the arm or elbow. Practice both playing evenly and with accented strums. Experiment with the *timbres* (colors or tonal effects) produced by playing near the neck or near the bridge and all points in between. Also practice strumming loudly and softly. Learn to have complete control of your right hand. This will come in handy when we start discussing various comping styles later in this series.

FINGERSTYLE CHORDS

Most guitar students place about ninety percent of their attention and efforts on their left hand. Limitations in their playing are usually blamed on some fault of the left hand only. The truth of the matter is that, with the exception of hammer-ons, pull-offs, trills and other decorative devices, it usually takes two hands to produce one note. Therefore, equal attention should be paid to both hands at all times.

With single-note playing, most guitarists have left hands that are faster than their right hands. When both hands are fully developed, the right hand actually "powers" the left. In chordal playing there are numerous ways to activate the strings.

There are actually many styles of fingerstyle playing. In the traditional methods the thumb and first three fingers are used. In certain folk styles, the thumb and two fingers work pretty well. I use all four fingers and the thumb. The chart on the right shows the right hand finger designations:

thumb = *p*
first finger = *i*
middle finger = *m*
third finger = *a*
pinkie = *c*

Generally, *p* controls the sixth and fifth strings, while *i* is on the fourth, *m* is on the third, *a* is on the second and *c* is on the first. If *p* is playing on the fifth or fourth strings, *i* plays the third, *m* plays the second and *a* plays the first. Different tunes and exercises will require some shifting of hand placement. It pays to be flexible.

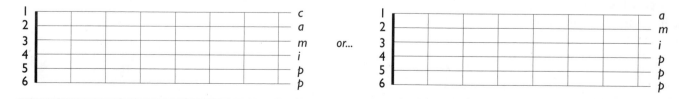

One advantage of playing fingerstyle chords is that you don't have to worry about muting strings or barring over a note that is unwanted in the chord. You pluck only the tones you want to hear. Playing fingerstyle also allows you to lower or raise the volume of individual notes in a chord. One other consideration is that playing fingerstyle is the only way to sound the voices simultaneously. When strumming with a pick or your thumb the notes will always appear one after the other. With fingerstyle techniques you sound harmonies much like a keyboard instrument—all the notes of a chord at the same moment. There are many great chords that are impossible to play with a pick. Spend time working on right hand techniques. It will pay off by giving you greater flexibility and versatility. It will allow you to play many more styles of music.

To play single-note lines fingerstyle, most jazz players either alternate their first two fingers, as in classical guitar technique. Some players alternate their thumb and second fingers. There are many good classical guitar books available. These should investigated by those wishing to pursue these styles of picking. I recommend *Pumping Nylon* by Scott Tennant, available at your local music store, as a great resource of information about classical guitar technique.

PICK AND FINGERS TECHNIQUE

In addition to using a pick and developing fingerstyle technique, it is also a good idea to practice using a pick along with your three remaining fingers. Most players do this once in awhile, and for many it is their primary way of playing.

Usually the pick is held between *p* and *i* fingers and takes care of the sixth, fifth and fourth strings while *m* covers the third, *a* covers the second and *c* handles the first.

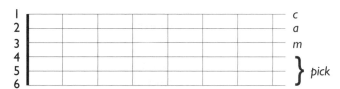

The advantage to this technique is that it allows you to switch from fingerstyle to using a pick with very little effort. When playing strictly fingerstyle, you either have to palm the pick, which can interfere with your right hand technique, or put it somewhere else (like in your mouth). The constant switching can be a hindrance. The only disadvantage is that you are pretty much limited to playing four-note chords, since two of your fingers are occupied with holding the pick. Like almost everything else with the guitar it is best to learn all techniques instead of relying on just one or two. This way you will be prepared for any musical situation that comes your way.

Practice

THE VALUE OF PRACTICING SLOWLY

A lot of students, especially at the beginning of their guitar studies, are very anxious to learn to play fast. While it is important to be able to play rapidly, it is even more beneficial to play accurately. Practicing something fast rarely leads to perfection, but working on accuracy always leads to the ability to play faster. You should never practice anything faster than you can play correctly. In other words, if you make a mistake, you are practicing too fast. Always.

Slow repetitions of what you are trying to learn is the way you program your brain for accuracy. When you make mistakes while practicing, you are programming the idea that it is OK to play sloppily and inconsistently. If you can play something twenty-five times in a row without a mistake, it's time to start working on speed and dexterity—but not until then. Playing fast has more to do with how well you know the "targets" you're aiming for than it does actual physical prowess. When you hear a great guitarist, you're hearing someone who has the patience and determination to work slowly and accurately.

LEARNING DIFFICULT CHORDS
AND CHANGING CHORDS

If you are having difficulty playing a chord, try moving your thumb around to different positions in behind the neck. Sometimes the slightest move can make all the difference.
If you are having trouble producing a good sound because of a difficult stretch:

1. Finger the chord as best you can by "relaxing" into it. Never try to force it. It is usually easier to plant your third and fourth fingers first and stretch with your first finger.
2. Hold the chord for a slow count of twenty.
3. Release slowly.

Repeat these three steps as many times as you want. Sometimes   chords will get gradually easier, but I find that most of the time the chord will suddenly "snap" into place. This will also take time so the key word here is patience.

When having difficulty switching from one chord to the next, stop and look at what each finger is doing during the switch. Practice moving each finger separately from the first chord to the second. Start with the first finger, then move on to the second, then the third and then the fourth. Close your eyes and experience how it feels to move from one string to the other. What is the distance covered? What do the strings feel like? Are you moving up or down the fingerboard? How far? Are you remaining on the same fret or string with any of your fingers? Be conscious of the actions you are trying to learn. The ideal move consists of all your fingers exiting the previous chord at the same time and landing on the following chord simultaneously. Until you can reach that ideal, try using one finger as a "pivot" finger, landing first to get yourself situated and letting the remaining fingers follow shortly after. Some classical guitar instructors teach that these movements should be learned like a "choreography" for the fingers, or like a "play" for a football team.

When learning a new chord form, always check to make sure that all of the voices in the chord are sounding. Sometimes students think they are sounding all the notes in a chord, but in reality they are accidentally muting one or more of the strings. Always check—what you get used to hearing, you will perceive as correct.

LEARNING SCALES TWO STRINGS AT A TIME

Instead of trying to learn an entire fingering at one time, many guitarists learn their patterns on only two strings at a time.

First practice the notes of a scale on only the sixth and fifth strings. Do this over and over until it feels very comfortable. The next step would be to practice the notes on only the fifth and fourth strings. When this feels easy, practice the pattern on the sixth, fifth and fourth strings over and over. Then practice the pattern on the fourth and third strings, later adding the notes on the sixth and fifth. Follow this pattern across to the first string. This makes learning new fingerings much less overwhelming and helps to see it with greater depth. This practice technique also works well with licks and arpeggios and will help you find more melodic possibilities.

THE VALUE OF LOCKED POSITIONS

For a long time, guitarists have learned to play by first learning the notes in open (or first) position, and later learning some scale fingerings that are moveable up and down the neck. In reality, most students could hardly wait to start playing "up the neck" because they never really saw their guitar idols play in the first position. Open position was definitely considered "kid stuff," especially by rock and jazz guitarists. Guitar playing as we know it is still in its infancy and new ideas are cropping up all the time. Methods that work well for some guitarists don't always get results for others. One objective of this series is to enable you to view and utilize the fingerboard in a variety of ways. With this in mind, we will deal with *locked positions* as well as single-string positions and open position.

Scales, arpeggios and licks are in *locked position* when they contain no open strings. This allows them to be moved around the fingerboard and played in other keys. The advantages to locked position ideas are that you can transpose them fairly easily and quickly. The disadvantage is that it keeps you stuck in *vertical* thinking. By vertical, I mean across the strings. Vertical thinking is not a bad thing. It's just that when you use it to the exclusion of horizontal thinking (for instance, playing along a single string and including open position) it can severely limit your improvisational ideas. After you get used to thinking in open and single string positions, you will find that your ideas will take on dramatic changes.

The biggest advantage to playing scales in locked positions is that, when using the six major scale fingerings shown earlier in this book, no matter what position you are in you can play in eleven different keys without shifting. This is really useful when you have to improvise through many key centers rapidly. We will be working with this concept a bit in the following books in this series. We define a position as the span of six frets. Your first and fourth fingers cover two frets and your second and third fingers each cover one. The following diagrams show the starting notes, or roots, of all the keys you can play in when in third and seventh position. With this in mind, starting at the third fret, you can play in all the keys indicated in the diagram at the top of page 92.

LOCKED POSITION KEYS IN THIRD AND SEVENTH POSITION

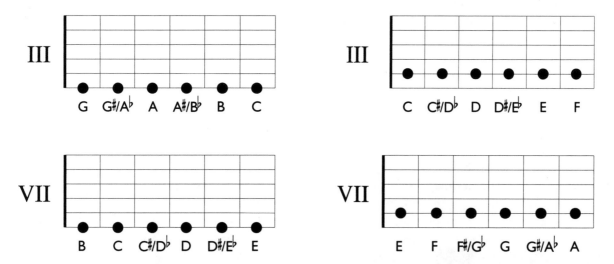

Note: there will always be duplication of one key when playing in one six fret area. There will always be one key *not* in position will be found one fret down on the sixth string or one fret up on the fifth string. It is a good idea to practice your scales in all positions like this.

PRACTICING THE MAJOR SCALES

By now, you should be realizing just how important the major scales are. Not only is it essential that you understand these scales, you must also work on getting from one scale to another physically. If you have been working on the six fingerings shown in this book, you are probably getting fairly proficient. Perhaps you are finding that drilling the scales can be tedious. Practicing scales is something you will probably do the rest of your life, so you need to come up with ways to keep it interesting. Here are some ideas.

1. Practice scales chromatically. Simply start the scale at the lowest fret possible. Play from the lowest note to the highest and back down. Move up one fret and do it again. Go all the way up the fingerboard this way, and then back down.
2. Practice the scales a whole step apart. Start the scale on the first fret and play it up and down. Then, skip the second fret and start the scale at the third fret. Continue the process of skipping very other fret. Once you have done this up and down the finger board, repeat the process starting on the second fret.
3. Practice the scales a minor 3rd apart. This is similar to the last idea except you are starting the scale two frets apart instead of skipping just one fret.
4. Practice the scales a 4th apart. Start with C, and then play F, B♭, E♭, A♭, D♭, G♭, B, E, A, D and finally G.
5. Practice the scales a 5th apart. Start with G and then play D, A, E, B, G♭, D♭, A♭, E♭, B♭, F and finally C.
6. All of the above ideas can be practiced another way as well: alternating ascending and descending scales. In other words, if you are practicing chromatically, you would first play the ascending scale, then move up to the next fret and play the descending scale. Move up again and ascend. Move up again and descend, and proceed up and down the fingerboard in this manner. The same approach should be used with whole steps, minor 3rds, 4ths and 5ths.

7. Instead of practicing the same fingering up and down the fingerboard all the time, it is a good idea to practice all the fingerings you know in one position. If you are on the first fret, play the F scale (6/1), then play the B♭ scale (5/1), then G♭ (6/2), then B (5/2), then A♭ (6/4) and finally D♭ (5/4). Proceed up and down the fingerboard, moving your hand one fret at a time.

8. Practice the scale with melodic patterns. Once you have learned and memorized a scale fingering, practicing it over and over can be a real waste of time. Pick a new melodic pattern each week and work with it.

9. Practice your scales in different *feels* and time signatures. You will eventually play what you practice in your solos. If you only practice with certain feels, your solos will always sound the same. Listen to different kinds of jazz to get ideas for different rhythms. Swing feels, straight eighth, Latin and rock rhythms are common ones that you want to get to know. Also experiment with 3/4, 4/4, 2/4, and 6/8 meters.

These ideas should also be applied to every scale you learn!

LIMITING RHYTHMIC OPTIONS

When learning to improvise over a new progression, most players will utilize a technique I call "limiting rhythmic options." During the first few passes through the progression, they will play with only whole notes. When comfortable with this they will use only half notes, then all quarter notes and finally a steady stream of eighth notes. This technique will help you really hear how the notes in a scale behave against the background chords. It will also help you to break out of finger patterns that you automatically fall into and let you use more of the rhythmic tools that are available. Later on, when working with very complex chord progressions, this technique will help you learn to find your way through rapidly changing tonal centers. Make limiting rhythmic options a regular way of practicing whenever you learn new material and you will make much faster progress and help to keep your creativity alive.

USING MELODIC PATTERNS

Melodic patterns are short melodies that are repeated from each note in a scale. (You will find examples of these in the "B" lessons in Chapter 2 of this book.) If you improvise using only melodic patterns, your solos will end up sounding like exercises. Used in the right places, melodic patterns can make your solos sound much more mature. Here are three ways you can apply these in your solos:

1. Use them as filler. Let's face it: we're human and sometimes the ideas just don't flow as easily as we would like them to. Using a melodic pattern during these moments will provide an easy way to fill a few bars with something melodically interesting while you are waiting for your next flash of inspiration.

2. Use them to connect other ideas together. If you play an idea in one area of the fingerboard and then get an idea that will occur in another area, you can use a melodic pattern to work your way over from the first idea to the second. This creates smooth, longer lines that are a sign of musical maturity.

3. Playing these patterns will expose you to the sounds that are possible within each scale. This is perhaps the most important reason to study melodic patterns. Each pattern breaks up the scale in ways you might not otherwise discover. This will expand your range of melodic possibilities. In the future, once you have learned and studied many melodic patterns, you will find yourself combining interesting melodic bits from one pattern with parts of another. You will start to realize that improvising melodies is an art that has no limit.

Use different patterns with the different scale fingerings you are learning so that your ideas change in your solos as you switch fingerings. Be sure to practice these in all available octaves on your instrument. Don't forget to do this in all twelve keys. Melodic patterns should be practiced with every scale you ever learn. This will help you master every scale's melodic possibilities.

Soloing

FORM: USING AN OPENING, BODY AND CONCLUSION

You now have a working knowledge of how the major scale is applied over diatonic chord progressions. Be sure to supplement the songs and exercises in this book with other songs from different sources. Try to work in all keys. The time you invest in this work will pay off in countless ways in terms of knowing your instrument and in your ultimate freedom as an improviser.

It is quite normal at this point to make comments like "I'm hitting all the right notes, but my solos don't really sound very interesting," or "all my solos sound like exercises and scales." Remember that there is a lot more to improvising besides knowing what notes to play against what chords. There is a wealth of information to absorb, and it does take time. Your patience will truly pay off. You can think of learning to improvise in terms of two very broad areas. They are: 1) technically, what scale and other devices work in different harmonic situations, and 2) how to encourage your own creativity, or how to come up with valid musical ideas.

One way to start playing more creatively is to think of your solos in terms of form. People tend to enjoy music that seems to start somewhere and go someplace. Random playing will bore your audience. If you want people to listen to your solos you need to grab their attention first. This is what the *opening* is all about.

Opening:
Start your solos with something that is easy for the listener to follow, or something startling, or something that is too soft or too loud. Maybe start with silence—that will always command attention. The opening is the time to play sparsely, to explore your ideas and moods and to see what your accompaniment is going to do. After you have set the tone for your solo it is time to build the *body* of your solo.

Body:
The body usually gets a little busier to develop themes you have initiated. This is the time to make your lines longer and to use melodic patterns or licks, and maybe change register, timbre or dynamics. Generally, this would be the longest part of your solo. It should culminate in the *conclusion*.

Conclusion:
The conclusion lets your listeners know the solo is ending, that you have made your statement, and now it's time to go. Players will sometimes save their "flash" element for this part of their solo. The use of repetition here is particularly helpful for adding intensity.

Many players see the opening, body and conclusion format as a way to control the contour of their solo as well. Maybe the opening is in the lower register leading to the body in the middle register and finally going to the higher register for the climactic conclusion. You could start very softly and end very loud or vice-versa. These form ideas are only suggestions and are not carved in stone. Listen to other player's forms and experiment!

FORM BASED ON MOTIF AND VARIATION

A motif is a short musical phrase. For instance, it can be a lick, a spontaneous idea, or a melodic pattern. For our purposes, a motif will mean a short phrase that becomes a *theme* in your solo. This theme becomes the basis for repetition or variation.

The concept of *variation on a theme* has many different meanings. If you have established a theme in your solo, examples of variation would include 1) maintaining the rhythmic figure but changing the pitches of the notes, or 2) maintaining the pitches of the notes and changing the rhythmic structure.

THE USE OF REPETITION IN YOUR SOLOS

Another element that is helpful in making your solos more interesting is the use of repetition. A phrase that is repeated over and over gives your listeners something to "hang on" to. When you never repeat a note or phrase, your solo can ramble. Sometimes this is the desired effect, but most good soloists employ repetition in their solos. Repetition also causes tension and keeps the listener's attention. Breaking the repetition eases the tension and resolution is achieved. This tension/release concept is central in almost all forms of improvisation and composition. A good solo is often the result of a tasteful treatment of tension and release.

Repetition tends to build intensity. This is why some players save this technique for the conclusion of their solo. There are many ways of achieving this effect. Sometimes you can fit a repetitive phrase through many chord changes. Sometimes it works better over static chord vamps (repetitions). Experiment to see what you like.

A guitarisitic approach to repetition is the use of scale/finger patterns. Repeat scale passages on adjacent strings (or skip strings) over and over. Below are some examples of this using this G Major scale fingering:

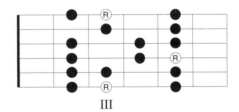

III

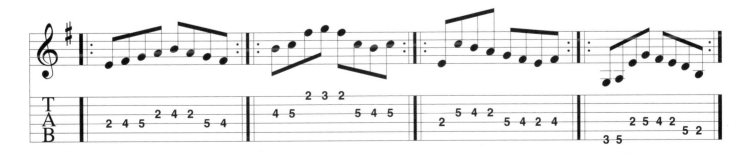

TAG ENDING (AFTERWORD)

You should realize that the skills you have been exposed to will take a while to master. Before moving on, you should be able to play all the tunes in this book. This means being comfortable playing the melodies in two or three octaves; playing chord changes in at least two areas of the fingerboard; improvising solos that reflect your understanding of the major scale and its modes; and melodic patterns with openings, bodies and conclusions. Strive for good tone and technique. Keep good time. These are some of the areas of study that all jazz musicians work on. Welcome to the club!

It is be a good idea to purchase one of the many jazz "fake-books" now available. A "fake" book is a very large anthology of standard jazz tunes. You can learn songs from that book using the same procedures you learned the ones in this book with. This would give you extra practice, and help you learn the jazz repertoire at the same time. Many of the tunes might be a little difficult at the beginning, but with further study you'll be swingin' in no time.

Try to play with as many other musicians as you can. This is of great value and cannot be overstressed. Listen to lots of music—there is quality in all styles, so don't be a jazz snob, you will only be limiting yourself. Listen to jazz played on other instruments as well. You may be surprised by what you can adapt to guitar. Most of all, enjoy what you are playing. There is a lot of work to do, so take your time and have fun.

Below, you'll find a list of guitarists you should hear. Listen to them and enjoy.

GUITARISTS

Kenny Burrell
Larry Carlton
Charlie Christian
John Collins
Al Dimeola
Joe Diorio
Herb Ellis
Ron Eschete
Tal Farlow
Bruce Foreman
Frank Gambale
Mick Goodrick
Ted Greene
Scott Henderson

Allan Holdsworth
Barney Kessel
Steve Khan
Pat Martino
John McLaughlin
Wes Montgomery
Oscar Moore
Joe Pass
Emily Remler
John Scofield
Django Reinhardt
Howard Roberts
Mike Stern
Gabor Szabo
George Van Eps

INTERMEDIATE JAZZ GUITAR

TABLE OF CONTENTS

00

Track
01

Companion online audio is included with this book to make learning easier and more enjoyable. The symbol shown on the left appears next to every example in the book that features an MP3 track. Use the MP3s to ensure you're capturing the feel of the examples and interpreting the rhythms correctly. The track number below the symbol corresponds directly to the example you want to hear (example numbers are above the icon). All the track numbers are unique to each "book" within this volume, meaning every book has its own Track 1, Track 2, and so on. (For example, *Beginning Jazz Guitar* starts with Track 1, as does *Intermediate jazz Guitar, Mastering Jazz Guitar: Chord/Melody* and *Mastering Jazz Guitar: Improvisation*.) Track 1 for each book will help you tune your guitar.

See page 1 for instructions on how to access the online audio.

INTRODUCTION

Welcome to the *Intermediate* section of *The Complete Jazz Guitar Method*. The format is the same as the *Beginning* section: each chapter is divided into lessons and each lesson is comprised of two sections. The "A" section of every lesson deals with chord work and harmonic concepts, while the "B" section contains information about single-line improvisation. The CODA section at the end of *Intermediate Jazz Guitar* discusses technique and a variety of other areas of interest to jazz guitar students.

To get the most out of the *Intermediate* section, you should already be familiar with major and minor pentatonic scales, triads and chords with extensions (such as 9ths, 11ths and 13ths), transposition, basic diatonic harmony, the modes of the major scale and melodic patterns. You don't need to be an expert in all of these areas, but a firm grasp of the concepts will certainly help you get through this section more easily.

Remember, it is important to supplement the information throughout this book with lessons, practice, and other instructional books and videos. Also, playing with others is very important for your development.

I wish you lots of joy as you absorb this information. I hope this book will help you find the self-expression you are looking for through music and the guitar.

CHAPTER 1

Lesson 1A: The *ii-V7-I* Progression

If you have been playing blues or rock guitar for any length of time, you should be quite familiar with the I-IV-V7 progression. It is the harmonic basis for countless songs and arrangements in many styles of music. In jazz, the ii-V7-I is the most important chord progression. The ii-V7-I progression is so important, and so common, because its sound establishes the key of the I chord.

In order to understand this more fully it might be helpful to think of the I chord in any key as a giant magnet. All of the diatonic chords in its key have varying levels of attraction back to it. For instance, in the key of C, if you play a G7 (V7) chord by itself, your ear feels unsatisfied. When you follow that G7 chord with a C Major chord (I) there is a feeling of resolution or completeness. The ii-V7-I progression implies the key center in a very powerful way because of the harmonic momentum set up by the ii and V7 chords, and the "pull" of the I chord on them. All chords eventually "want" to return to I, but they also have an attraction to other chords in the key (and sometimes outside the key) as well. The following chart shows the most common chord movements.

Chord	Attraction
I	Establishes key center
ii	Moves to V7 or $^\flat$ii
iii	Moves to vi or $^\flat$iii
IV	Moves to V7 or I
V7	Moves to I
vi	Moves to ii or $^\flat$vi
vii	Moves to I

Many songs in the standard jazz repertoire consist of various ii-V7-I progressions traveling through many keys. We will call these "traveling ii-V7-I's." It is important to note that the ii and the V7 chord will still establish the key center regardless of whether the I chord is present or not. As you will see, this is a common situation. The following chord progression is based on *"Tune Up"* by Miles Davis, and illustrates the idea of the traveling ii-V7-I. The circled letters indicate the established key center.

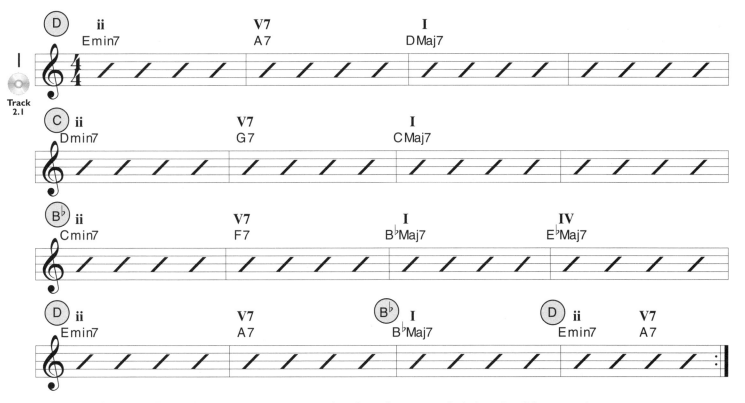

Track
2.1

Any and all chords in a ii-V7-I progression can be altered or extended. It will still be considered a ii-V7-I. For instance, Dmin9-G11-CMaj13 would still be considered a ii-V7-I in C. As long as the roots are a perfect 4th apart and the qualities appear as minor, dominant and major respectively, a ii-V7-I exists.

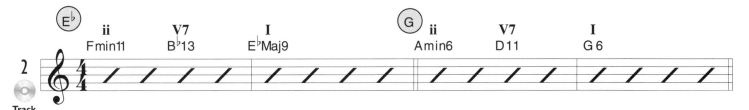

Track
2.2

Since so many songs consist of traveling ii-V7-I progressions, you can see that memorizing a lot of songs isn't such a big deal. You simply remember the key centers that appear in the overall progression. In almost every song you'll learn there will be sections that do not fall into this ii-V7-I pattern. These sections are generally the parts that add interest to the song and make it distinctive. Obviously, you must know what the ii-V7-I progressions are in every key so that you can pick them out easily. Here they are—memorize them!

Key	ii	V7	I	Key	ii	V7	I
C	Dmin7	G7	CMaj7	G♭	A♭min7	D♭7	G♭Maj7
F	Gmin7	C7	FMaj7	B	C#min7	F#7	BMaj7
B♭	Cmin7	F7	B♭Maj7	E	F#min7	B7	EMaj7
E♭	Fmin7	B♭7	E♭Maj7	A	Bmin7	E7	AMaj7
A♭	B♭min7	E♭7	A♭Maj7	D	Emin7	A7	DMaj7
D♭	E♭min7	A♭7	D♭Maj7	G	Amin7	D7	GMaj7

For more information concerning the ii-V7-I progression check out *Mastering Chord Melody*, also from this series.

Lesson 1B: Improvising Over Diatonic ii-V7-I Progressions

The rule for improvising over diatonic ii-V7-I progressions is quite simple, at least at this stage of the game: use the major scale of the I chord. If the progression is Gmin7-C7-FMaj7, improvise using the F Major scale; for Cmin7-F7-B♭Maj7, use the B♭ major scale, etc. Be sure the chords in the ii-V7-I are not altered. In other words, all chords with a raised or lowered 5th (♯5, ♭5), 9th (♯9, ♭9) or 11th (♯11, ♭11) would make this rule inapplicable, because these altered tones are not diatonic (not in the major scale). After we get a handle on using the major scale, we will learn how to handle non-diatonic situations.

Example 3 will help you get used to the ii-V7-I sound, and train you to get around from key to key. Use the audio that accompanies this book, or record the chord progressions, and play along. Simply practice improvising over the entire progression without stopping. Each ii-V7-I progression is repeated twice and then moves on to the next key. Use all the major scale fingerings that you know in all areas of the fingerboard. For some general tips on how to get started improvising, check out the CODA section of *Beginning Jazz Guitar* (page 86).

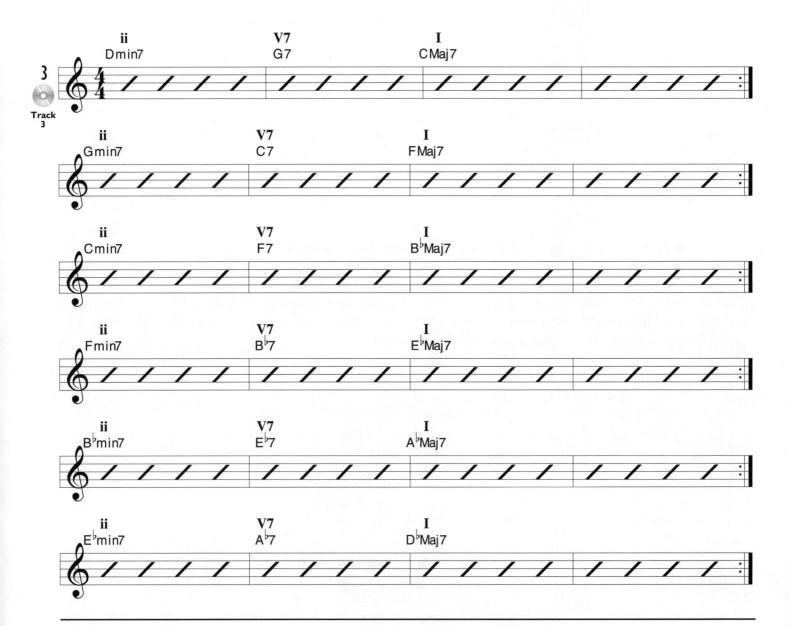

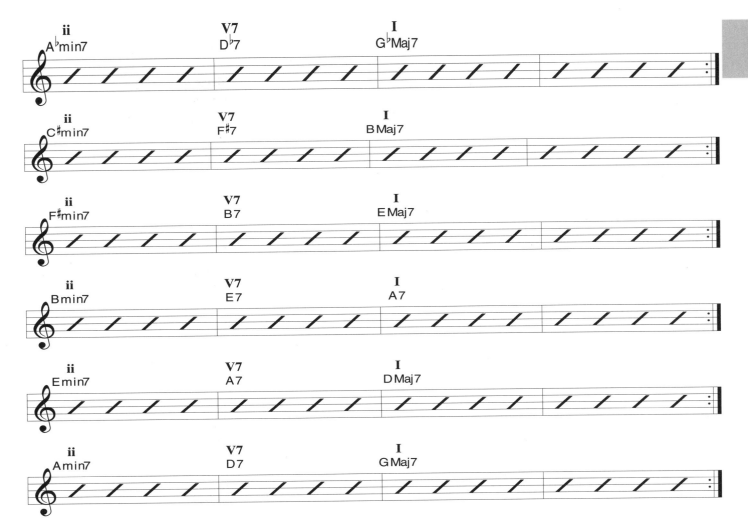

The following progressions will give you some practice dealing with traveling ii-V7-I progressions. To do this effectively, you must be able to pick out the individual ii-V7-I patterns and improvise using the major scale of the current I chord. Practice these until you can improvise freely using several different major scale fingerings up and down the fingerboard. After that, make up your own exercises that follow the same idea.

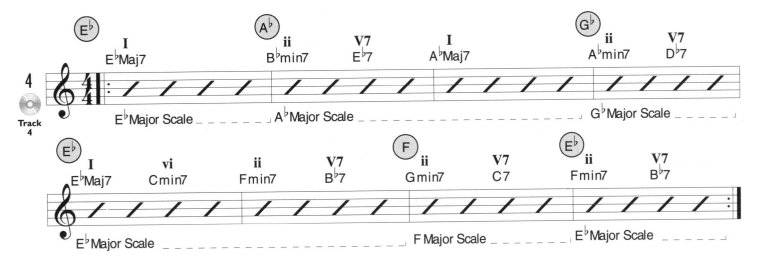

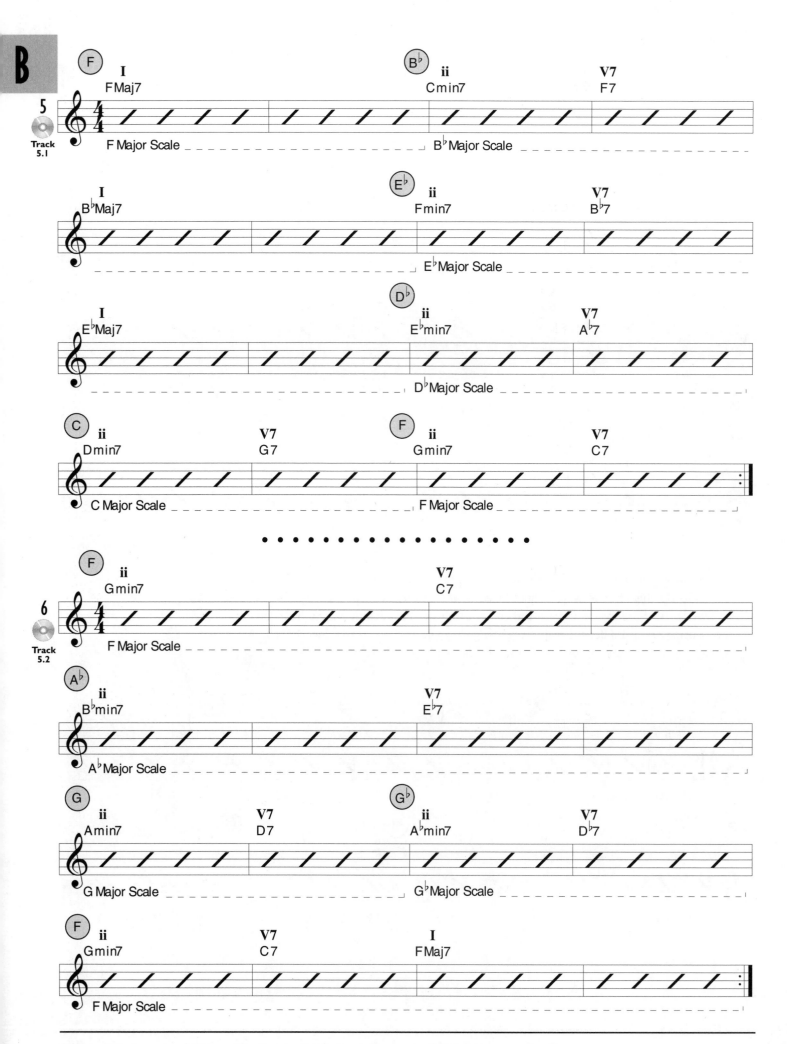

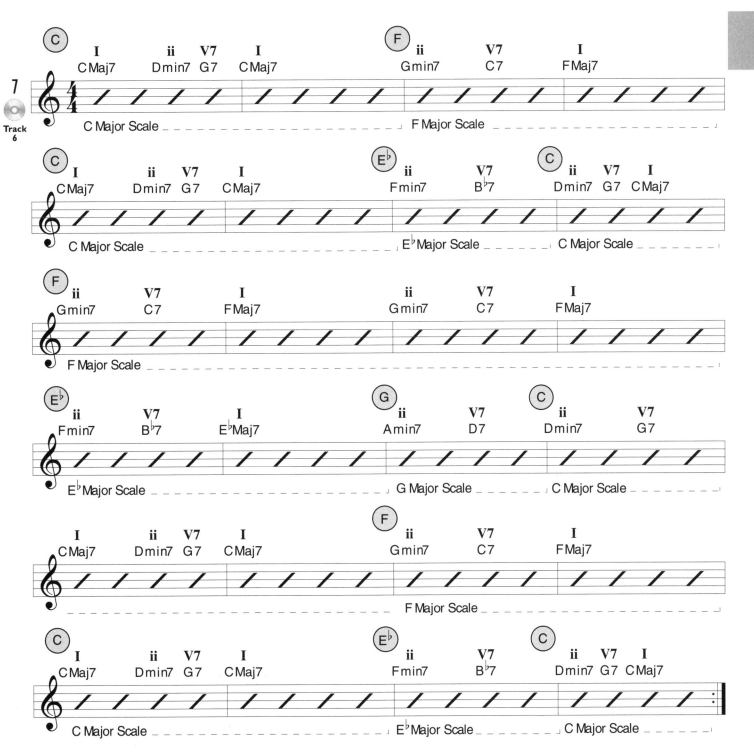

Lesson 2A/2B: Diatonic Arpeggios

George Van Eps once said "arpeggios are melted chords and chords are frozen arpeggios." That is pretty accurate. Arpeggios are simply the notes of a chord sounded one at a time rather than simultaneously. As you will see, it is very important to know arpeggios because they will help you gain more control over your solos. They are also an important ingredient in understanding harmony, which is why this is both an "A Lesson" and a "B Lesson."

The following diatonic arpeggios are based on the major scale fingerings first introduced in *Beginning Jazz Guitar*. The diagrams that follow show the arpeggio fingerings preceded by the major scale fingering on which they are based. Note that all the arpeggios begin on the lowest chord tone in the scale fingering, and not necessarily on the root. For the most part, the fingerings for each arpeggio are consistent with the scale fingering from which it was derived. Pick one or two sets of these arpeggios and memorize them. Come back to this lesson later, and memorize some more.

The scale fingerings are named for the position of lowest root in the fingering. For instance, 6/2 means that the lowest root in the fingering is on the sixth string, and played with the second finger. Read the scale and arpeggio fingerings from left to right, starting on the lowest string and moving to the highest.

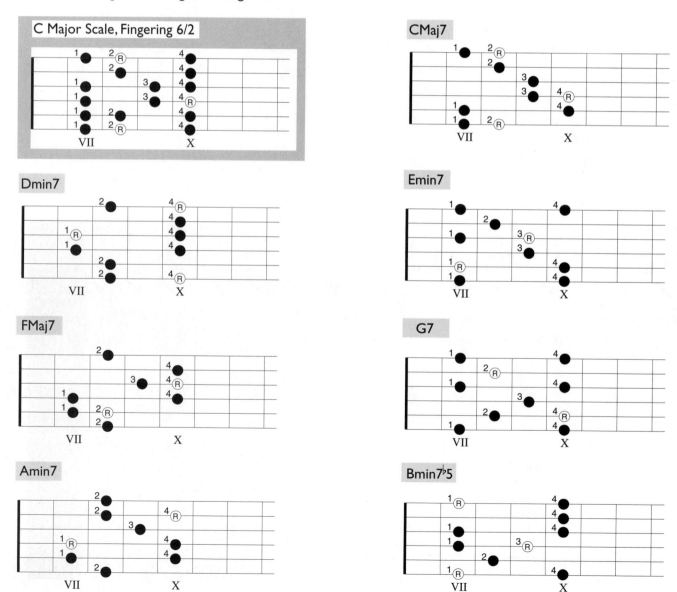

C Major Scale, Fingering 6/2 · CMaj7 · Dmin7 · Emin7 · FMaj7 · G7 · Amin7 · Bmin7♭5

C Major Scale, Fingering 6/4

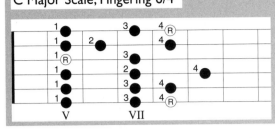

CMaj7

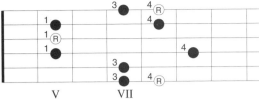

Dmin7

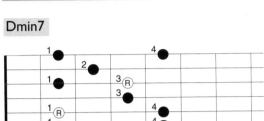

Emin7

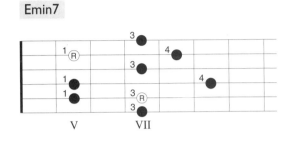

FMaj7

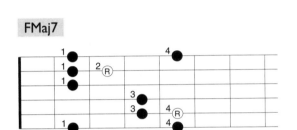

G7

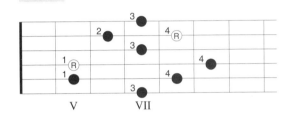

Amin7

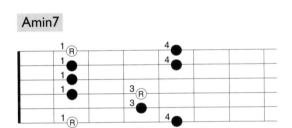

Bmin7♭5

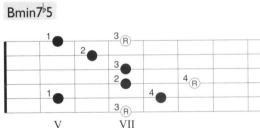
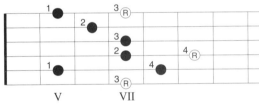

Joe Diorio (b. 1936) has performed with such artists as Sonny Stitt, Eddie Harris, Ira Sullivan, Stan Getz, Pat Metheny, Horace Silver and Freddie Hubbard. Respected as both a player and a pedagog, he has also recorded with modern performers like Robben Ford, Gary Willis, David Becker and fellow respected guitar educator Mick Goodrick.

PHOTO • COURTESY OF JOE DIORIO

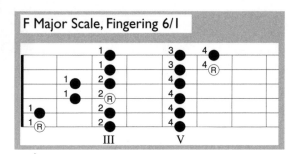

F Major Scale, Fingering 6/1

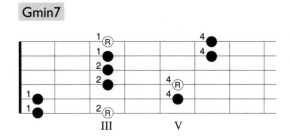

Gmin7

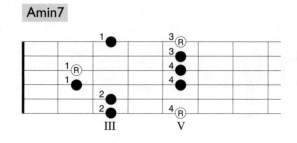

FMaj7

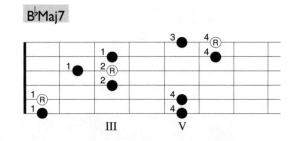

B♭Maj7

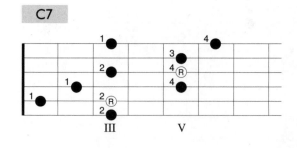

Amin7

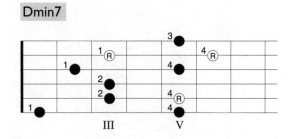

Dmin7

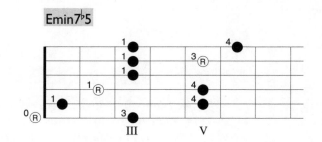

C7

Emin7♭5

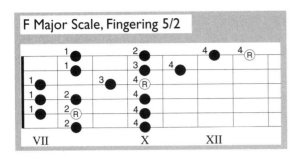

F Major Scale, Fingering 5/2

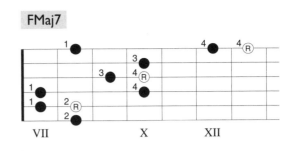

FMaj7

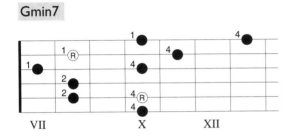

Gmin7

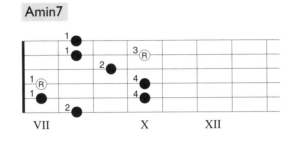

Amin7

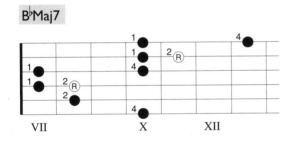

B♭Maj7

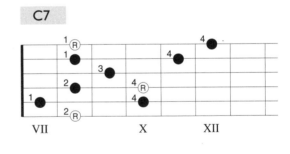

C7

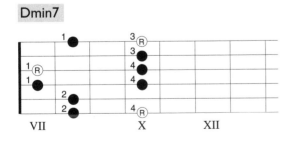

Dmin7

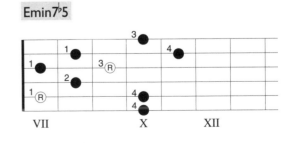

Emin7♭5

F Major Scale, Fingering 5/4

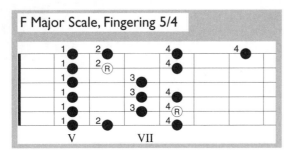

FMaj7

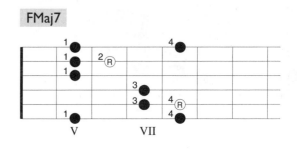

Gmin7

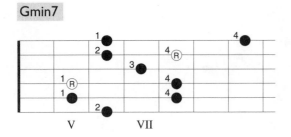

Amin7

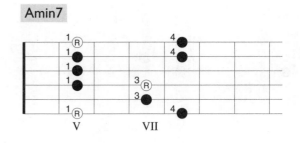

B♭Maj7

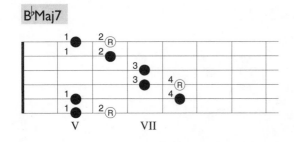

C7

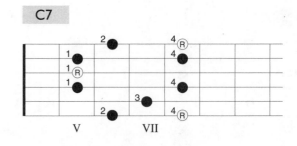

Dmin7

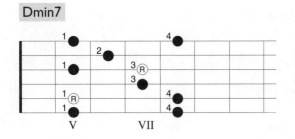

Emin7♭5

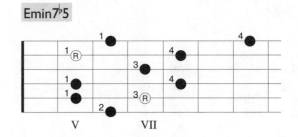

C Major Scale, Fingering 5/1

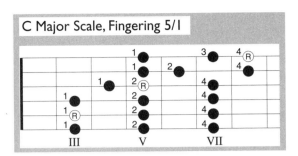

CMaj7

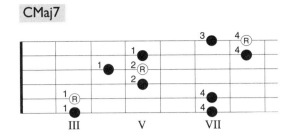

Dmin7

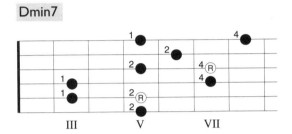

Emin7

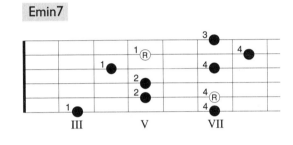

FMaj7

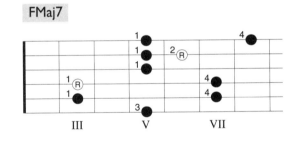

G7

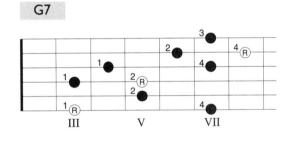

Amin7

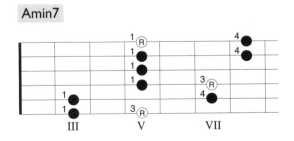

Bmin7♭5

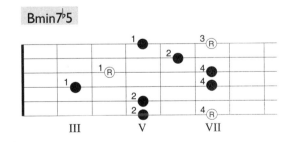

CHAPTER 2

Lesson 1A: Altered Chords

One of the most distinctive sounds in jazz, and part of what makes jazz different from other forms of music, is the liberal use of altered chords. Up to this point, the examples in this series have contained all unaltered diatonic chords, which tend to sound a little bland. It is important, however, to get a handle on straight diatonic harmony before worrying too much about altered sounds.

All types of chords may be altered, but altered dominant chords are by far the most common. At first, these formulas and symbols may seem intimidating, but you will see that the only notes that can be altered in any chord are the 5th, 9th and the 11th.

Remember that the two most essential notes in any chord are the 3rd and the 7th because they distinguish major, minor and dominant chords from each other. It is common to omit roots, 5ths, 9ths and 11ths in certain situations. (There will be many examples of this on the pages to come.) These possibilities, along with virtually endless voicings, keep the search for great chords interesting.

Over the next several "A" lessons you will learn fingerings for various altered chords. Because space limits the number of examples that can be shown, it is a good idea to supplement your chord vocabulary with a good chord dictionary. I recommend Alfred's *Guitar Chord Encyclopedia*.

DOMINANT 7TH ♭5 CHORDS

The dominant 7♭5 chord is an extremely important sound in jazz. It is constructed from the following formula: Root-3-♭5-♭7. In the key of C this is C-E-G♭-B♭. In F it's F-A-C♭-E♭. In other words, it's the old familiar V7 chord, but with a ♭5.

Here are some sample voicings for you to work with. Try substituting these for ordinary dominant chords in songs you already know. These will give your progressions a distinctively jazz flavor. When you are comfortable with these sounds, try flatting the 5th in the dominant 9th, 11th and 13th chords you know.

C7♭5:

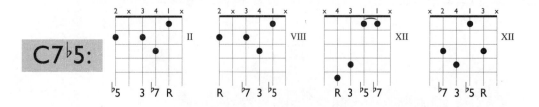

Here is an etude loosely based on the chord changes of the standard *The Nearness of You* that uses some $7\flat5$ sounds.

THE CLOSER YOU ARE

Track 7

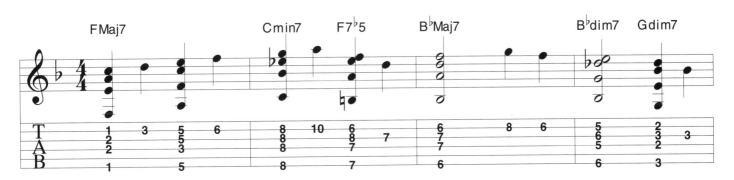

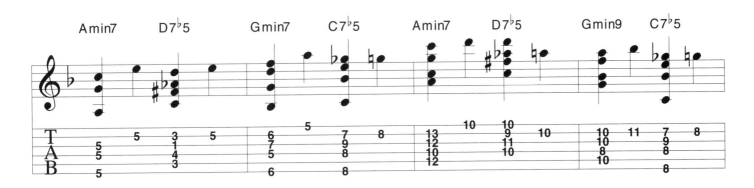

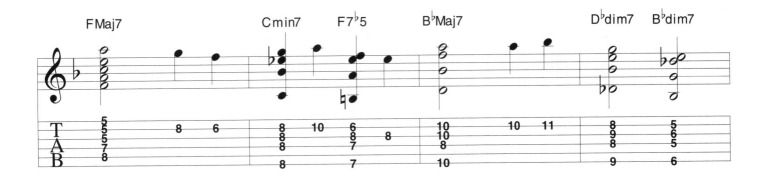

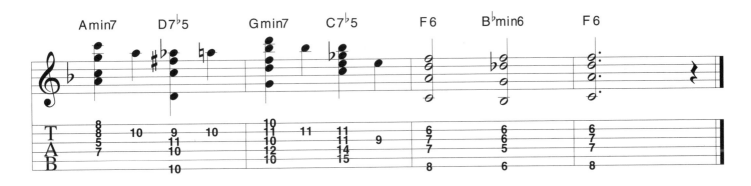

Lesson 1B: Practicing Arpeggios

If you have memorized a set of arpeggios then it's time to start practing them in a way that will help you get some mileage out of them. As you will see in the next several "B" lessons, arpeggios can help you spell out the chord changes of a tune. This will enable you to control the contour of your solos in a very melodic way. Flexibility with arpeggios is the key. The following routine has helped many students master their arpeggios.

Exercise Routine

1. Memorize at least one set of diatonic arpeggios from pages 108 through 113 of this book.

2. Practice moving each arpeggio fingering <u>chromatically</u> up and down the finger board. In other words, after playing through it in the original key, move up one half step and play through it again. Continue as far as the fingerboard of your guitar allows, and then descend as far as you can in the same manner.

3. Practice moving each arpeggio fingering in <u>whole steps</u> up and down the finger board.

4. Practice moving each arpeggio fingering in <u>minor 3rds</u> up and down the finger board.

5. Practice moving each arpeggio fingering in <u>4ths</u> up and down the fingerboard.

6. Practice moving each arpeggio fingering in <u>5ths</u> up and down the fingerboard.

7. Practice all of the preceding, alternating ascending and descending forms of the arpeggios. For example, play an ascending GMaj7 arpeggio followed by a descending G♯Maj7 arpeggio. Then play an ascending AMaj7 arpeggio followed by a descending B♭Maj7 arpeggio, etc.

This should give you plenty of practice with individual fingerings. The next step is to learn to think of them in groups of "like" quality.

Exercise Routine

1. Practice playing all the <u>major 7th</u> arpeggio fingerings you know, using the same root, from the lowest point on the fingerboard to the highest. Do this using all twelve roots.

2. Practice playing all the <u>minor 7th</u> arpeggios you know, using the same root, from the lowest point on the fingerboard to the highest. Do this from all twelve roots.

3. Practice playing all the <u>dominant 7th</u> arpeggios you know, using the same root, from the lowest point on the fingerboard to the highest. Do this from all twelve roots.

4. Practice playing all the <u>min7♭5</u> arpeggios you know, using the same root, from the lowest point on the fingerboard to the highest. Do this from all twelve roots.

Lesson 2A: More Altered Chords

DOMINANT 7♯5 CHORDS

The dominant 7♯5 chord is another very common sound in jazz. It is immediately recognizable. You will see it written a variety of other ways, such as 7+, 7aug and 7♭13. The addition of the 9th is also common, in which case 9♯5 or 9+ are the usual symbols. The formula for this chord is Root-3-♯5-♭7. In the key of G, this would be G-B-D♯-F. In the key of D it's D-F♯-A♯-C.

Here are some common voicings for you to use. Once again, realize that all chords have many different fingerings on the fingerboard. You should experiment to find your own voicings and check out the various chord books that are available to expand your vocabulary as much as possible.

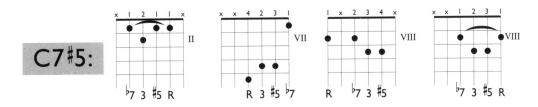

This etude is based on the chord changes from the song *She's Funny That Way* and will help you get to know the 7♯5 sound.

FUNNY

Track 8

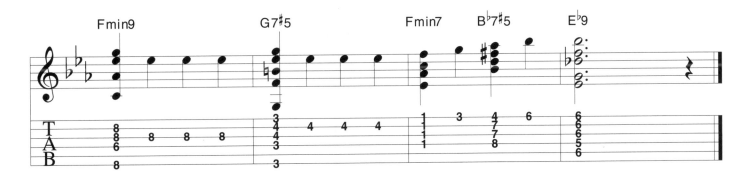

Lesson 2B: Progressions for Practicing Arpeggios

In the coming lessons you will be learning how to "spell out" the chord changes as they go by while you solo. You will start to realize how important it is to know your arpeggio fingerings on an intuitive level. Play along with these progressions using the audio that accompanies this book, or record them yourself. Improvise using only chord tones. The sound will be rather bland, but what you are trying to do is make the chord tones to each chord you hear very familiar, so that they sort of "light up" all over the fingerboard. You should come up with some of your own practice progressions as well. Practice slowly and remember—chord tones only! Starting with Example 9, the chord tones will be shown at every change of harmony. You can use these tones in any octave, using arpeggio fingerings you have learned. Example 8 shows how this is done.

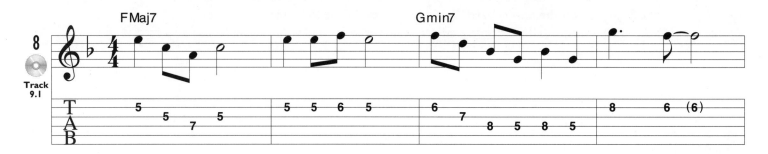

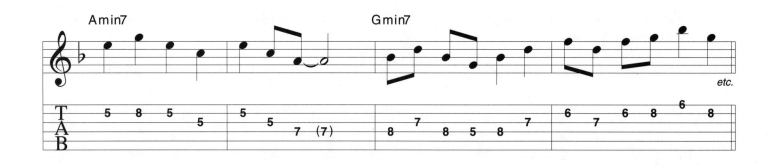

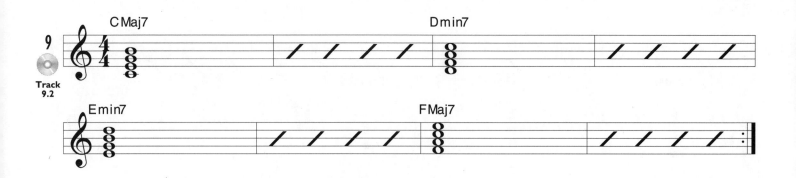

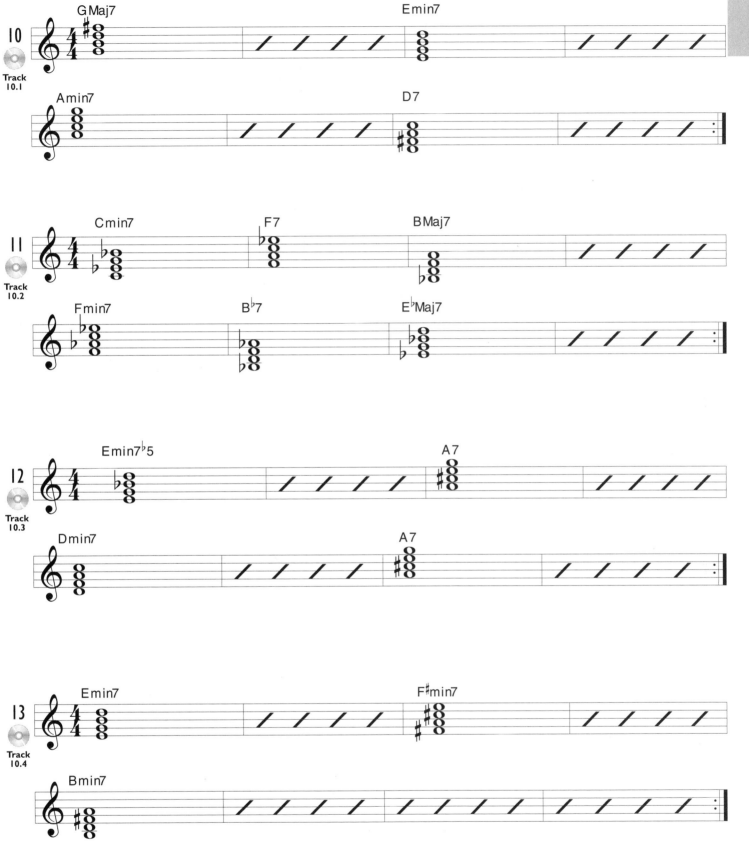

Lesson 3A: Altered Chords, Continued

DOMINANT 7♭9 CHORDS

Adding a lowered 9th to any dominant chord (7♭9) gives a chord progression a very distinctive sound. Check out the formula: Root-3-5-♭7-♭9. In the key of E this is E-G♯-B-D-F. In A it's A-C♯-E-G-B♭.

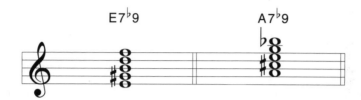

Learn these voicings and try substituting them for the dominant chords in progressions you play.

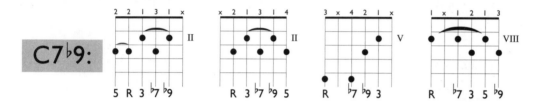

One interesting aspect of a 7♭9 chord is that, when you drop the root, you can move the same fingering around the fingerboard at intervals of a minor 3rd without changing the chord's quality.

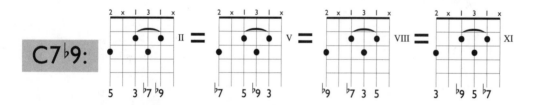

Also, notice that 7♭9 chords without a root are identical to diminished 7th chords. These chords also remain the same when moved around in minor 3rds. For more information about diminished 7th chords check out *Mastering Chord Melody* in this series.

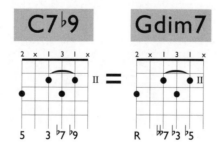

Here is an etude, based loosely on the changes to *Just Friends*, by Klemmer and Lewis, illustrating the use of dominant 7♭9 chords.

FRIENDLY

Track 11

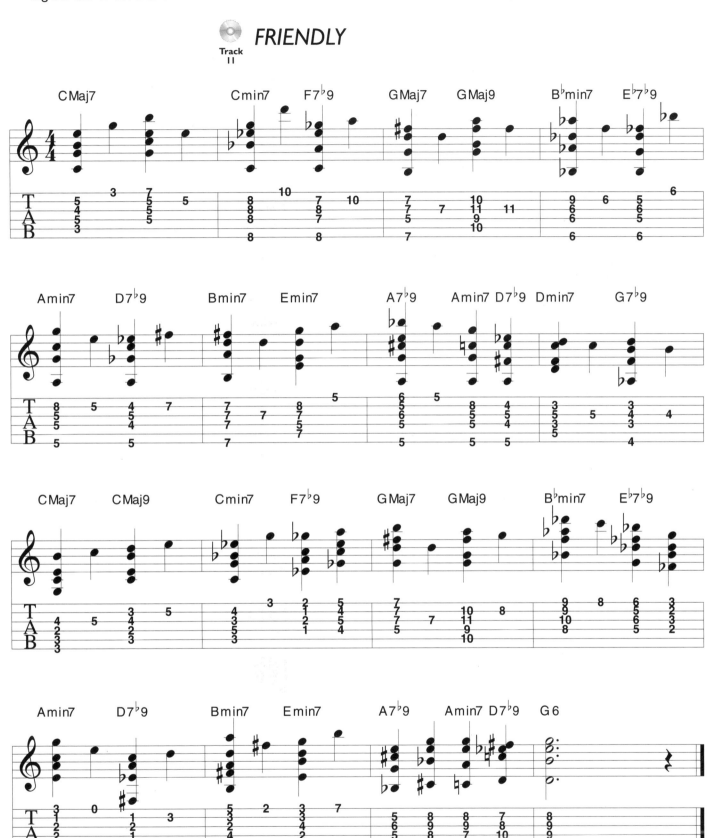

Lesson 3B: Creating Lines #1

SPELLING OUT THE CHANGES

So far, you have been improvising with the major scale in a *progressional* manner—freely using the appropriate scale in a fairly random manner over the diatonic chords. When you listen to an accomplished improvisor, however, you can actually hear the chord changes being *spelled out* in their solos. This is accomplished by combining what you know about arpeggios with what you know about the major scale. Instead of randomly playing the major scale over a progression, try to begin each phrase you play with a note of the chord that you are improvising over. This is called *spelling out the changes*, *targeting* chord tones, or using *target notes*.

You may start your phrases from roots, 3rds, 5ths or 7ths of the chord. You will still use the major scale to improvise, it's just that the first note of each phrase will be a chord tone. Improvisors tend to use 3rds and 7ths the most, because these notes are what give a chord its distinctive quality, but feel free to utilize roots and 5ths as well. This technique will help give the effect of playing "through" the changes instead of just "over" them.

SWING FEEL

In jazz it is standard practice to play eighth notes with a *swing feel*. While the music may be written as standard eighth notes, they will feel and sound like a series of eighth note triplets with a tie between the first two notes. When played in this manner, they are referred to as *jazz eighths* or *swing eighths*. Eighth notes played in a traditional manner are called *straight eighths*.

"Straight" Eighths

"Swing" Eighths

This is as close to the swing feel as music notation will allow. To simplify things, we just write them as eighth notes. Jazz players need to be proficient at playing and reading both styles. Keep this in mind when learning the examples in this book.

Study the following examples to practice spelling out the changes of a chord progression.

Using Roots as target chord tones

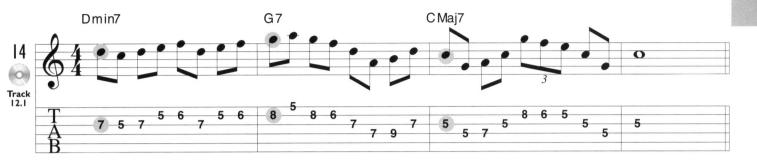

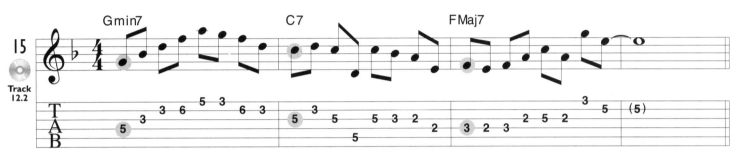

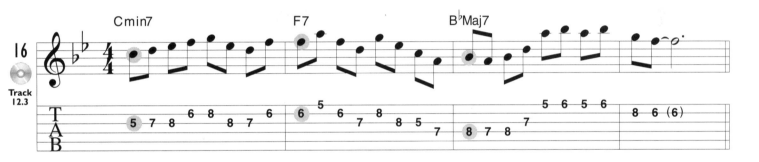

Using 3rds as target chord tones

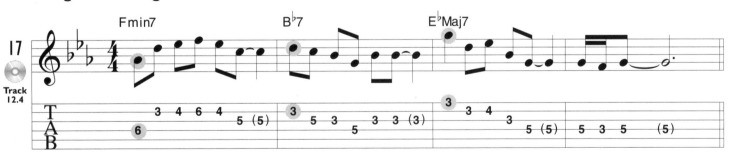

♩ = Target chord tones

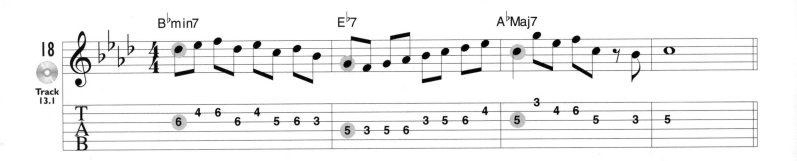

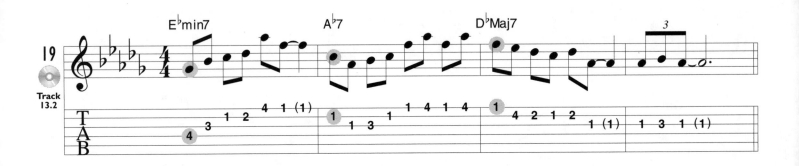

Using 5ths as target chord tones

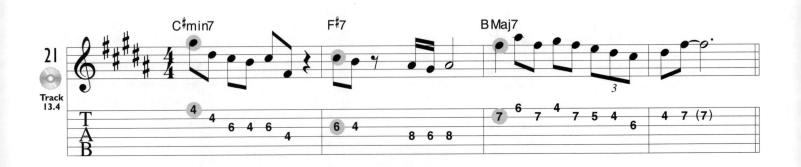

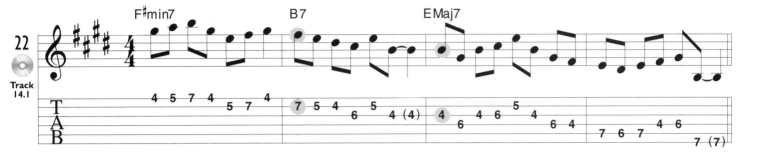

Using 7ths as target chord tones

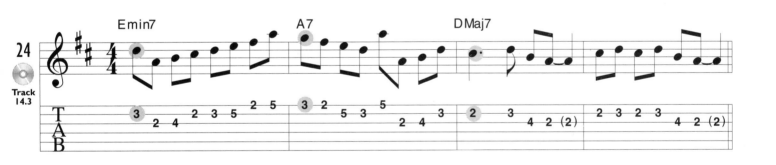

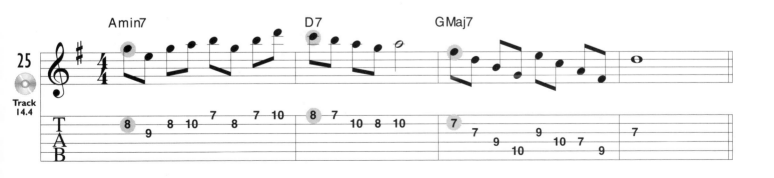

Lesson 4A: More Altered Chords

DOMINANT 7♯9 CHORDS

Dominant 7♯9 chords are also very common in jazz. They add a certain funkiness to a progression. Here is the formula for dominant 7♯9 chords: Root-3-5-♭7-♯9. In the key of F that's F-A-C-E♭-G♯. In B♭ it's B♭-D-F-A♭-C♯.

Once again, try substituting the dominant chords in progressions you know with some of the following voicings.

C7♯9:

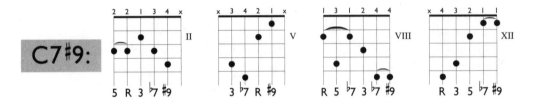

This etude is based on the changes to *Moonlight in Vermont,* by Karl Suesseorf, and illustrates the use of dominant 7♯9 chords.

💿 *BY THE LIGHT OF THE MOON*

Track 15

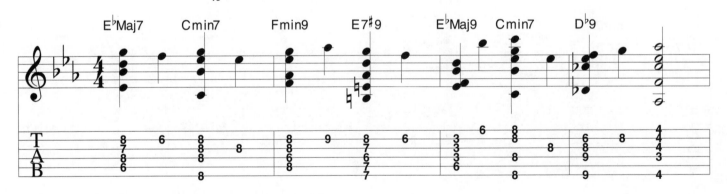

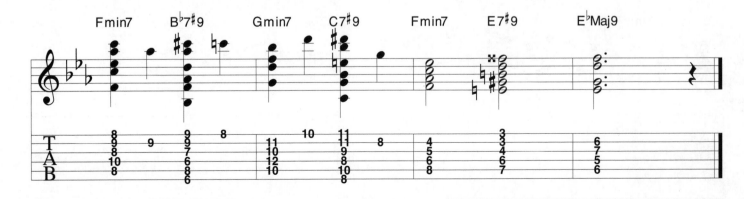

Lesson 4B: Creating Lines #2

NEIGHBOR TONES APPROACHING THE ROOT

If you are comfortable with your arpeggios and beginning phrases on the various chord tones, you are ready to go on. The next step is learning to use *neighbor tones*. These are notes that an improviser uses to approach targeted chord tones. By far, the most common neighbor tones are the notes one half step below and above the chord tone. Neighbor tones a whole step below and above are common too.

This technique requires "looking ahead" in your solo. Targeted chord tones are generally played on the strong beats of the measure, so you need to apply neighbor tones either one beat or half a beat before the chord tone. Neighbor tones can really appear anywhere in the measure, but since the examples that follow will emphasize chord tones occurring on the first beat of each measure, we'll look at the neighbor tones right before the downbeats. This is an excellent way to emphasize a chord change and extend the length of your melodic line as well.

You should memorize several of the examples that follow and transpose them to other keys and octaves. Doing this will help you internalize this technique. Any chord tone may be approached with neighbor tones, although most players tend to use 3rds and 7ths. In this book we will study this technique with all the basic chord tones (roots, 3rds, 5ths and 7ths), but this lesson will deal with approaching roots only.

One half step below the root

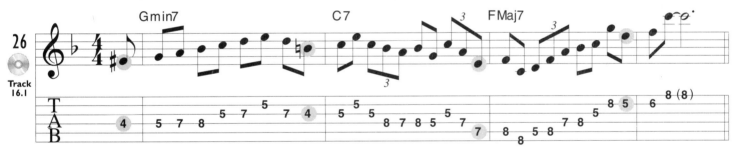

One half step above the root

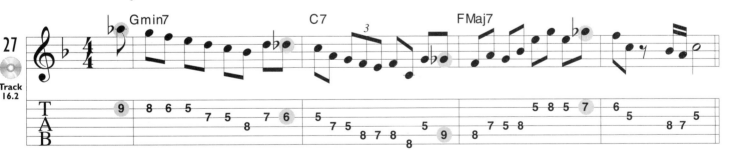

♪ = Neighbor tones

One half step above and below the root

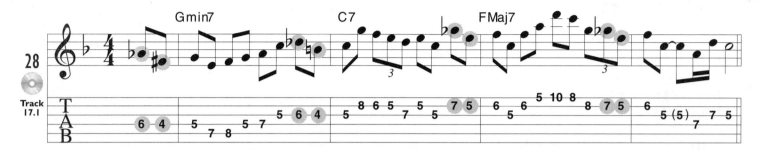

One half step below and one whole step above the root

Multiple neighbor tones: root, half step below root, whole step above root, half step below root

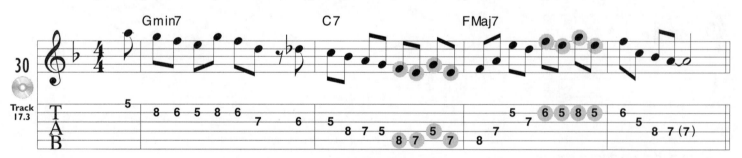

Multiple neighbor tones: root, whole step above root, half step below root, whole step above root

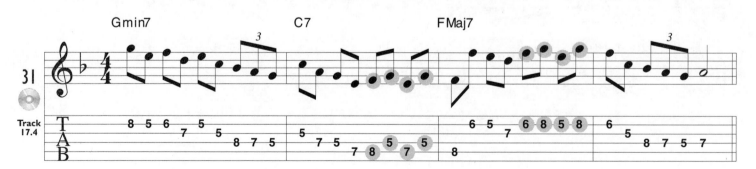

Mixed approaches to the root

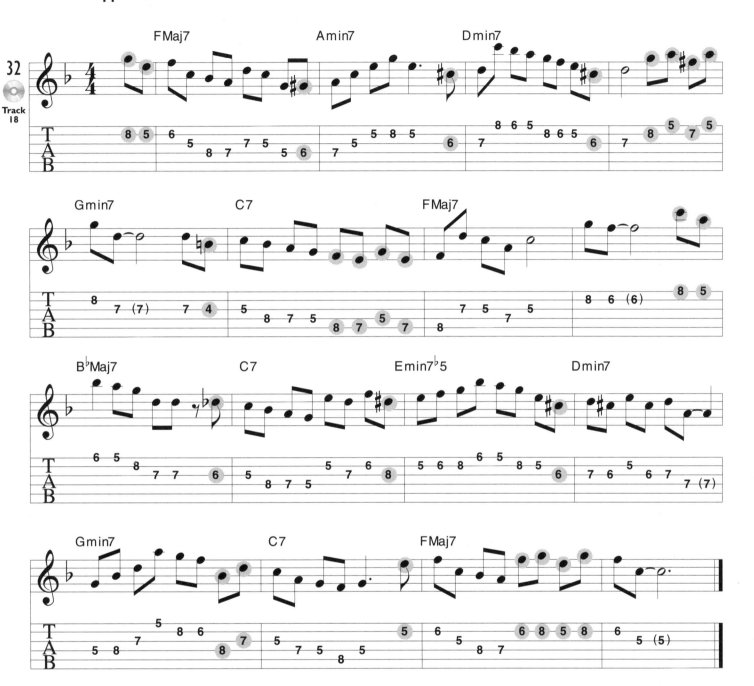

Lesson 5A: Chords with Combined Alterations

In the previous "A" lessons you have been introduced to the basic types of altered dominant chords. Remember, you need many more voicings for these chords than there is space to show in a method book. You should start collecting chord encyclopedias. You will reap many rewards by exploring other ways to produce these chords. Strive to develop a large palette of sounds from which to choose.

In addition to adding altered 5ths and 9ths to dominant 7th chords, you can also combine these alterations. The following examples show some of the possible ways to combine altered tones. These are just some new combinations of the alterations that are already familiar to you. These sounds, though very common in jazz, may be new for you. They may even sound strange at first. With continued exposure and study, your ears will become accustomed to them.

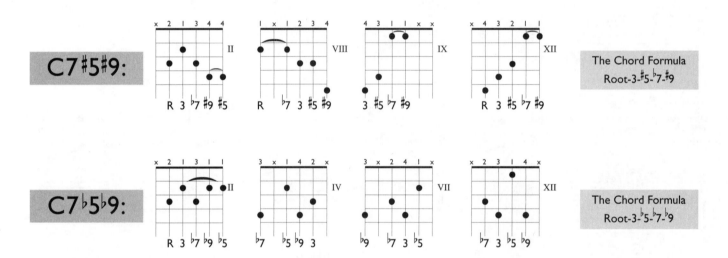

Where do we use all these altered dominant sounds? In jazz, we often substitute the original harmony of a song with more sophisticated chords. When a jazz player sees a C Major chord he or she knows that it may be possible to use a C6, CMaj7, CMaj9, CMaj13, or a host of other major type chords with the same root. The same concept holds true for minor and dominant chords as well. In the case of dominant chords, altered 5ths and 9ths are added to the list of possible substitutions.

Remember that when enhancing or substituting chords, context is everything. Just because a substitution is "theoretically correct" doesn't mean it sounds good in every instance. Experimentation is the way we find out what works, and is a large part of the fun. Have patience.

Example 33 shows some of these voicings in the context of ii-V7-I progressions.

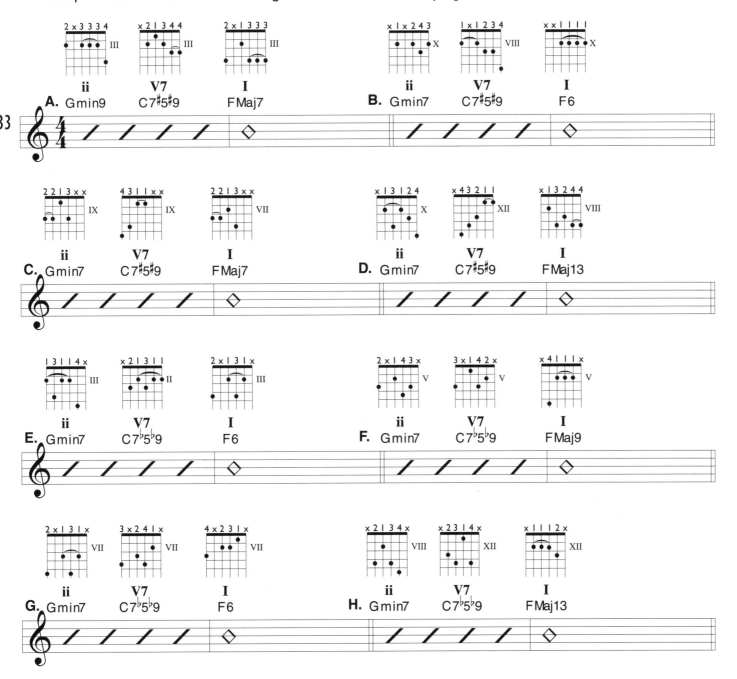

Lesson 5B: Creating Lines #3

NEIGHBOR TONES APPROACHING THE 3RD

In this lesson we will deal with neighbor tones approaching the 3rd of the chord. As in lesson 4B, you should learn several of these examples and transpose them to other keys. Targeting 3rds is a great way to point out the difference between major and minor chords. Often, we will approach chord tones with multiple neighbor tones as some of the following examples illustrate. Of course, this means you must start your approach earlier in the previous measure.

One half step below the 3rd

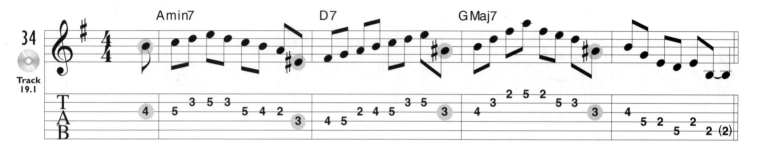

One half step above the 3rd

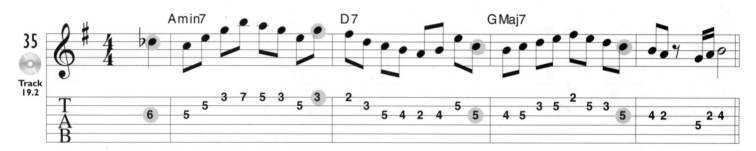

Multiple Neighbor tones: half step above the 3rd, half step below the 3rd

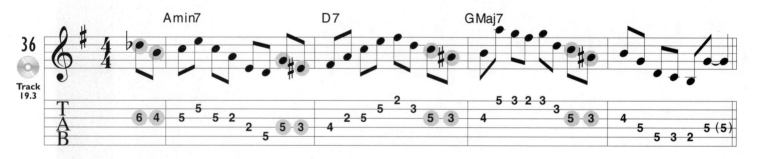

= Neighbor tones

Mixed half step and whole step approaches to the 3rd

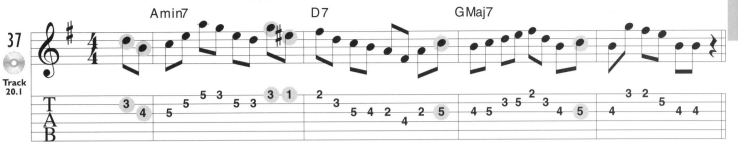

Multiple neighbor tones: mixed half step and whole step approaches to the 3rd

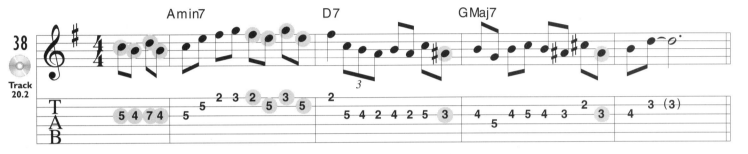

Multiple neighbor tones: mixed approaches to the 3rd

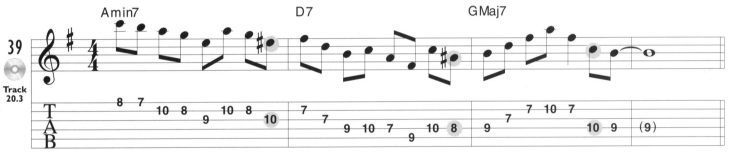

Jim Hall's (b. 1930) live and recorded collaborations with Bill Evans, Paul Desmond and Ron Carter have become legendary. He has also played with Sonny Rollins, Art Farmer, the Chico Hamilton Quintet, the Jimmy Giuffre Trio, and Ella Fitzgerald, among others. In addition, he is respected for his compositions, and in 1997 was awarded the New York Jazz Critics Circle Award for Best Jazz Composer/Arranger.

Multiple neighbor tones: mixed half step and whole step approaches to the 3rd

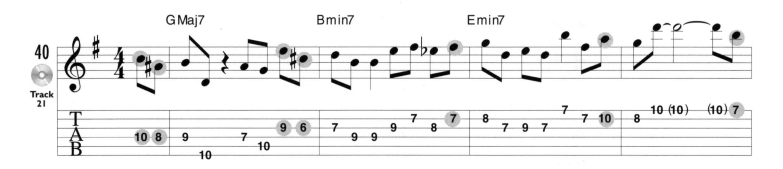

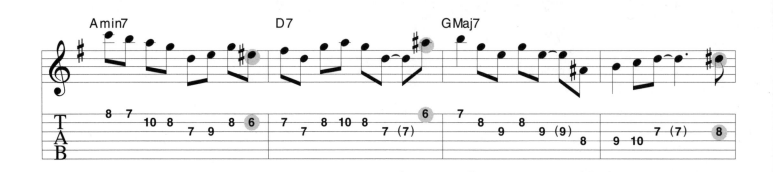

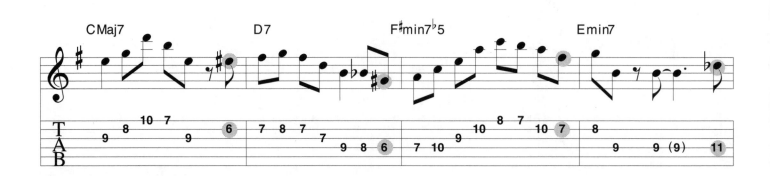

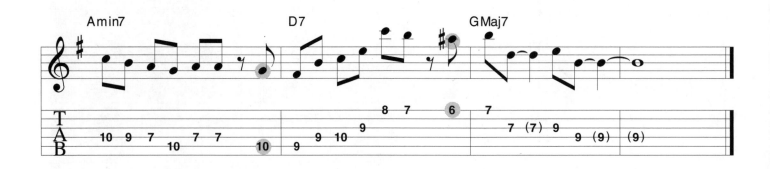

Lesson 6A: More Chords with Combined Alterations

Here are some more dominant chords with combined alterations for you to sink your teeth into. Enjoy exploring these new sounds.

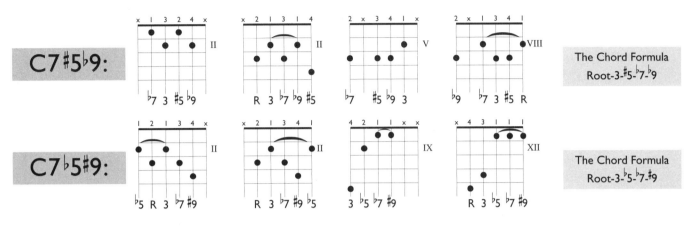

C7#5♭9:

The Chord Formula
Root-3-#5-♭7-♭9

C7♭5#9:

The Chord Formula
Root-3-♭5-♭7-#9

Example 41 shows these chords in the context of ii-V7-I progressions.

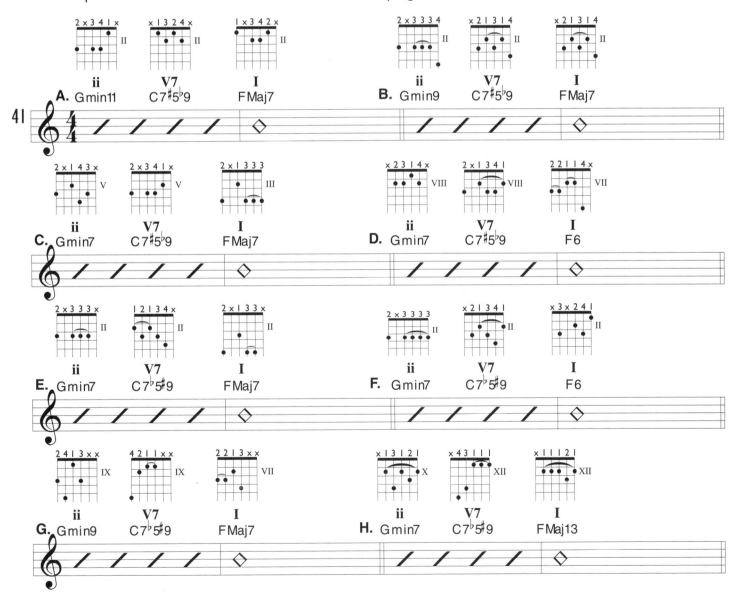

Lesson 6B: Creating Lines #4

NEIGHBOR TONES APPROACHING THE 5TH

The following are examples of neighbor tones approaching the 5th. Memorize some or all of them, transpose them to all the other keys and use them in your improvisations.

♪ = Neighbor tones

One half step below the 5th

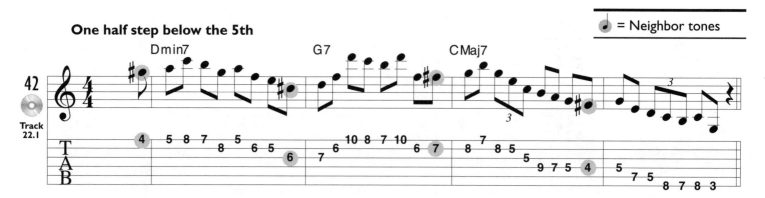

One half step above the 5th

Multiple neighbor tones: half step above the 5th, half step below the 5th

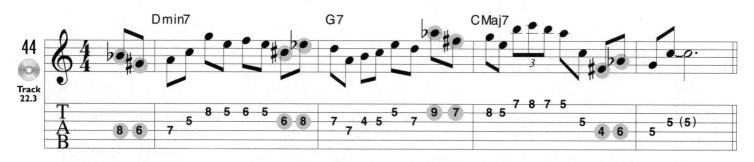

Multiple neighbor tones: whole step above the 5th, half step below the 5th

Multiple neighbor tones: mixed approaches to the 5th

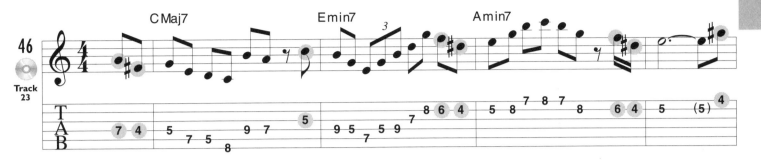

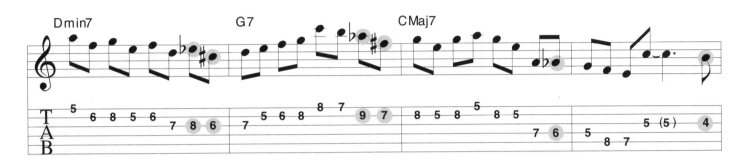

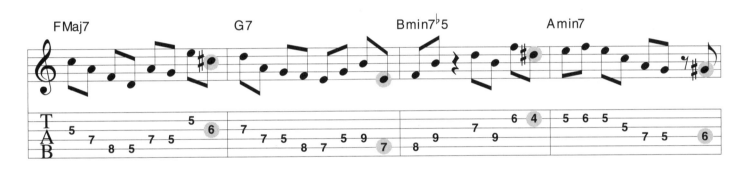

Lesson 7A: Other Important Chords and
ii-V7-I Fingerings

A 7#5♭5 chord is sometimes called 7♭5♭13, because a ♭13 is an octave higher than a #5.

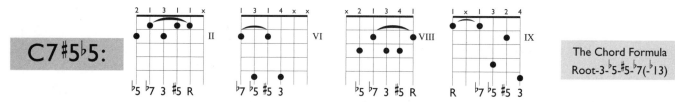

C7#5♭5:

The Chord Formula
Root-3-♭5-#5-♭7(-♭13)

While dominant 13 chords with ♭9's (13♭9) are not "combined" alterations, they are important to take a look at now. They are very common but have a distinctive sound.

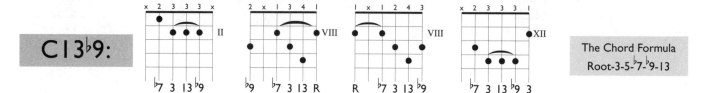

C13♭9:

The Chord Formula
Root-3-5-♭7-♭9-13

SLASH CHORDS

You will often see chord symbols with a slash (/) in them. This has two meanings. For instance, "F/G" means that an F chord is to be played, but with the note G added in the bass. Another usage of the slash, however, refers to quality. C6/9 means that the 6th and 9th degrees of the scale have been added to a C Major triad. C7/6 shows a C7 chord that also contains a 6th. From here on, you will find various slash chords in the examples.

Here are some ii-V7-I progressions to practice with your new chords.

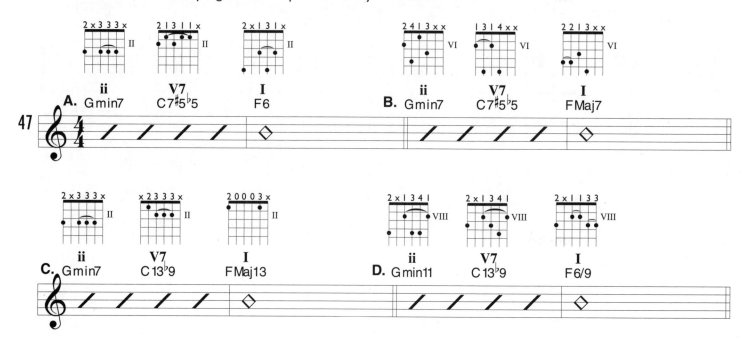

ii-V7-I FINGERINGS

It's often said that you are only as good a jazz player as the number of ii-V7-I progressions you know. There is some truth to this. Knowing lots of fingerings will allow you to play with greater taste and variety. The various sounds that the changes produce will also ensure newer, fresher ideas for improvisation. You can literally learn a new progression every day for the rest of your life and still feel like you need more variety. The following fingerings should get you off to a good start. You may want to practice the ii-V7-I progressions from the previous lessons using some of these fingerings, or better yet, buy a fakebook and learn some tunes while you put putting some of this material to work. Enjoy the sounds!

Play from left to right.

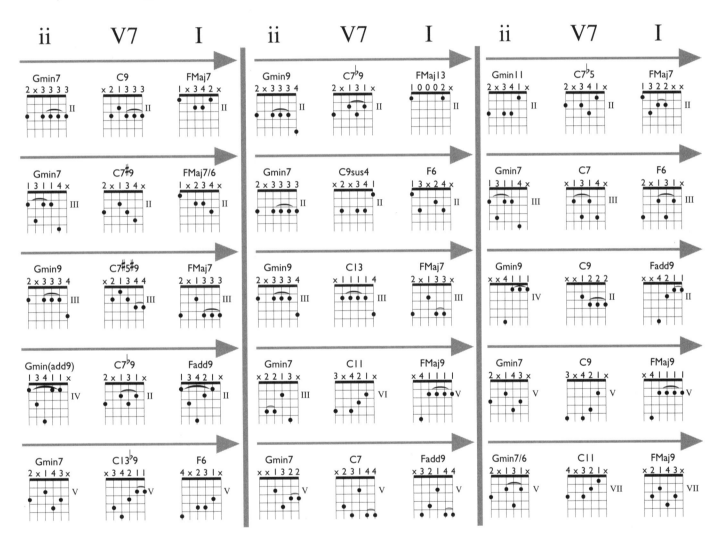

Turn the page for even more ii-V7-I ideas!

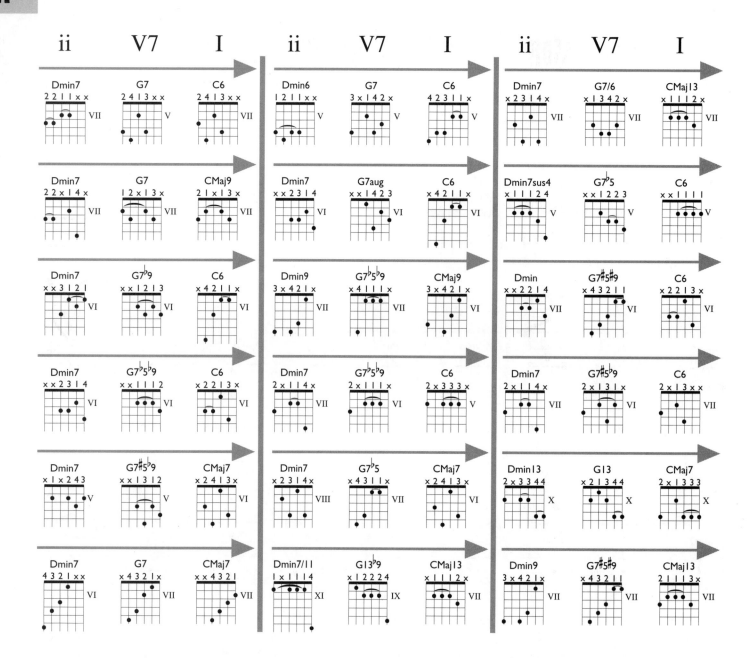

Exercise

Try combining a ii chord from one progression with a V7 chord from another and a I chord from yet another. The possibilities are endless. Be sure to transpose the ones you like to other keys!

Lesson 7B: Creating Lines #5

NEIGHBOR TONES APPROACHING THE 7TH

Even though approaching the 7th of a chord with neighbor tones has a slightly more limited application, it is well worth your time to explore this sound. Learn some of the examples and make up your own. Eventually, you will need this technique to be second nature. Note the B♭♭'s in this tune—just lower the B two half steps (one whole step).

Mixed approaches to the 7th

♪ = Neighbor tones

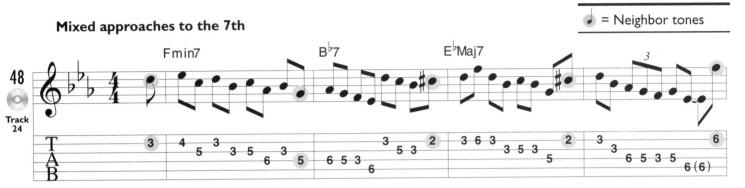

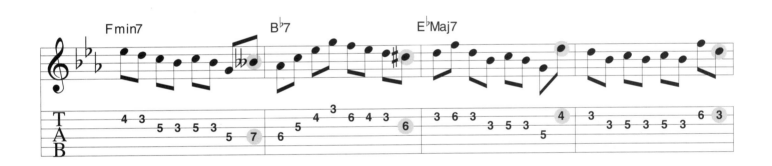

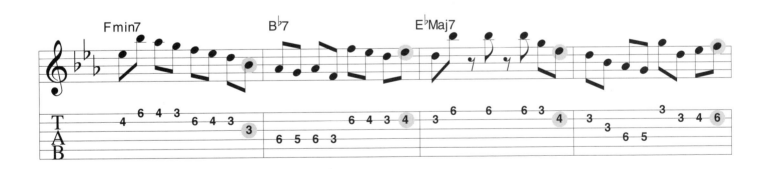

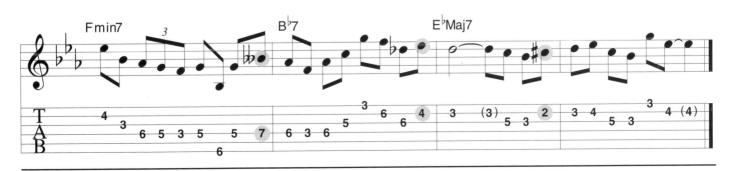

B

More mixed approaches to the 7th

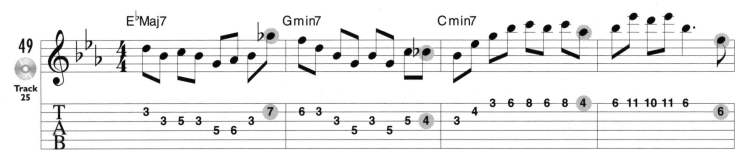

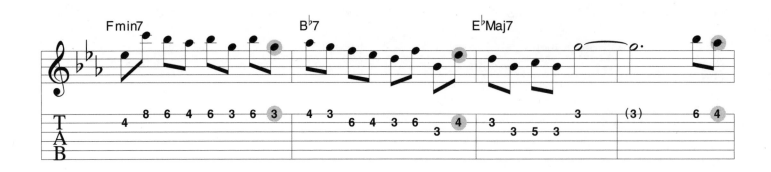

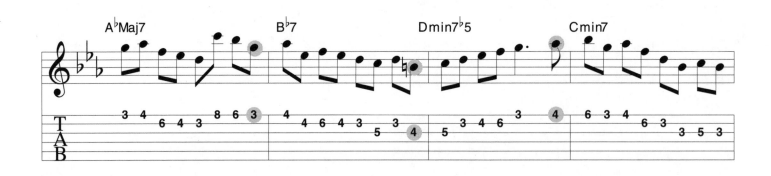

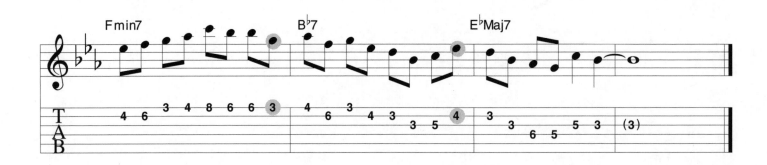

CHAPTER 3

Lesson 1A: Comping Swing Feels

Comping is the term used to describe *accompanying*, or complimenting with chords. This is what jazz guitarists do when other players are soloing. We provide a harmonic background. When playing with a keyboard player, it is preferable to take turns comping behind the soloist. If both the guitarist and the keyboard player comp freely at the same time the tune will become like a harmonic can of worms. Always listen carefully to what is going on around you.

It's a good idea to strum down ⊓ on the downbeats and to strum up ∨ on the upbeats. This will help you keep your place in the measure. Also, try to *damp* the strings so that the chords don't sustain during the rests. Damping is accomplished by either releasing pressure with the left hand, thereby halting the sound, or by stopping the vibrating strings with the palm or wrist of the right hand. Different methods work depending on the situation. Experiment.

Early in the twentieth century, the *swing feel* was one of the first elements that separated jazz from other styles of music. Jazz style syncopation was introduced and the first *jazz eighths* or *swing eighths* were heard. Even though they are written like straight eighth notes, they have the feel of three eighth note triplets with the first two tied. Refer to page 122 if you are unclear about swinging eighths.

Unlike rock, pop and country music, the rhythm in a swing feel is implied. The beat is often suggested by the guitarist. Predictable rhythm parts are considered to be trite, so the guitarist is left to accent various parts of each measure, usually with an element of surprise and with a spirit of improvisation. The best way to learn this feel is to listen to a lot of jazz guitarists. Listen to how they comp. Listening to a pianist's left hand is also a good source of comping ideas. Chick Corea, Herbie Hancock or Keith Jarrett are some of this century's great accompanists. Think of swing style comping as similar to the brass "punches" in big band arrangements. Even though this feel is basically improvised, Examples 50 through 60 will give you a good idea of what this is all about.

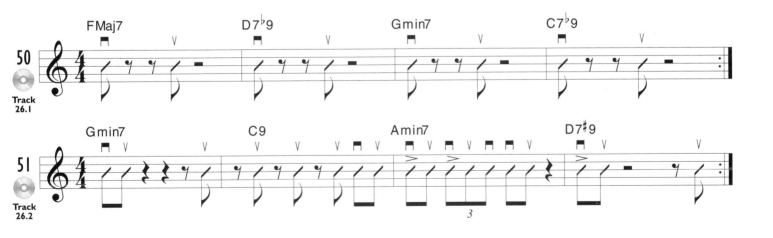

Lesson 1B: Major 7th Extensions

This is a nice little trick that is used by most jazz players. It adds a little variety and smoothness to the lines over the V7 chord. Simply play the notes of a major 7th arpeggio rooted on the ♭7 degree of the V7 chord in any ii-V7-I progression.

For example, if the V7 chord is G7, you can play an FMaj7 arpeggio because F is the ♭7 of the G7. Notice that this technique works nicely because you are actually just playing the upper extensions of the G7 chord: A is the 9th, C is the 11th and E is the 13th.

Examples 62 and 63 illustrate this technique. Try putting this to use in your solos.

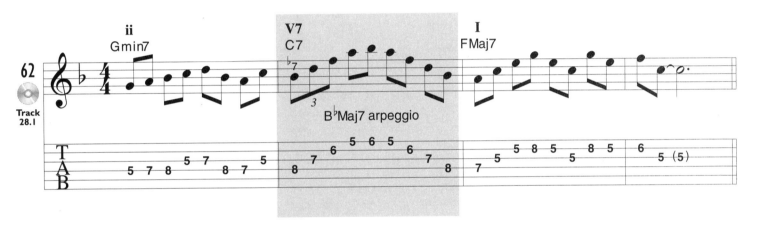

Notice that you don't have to start the major 7th arpeggio on the root of the Maj7 chord.

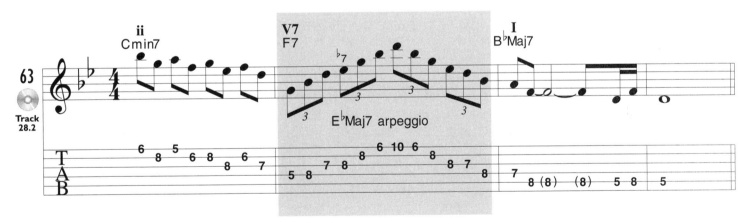

Lesson 2A: Comping Latin Feels

In today's jazz, many rhythms are borrowed from other cultures and styles of music. There are many different feels that are called *Latin*. In fact, there are so many of them that we could never cover all of them in this book. The term *Latin* refers to rhythms borrowed from or influenced by the music of South America. This lesson will introduce you to some of the most common Latin feels. There is a great wealth of Latin flavored jazz in the world, and you should try to explore it all. Lee Ritenour is a good example of someone who uses Latin feels extensively.

Lesson 2B: Diminished Extensions

This is another way to add interest to a line. Play a diminished triad starting at the 3rd, 5th or 7th degree of the V7 chord in any ii-V7-I progression. For instance, if the V7 chord is G7, you can play a Bdim arpeggio, a Ddim arpeggio or an Fdim arpeggio. These tones will resolve nicely into the I chord. This technique produces extensions of the G7 chord, some of which are altered: A♭ is the ♭9 and C♭ is the ♭11 (enharmonically the same as the 10, which is an octave above the 3).

Practice this technique in all octaves, keys and fingerings. Listen for this sound when you listen to jazz—it is a very commonly used part of our vocabulary.

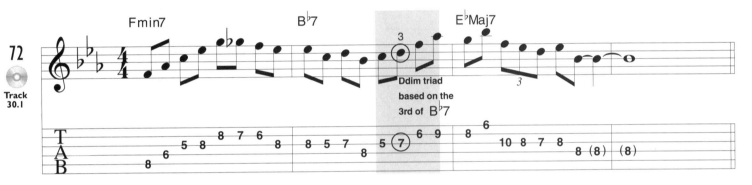

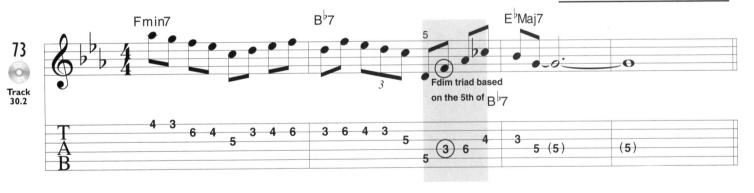

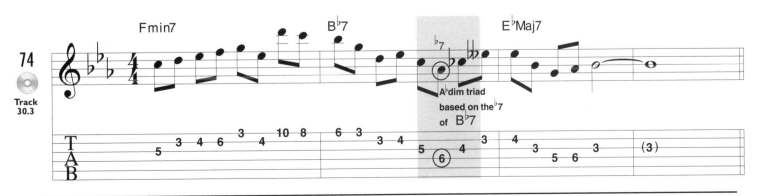

Lesson 3A: Comping Funk Feels

The use of *straight eighths* in jazz started in the 1960's when a lot of the rock feels were being investigated by jazz artists. Today, straight eighths and funk feels are standard fare in jazz. Listen to The Rippingtons, Yellowjackets and Fourplay to hear this style played well. Also, listen to the classic funk sounds of Tower of Power and James Brown. Here are some examples of modern funk feels.

Lesson 3B: Ascending Lines from Chord Tones

This is a very common melodic device. Simply play ascending scale-wise patterns starting from chord tones. Experiment on your own. Most players find this a very easy technique to incorporate.

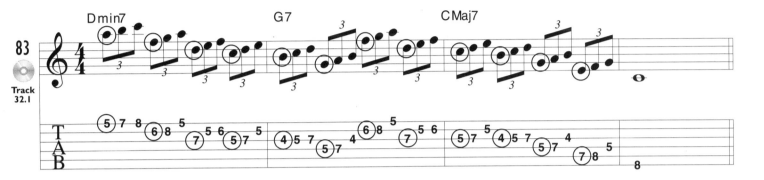

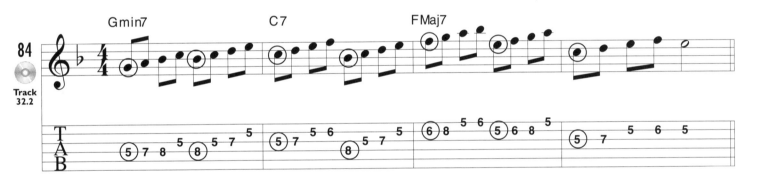

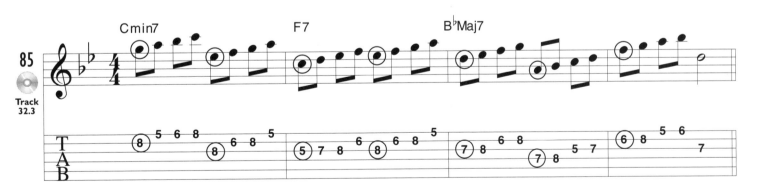

♩ = chord tone to begin an ascending line

Lesson 4A: Comping Ballads

Accompanying with a ballad feel requires listening very carefully to what is going on around you. Generally, it is a good idea to play only when there is a sustained note or a complete break in the melody. This applies mostly to "standards." For a rock ballad feel, you may be asked to keep a steady rhythm going, as in "pop" oriented jazz. Here are some examples of different ballad feels.

Lesson 4B: Descending Lines from Chord Tones

This technique calls for simply playing scale-wise patterns downward from the chord tones.

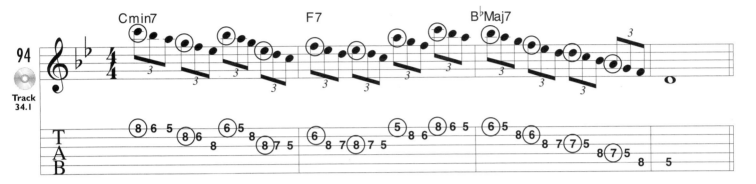

Alternating ascending and descending patterns will give your line a more interesting contour.

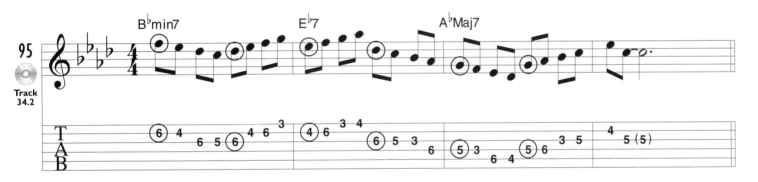

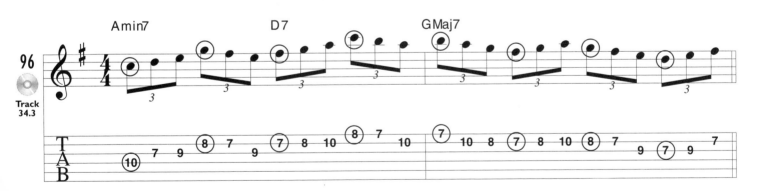

♩ = chord tone for beginning descending lines

CHAPTER 4

Lesson 1A: Chord Connections

PHOTO · INSTITUTE OF JAZZ STUDIES

Wes Montgomery (1923–1968) was one of the most important jazz guitarists, emerging after such seminal figures as Django Reinhardt and Charlie Christian. He influenced countless others, including Pat Martino, George Benson, Emily Remler, Kenny Burrell and Pat Metheny.

Over the next four "A" lessons you will be exposed to a system of learning and organizing chords according to string sets and voicings. While you will be shown this using a very specific set of chords, understand that this type of organization should be applied to other chords and chord types as well.

We will divide the six strings of the guitar into three string sets (6-5-4-3, 5-4-3-2 and 4-3-2-1 with 6 as the low E string and 1 as the high E string), and find the different inversions of specific chords going up, down and across the fingerboard. For examples, we will use Dmin9 (ii), G9 (V7), CMaj7 (I) and C6 (also I) as the material for ii-V7-I progressions.

Armed with the knowledge gained from this study, you will be able to arrange comping parts and chord melody arrangements with much more artistry and variety. You won't be stuck using the same tired voicings over and over, and you will be exposing your ears to chord sequences that could inspire you to write your own tunes. The more you know, and the more control you have over the elements of music, the more "in tune" your self- expression will be.

The first step is simply to familiarize yourself with these voicings and this system of organization.

Note that the roots have been omitted from both the Dmin9 and G9 voicings. This is to allow the use of more interesting chords. It will also give you experience organizing chords that have no root. Playing rootless chords often permits the use of more extensions in chord voicings. The various voices can actually "imply" the sound of the root. Try to "hear" the root in your head when playing these chords. If you play in a group setting, the bass player can take care of playing the roots. Sometimes a bigger sound can be obtained this way.

Transpose and "hang-out" with the following chords until they are familiar to you. We'll be putting these to use in the following lessons.

Dmin9 (ii)

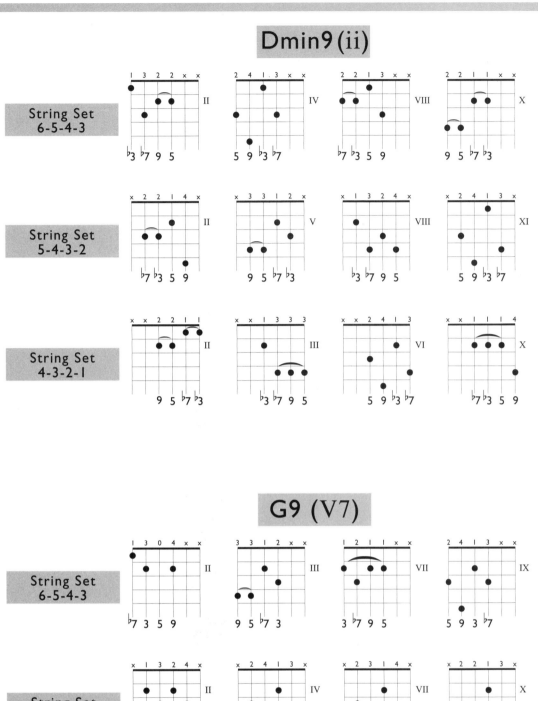

G9 (V7)

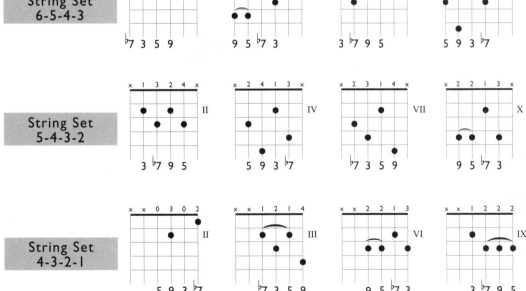

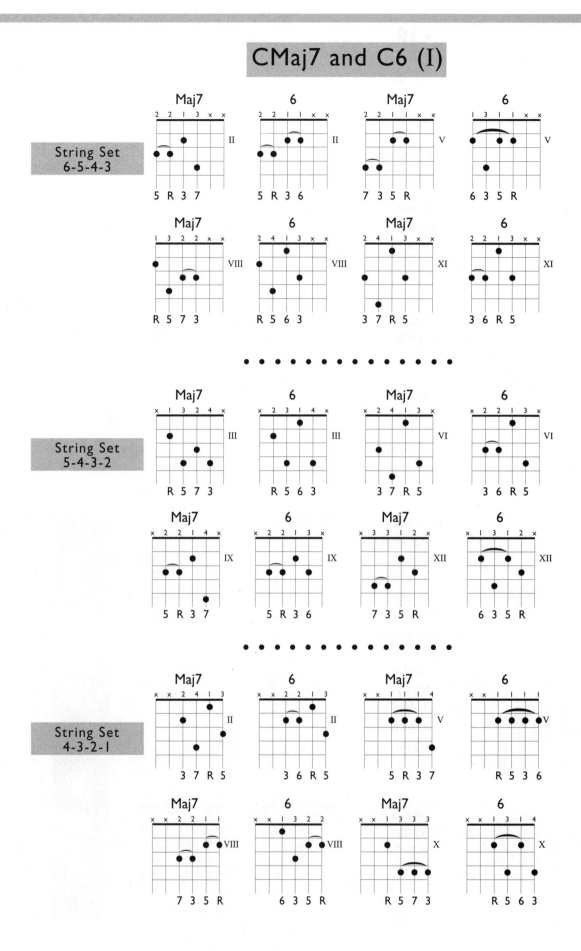

CMaj7 and C6 (I)

Lesson 1B: Learning Licks #1

The ideal in the art of improvisation is to hear music in your head and then execute it on your instrument. Some players would like you to believe that all of their ideas are totally spontaneous. Actually, many devices and concepts go into creating a good improvised solo. Scales, modes, arpeggios, melodic patterns and licks all play a certain part, along with moments of spontaneity and true inspiration. To a large extent, improvisation is really the "creative reorganization" of things you already know.

Licks are a very important part of your vocabulary. If scales can be compared to our alphabet, then licks are comparable to words or sentences. Licks are groups of notes, phrases or runs that an improviser can use in solos. These are pre-planned phrases that the improviser knows will work over a particular chord or chord progression. There are two main reasons for having a large vocabulary of licks:

1. Knowing a lot of licks from different styles of music will make it possible for you to play in a greater variety of venues. You will become more employable as you learn to play more convincingly in those styles.

2. A person cannot be 100% creative four hours per night, five nights per week. It's nice to have some ideas to fall back on.

Everyone uses licks. It is part of your style and identity. Some players' styles consist of merely running all their licks together, one after the other. This is not improvisation. Licks are important, but don't overuse them!

Where do you learn licks? The best source is recorded music. When you hear a phrase you like, stop, learn the lick and figure out the various chords it can work over (there are usually many). Other good sources are the many "lick books" and solo transcriptions that are available. As you mature as a soloist, you will find yourself combining all sorts of licks from many sources, and coming up with new and interesting sounds. The sample licks that follow are based on the major scale, and they represent the basis for developing the spicier licks you hear when you listen to players like John Scofield, Wes Montgomery, Mike Stern and all the other jazz guitar greats. When you proceed to *Mastering Jazz Improvisation* you will learn licks based on more exotic scales.

PHOTO • COURTESY OF ATLANTIC JAZZ/TROPIX INT.

__Mike Stern__ (b. 1953) has been considered an important jazz guitarist since his early 1980s stint with Miles Davis. He has played with such jazz icons as saxophonists George Coleman and Joe Henderson, bassist Jaco Pastorius, guitarists Jim Hall and Pat Martino, and trumpeters Tom Harrell, Arturo Sandoval and Tiger Okoshi. His most important work, however, has been as a bandleader-composer and recording artist.

MAJOR CHORD LICKS

Here are eight sample licks that work well over major-type chords. Transpose them and start using them immediately in songs you are learning. These licks are labeled with major 7th chords but will work equally well with major 6th, major 9th and major 13th chords. Experiment and let your ear be your guide.

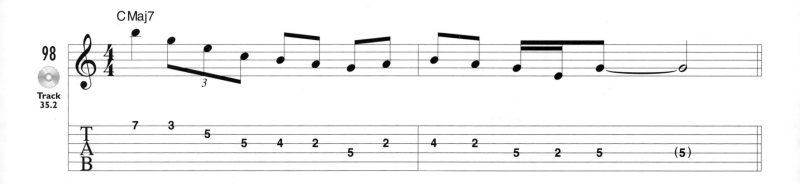

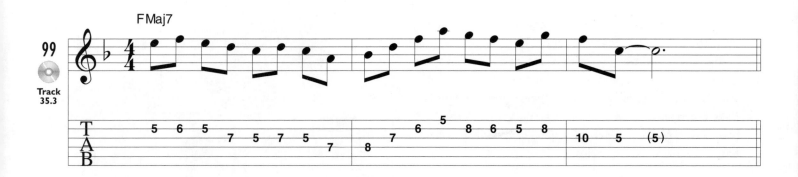

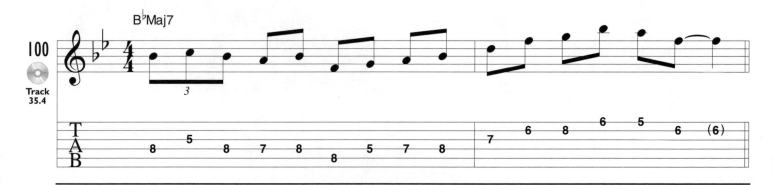

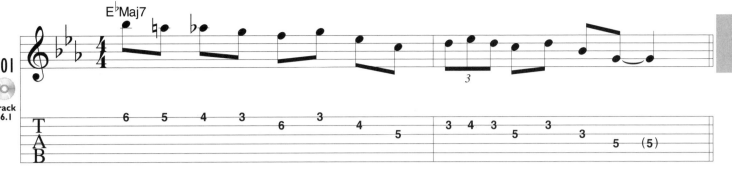

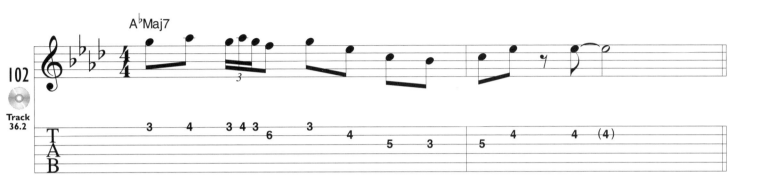

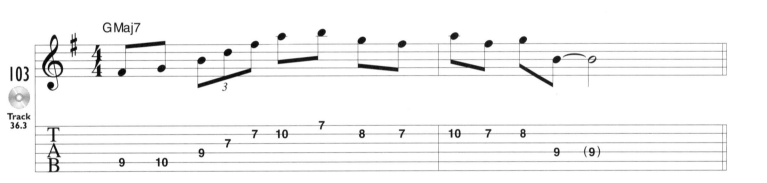

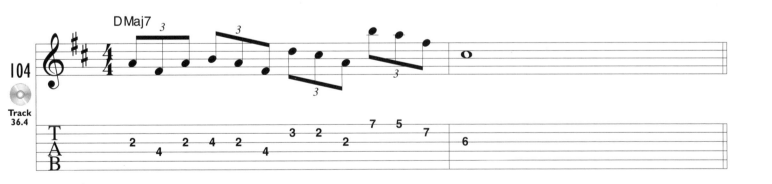

Lesson 2A: Chord Connections #2

In this lesson, the chords you were working with in Lesson 1A have been organized into ii-V7-I patterns. Each chord receives one beat. Be sure to transpose these progressions to all twelve keys. Have patience, and enjoy the process. It can take some time to get comfortable with these chord connections.

STRING SET 6-5-4-3

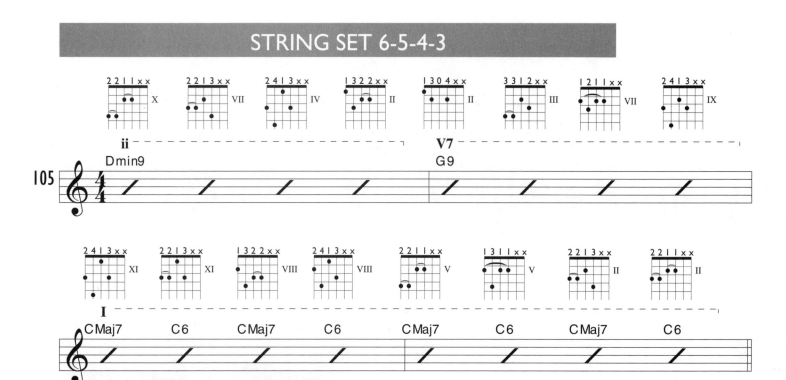

Steve Khan (b. 1947) is known for his work with artists such as Steely Dan, Billy Joel, Michael Franks, Hubert Laws, Billy Cobham, Jack DeJohnette, James Brown, Maynard Ferguson, and Weather Report.

PHOTO • COURTESY OF STEVE KHAN

STRING SET 5-4-3-2

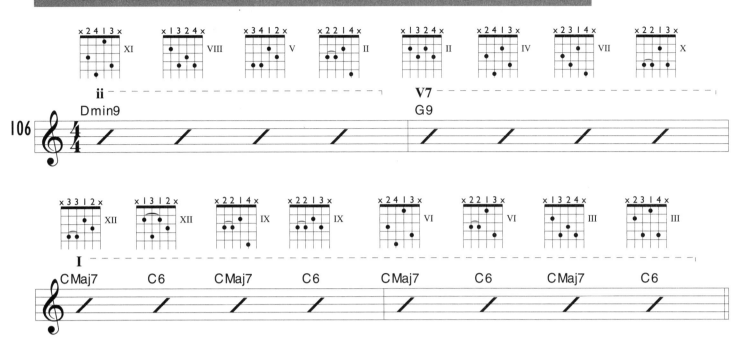

STRING SET 4-3-2-1

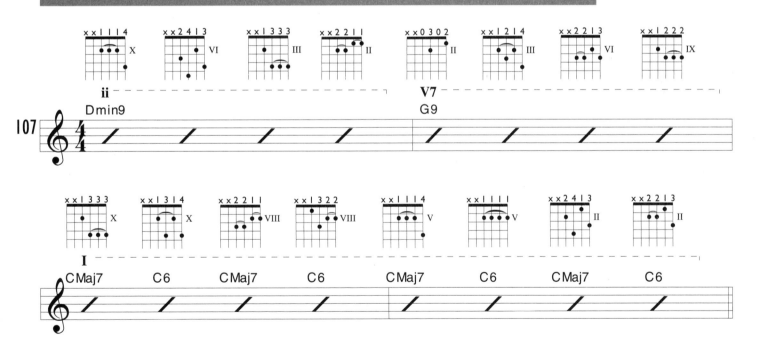

Lesson 2B: Learning Licks #2

MINOR LICKS

Here are some sample licks to use over minor chords. Once again, learn, transpose and insert these into your solos as soon as possible!

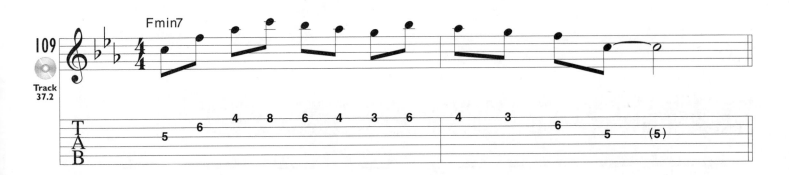

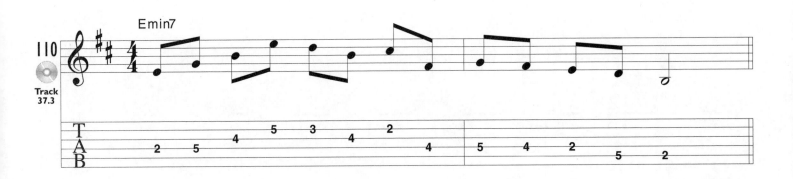

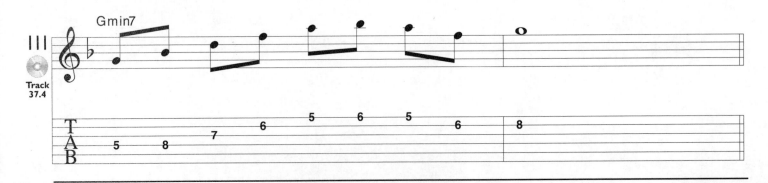

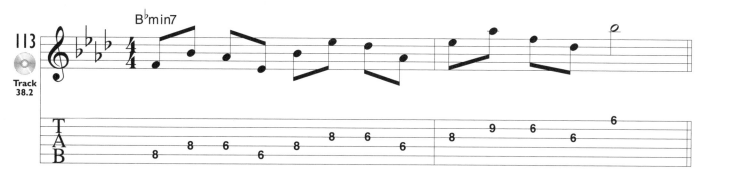

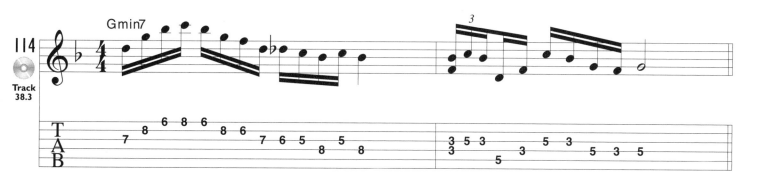

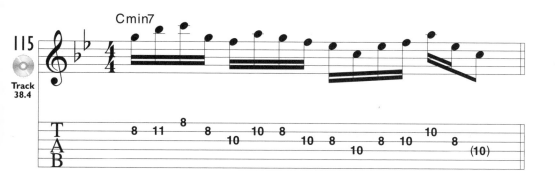

Lesson 3A: Chord Connections #3

MOVING ACROSS THE STRING SETS

By now, these chords are surely getting easier for you to handle. The following ii-V7-I progressions move across the string sets. Once again, each chord receives one beat. Transpose these to all twelve keys.

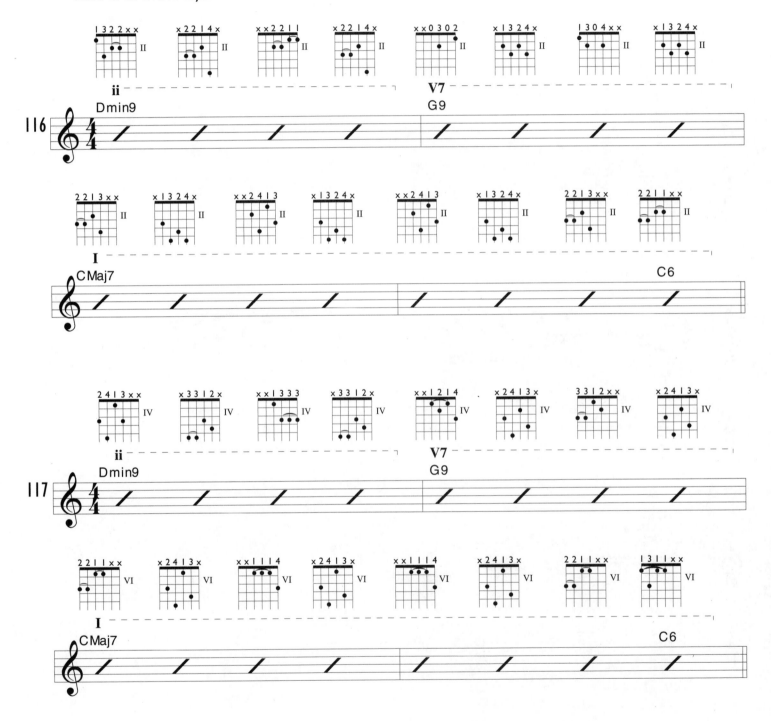

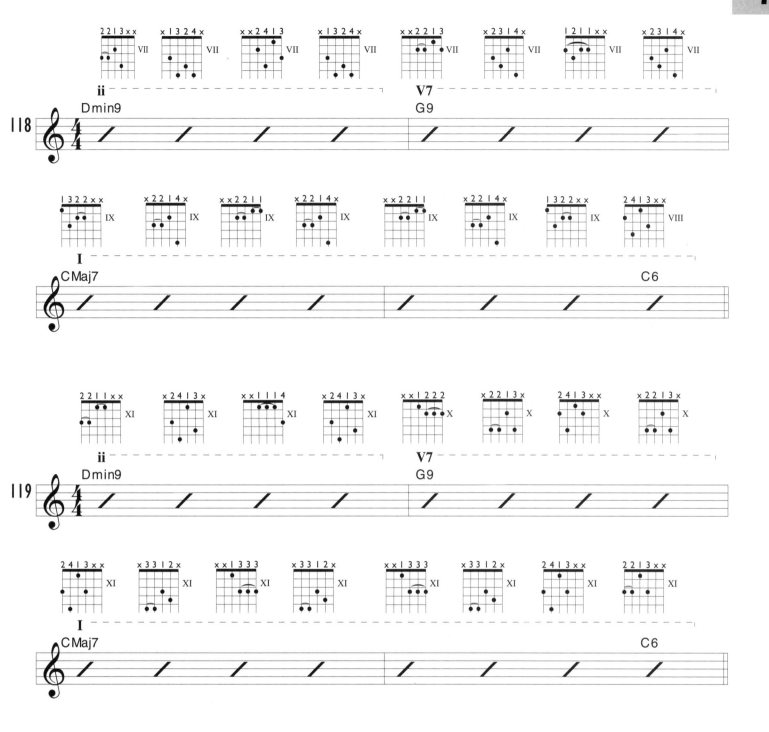

Lesson 3B: Learning Licks #3

DOMINANT LICKS

Here are some licks that will work well over unaltered dominant chords. Try using them over dominant 9th, 11th and 13th chords as well. Transpose them and apply them to your solos.

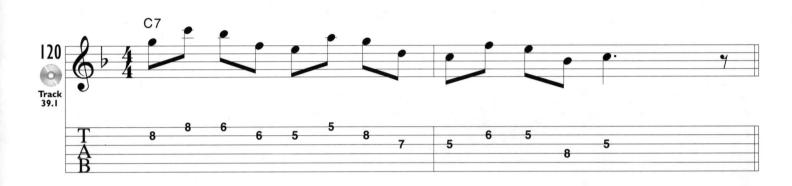

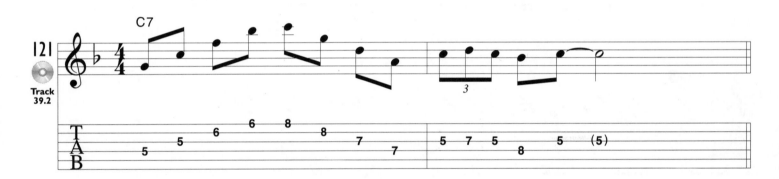

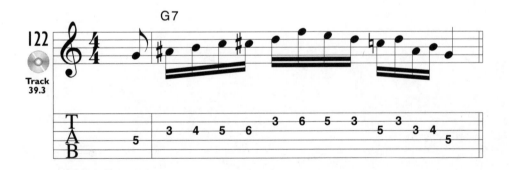

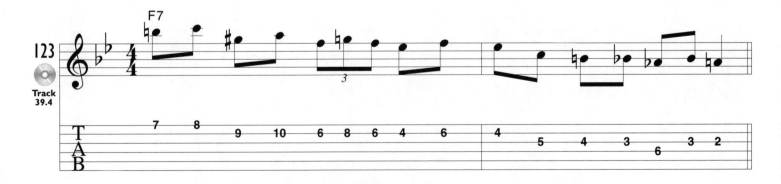

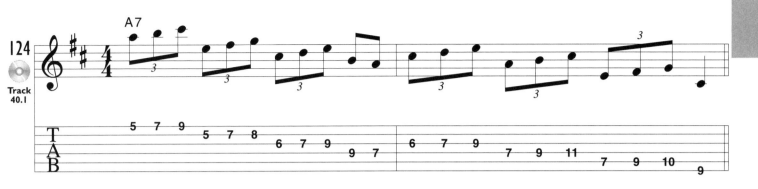

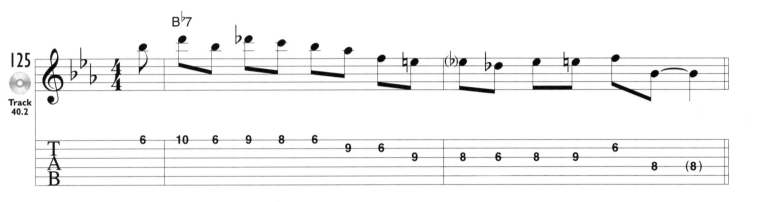

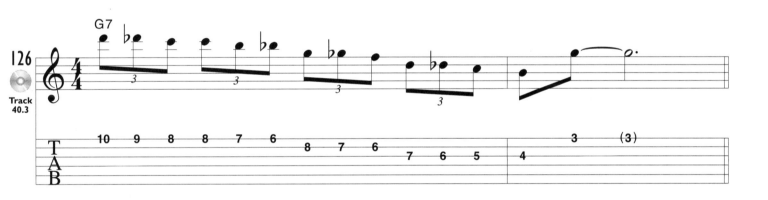

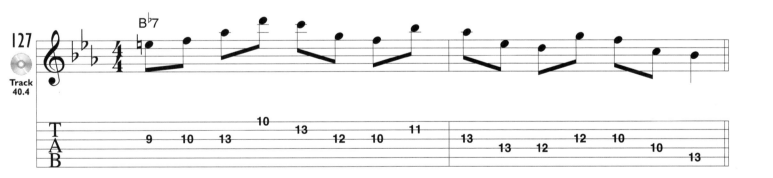

Lesson 4A: Chord Connections #4

Once the examples in Lesson 3A get easier, challenge yourself with these. They are arranged in one-measure ii-V7-I patterns. Take your time learning each example and then transpose them.

STRING SET 6-5-4-3

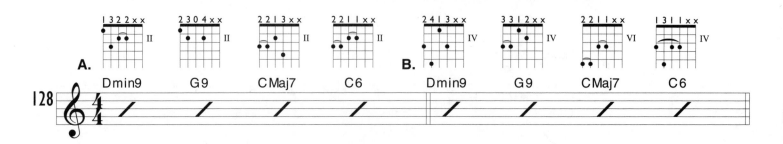

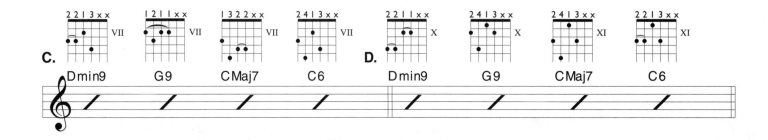

STRING SET 5-4-3-2

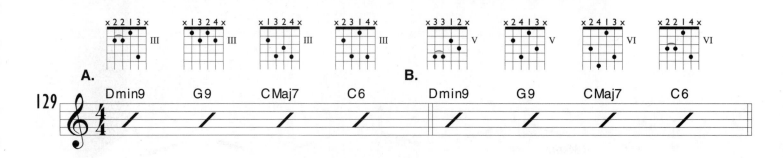

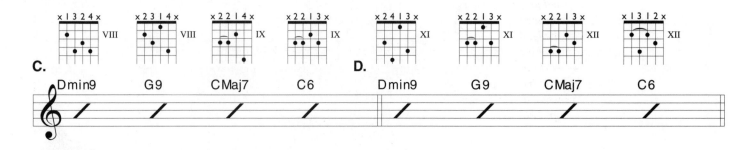

STRING SET 4-3-2-1

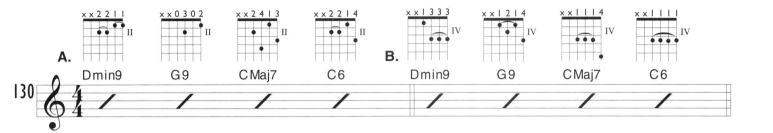

A.
xx2211 II — Dmin9
xx0302 II — G9
xx2413 II — CMaj7
xx2214 II — C6

B.
xx1333 IV — Dmin9
xx1214 IV — G9
xx1114 IV — CMaj7
xx1111 IV — C6

130

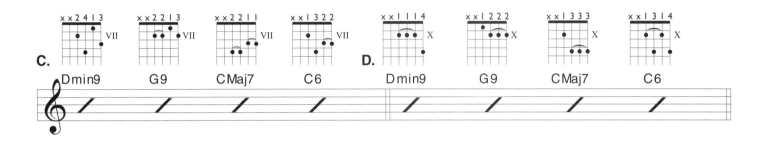

C.
xx2413 VII — Dmin9
xx2213 VII — G9
xx2211 VII — CMaj7
xx1322 VII — C6

D.
xx1114 X — Dmin9
xx1222 X — G9
xx1333 X — CMaj7
xx1314 X — C6

Pat Metheny (b. 1954) is one of the most successful and critically acclaimed jazz musicians to come to prominence in the 1970s and '80s. He is the leader of the Pat Metheny Group and is also involved in duets, solo works and other side projects. His style incorporates elements of progressive and contemporary jazz, post-bop, Latin jazz and jazz fusion.

Lesson 4B: Learning Licks #4

min7♭5 LICKS

There are many ways to improvise over min7♭5 (half-diminished) chords. Here are just a few licks to help you get used to the sound.

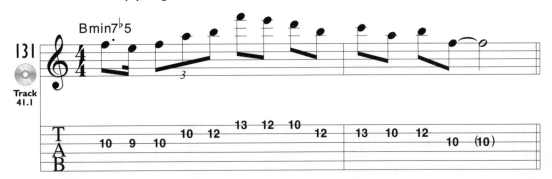

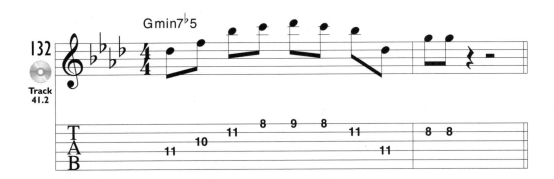

135

Track 42.1

136

Track 42.2

137

Track 42.3

138

Track 42.4

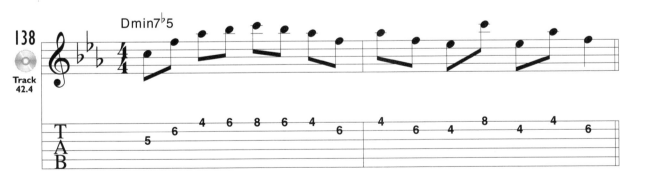

CHAPTER 5

Lesson 1A: The Blues Progression

The blues is a style of music unto itself. It is also a very important part of the jazz vocabulary. You may have heard about the various styles of blues, like Delta Blues, Chicago Blues, Country Blues, Urban Blues, English Blues and Rock Blues among others. Each blues style can be thought of as a different dialect of the same basic language. If you are interested in learning about the many different kinds of blues styles check out *Beginning*, *Intermediate* and *Mastering Blues Guitar*, available at any music store.

For our purposes, the blues will be thought of as a *form*; it is a twelve measure chord progression that is based around a I-IV-V7 progression. As you will see, the blues progression can be very simple or very complex. In fact, if you compare the first few progressions in this lesson with the later ones, you might be hard pressed to find any similarity at all. Jazz blues progressions tend to use quite a few substitutions and passing chords. There are many examples of this with detailed explanations in *Mastering Jazz Guitar Chord/Melody*. You should try to learn as many blues progressions as possible.

Example 139 is a basic blues, and the examples that follow show how jazz players might elaborate on the form.

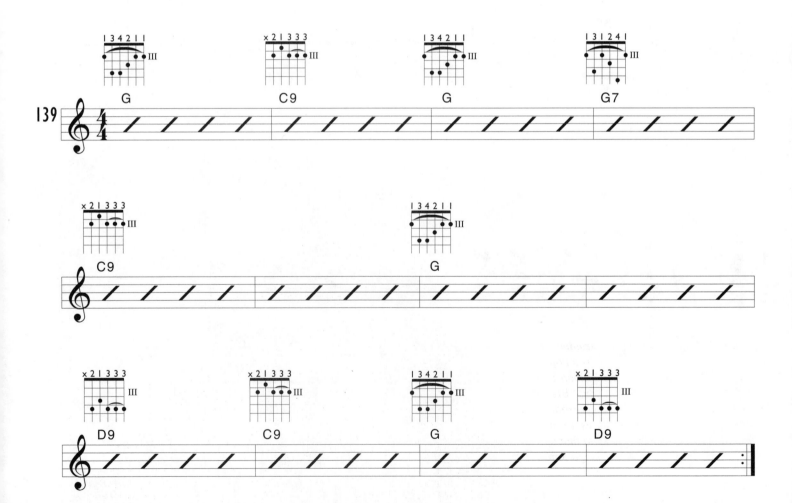

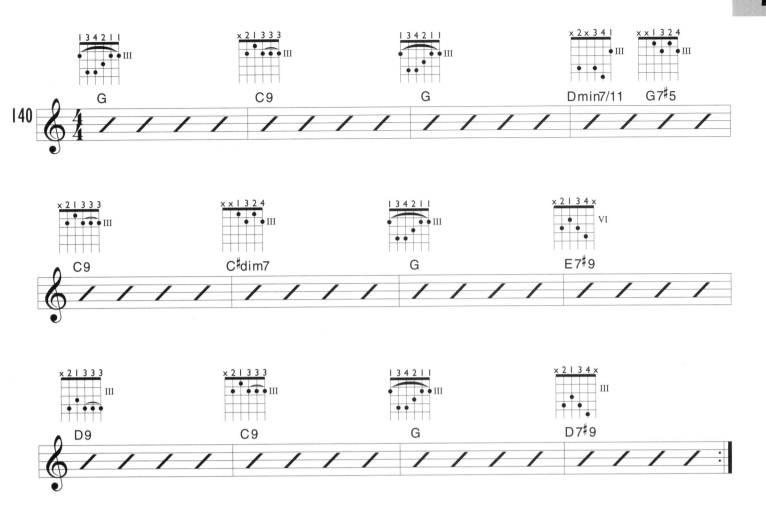

George Benson *(b. 1943) is a Grammy Award-winning jazz guitarist also known as a pop, R&B, and scat singer. He topped the Billboard 200 in 1976 with the triple-platinum album, "Breezin' ". The most influential player in the generation after Wes Montgomery's, Benson uses a rest-stroke picking technique very similar to that of gypsy jazz players such as Django Reinhardt.*

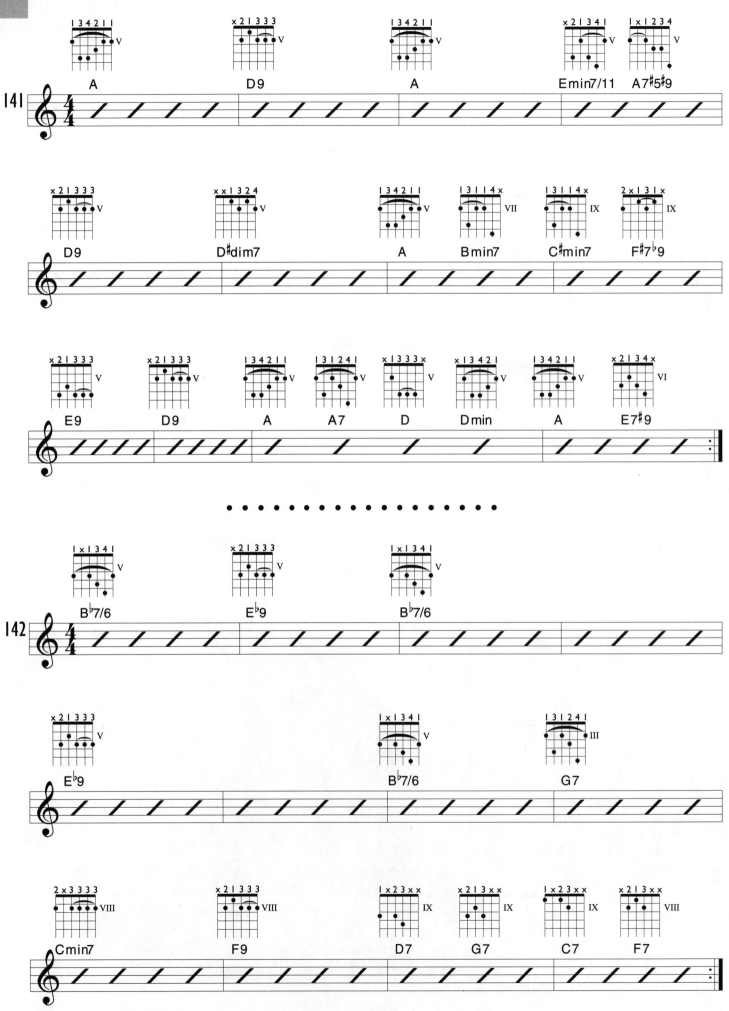

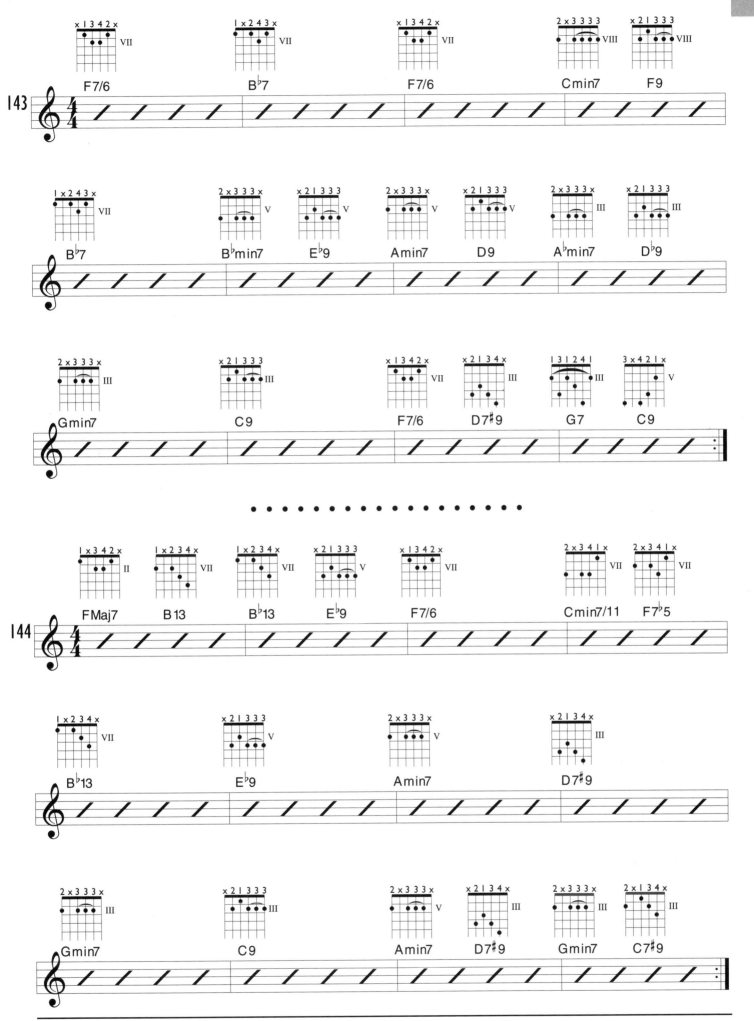

Lesson 1B: Soloing Over Blues Progressions

You have probably had some experience improvising over basic blues progressions. This lesson begins with a review of the minor pentatonic scale, blues scale and Mixolydian mode fingerings. They appear here in the key of C, but you should practice transposing them. Just move to any other root of your choice and work through the same fingerings.

C MINOR PENTATONIC FINGERINGS

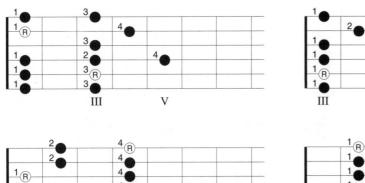

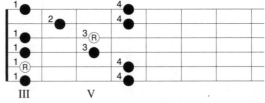

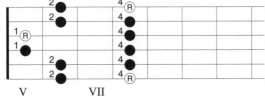

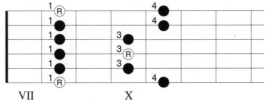

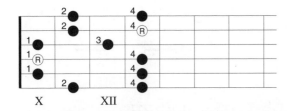

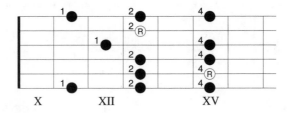

B.B. King, the undisputed "King of the Blues," was born in 1925 and raised in Itta Bena, Mississippi. He had his first hit in 1951 with the Lowell Fulson song "Three O'Clock Blues."

C BLUES SCALE FINGERINGS

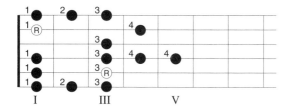

I   III   V

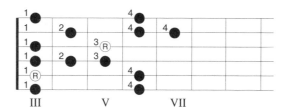

III   V   VII

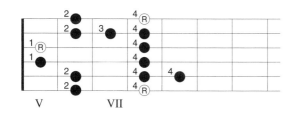

V   VII

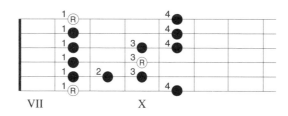

VII   X

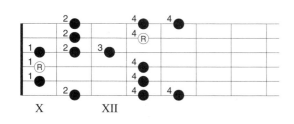

X   XII

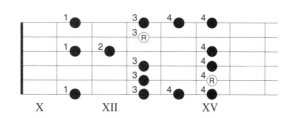

X   XII   XV

C MIXOLYDIAN FINGERINGS

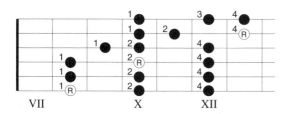

VII   X   XII

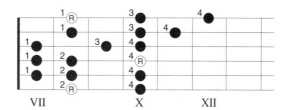

VII   X   XII

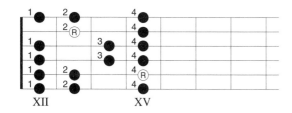

XII   XV

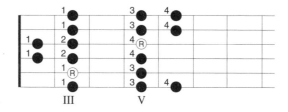

III   V

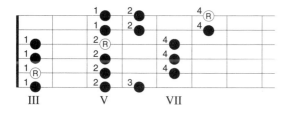

III   V   VII

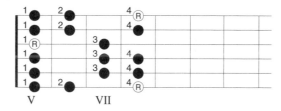

V   VII

SAMPLE BLUES SOLOS

There is a big difference between learning improvisational tools, such as scales, and actually putting them to use. At first, we tend to organize them into patterns in different areas of the fingerboard. In actual practice, we usually combine the various tools and utilize the entire fingerboard. This is because the ideas we hear in our heads don't always conform to organized fingering patterns. In the sample blues solos that follow, you will find that the scales being used jump around to various parts of the fingerboard. Study these solos and memorize the parts that you enjoy so you can use them in your own solos.

BLUES SOLO #1

Track 43

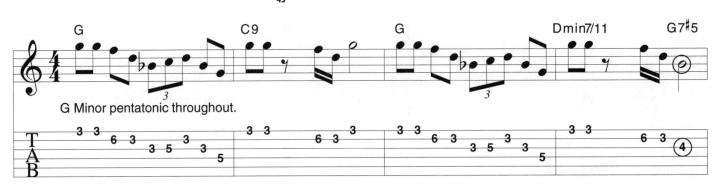

G Minor pentatonic throughout.

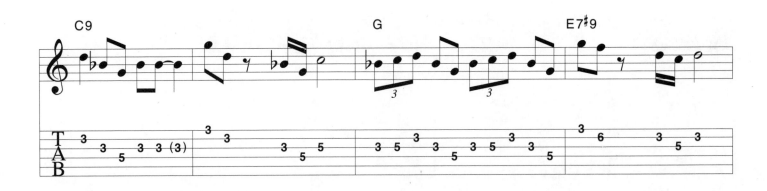

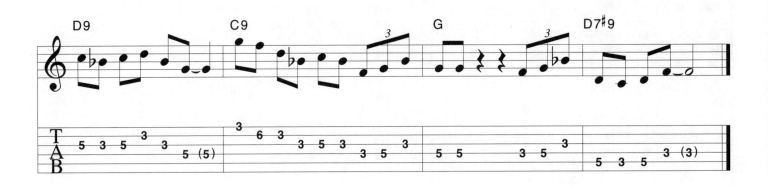

𝅗𝅥 = Target chord tones

BLUES SOLO #2

Track 44

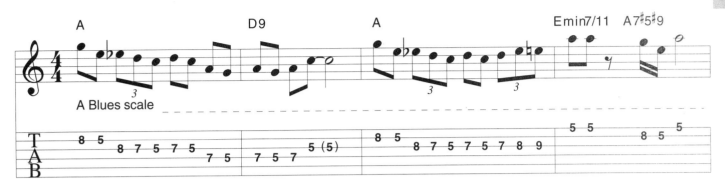

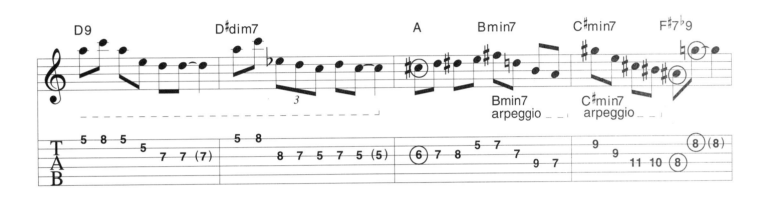

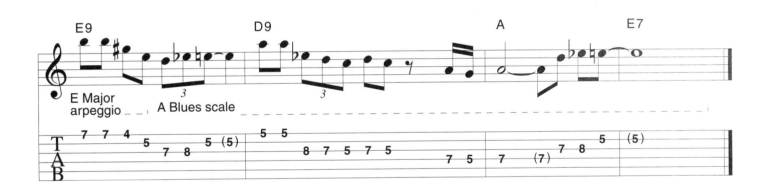

BLUES SOLO #3

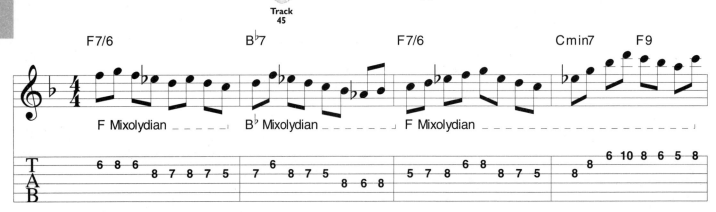

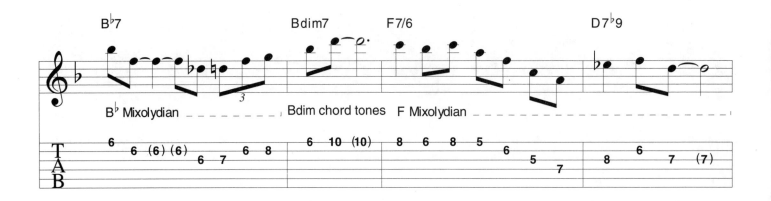

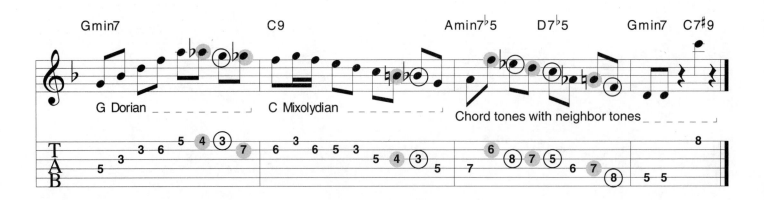

♩ = Neighbor tones

𝅗𝅥 = Target chord tones

CHAPTER 6

Lesson 1A: Rhythm Changes

Just as the blues form is part of our "stock and trade," *rhythm changes* are a very important part of our vocabulary. This chord progression was originally found in the song *I've Got Rhythm* by George Gershwin. It has been the basis for literally dozens of songs, and has been a favorite progression of improvisers for decades. *Oleo*, by Sonny Rollins, *Anthropology* by Charlie Parker and *The Flintstones* would be examples of songs based on these changes. There are actually many variations on this progression, but the example below represents its most basic form.

RHYTHM

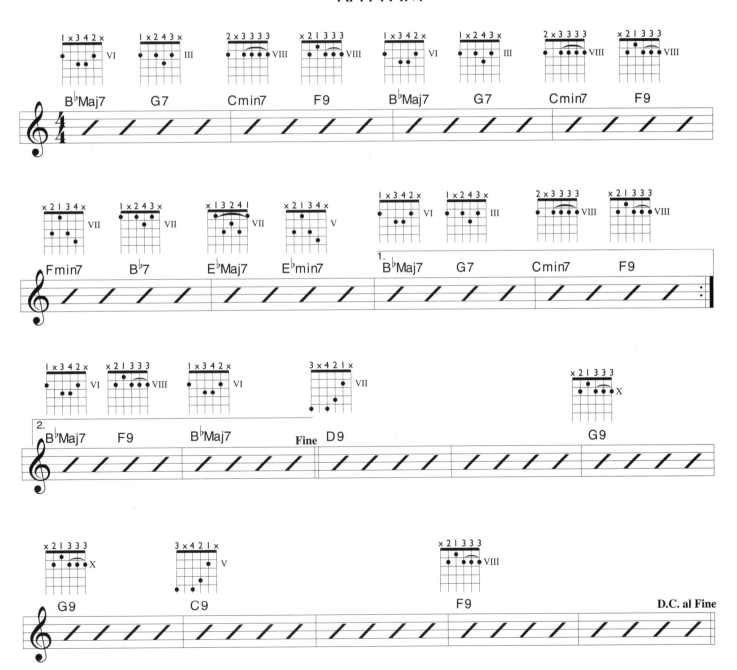

D.C. al Fine = Return to the beginning and play until the *Fine*.

Lesson 1B: Soloing Over Rhythm Changes

This solo utilizes scales that you learned in both this book and *Beginning Jazz Guitar*. As you progress, you'll find that rhythm changes are usually highly altered and extended, so that more interesting scales and improvisational devices can be used. For now, just become familiar with the sound of this progression. Use the audio that is available with this book, or record yourself playing the changes, so that you can practice playing along and improvising your own solo.

RHYTHM SOLO

Track 46

CHAPTER 7

Lesson 1A: Turnarounds

A *turnaround* is a two- or four-measure section at a first ending, or at the end of a tune. A turnaround creates a smooth harmonic transition back to the first measure. You will find turnarounds in most jazz tunes. Generally, the guitarist can choose to play any one of the many kinds of turnarounds possible and it's up to the other players to react. For variety's sake, it pays to know a lot of different turnarounds. Using a variety of turnarounds will create unexpected twists and turns in an arrangement. They also make good intros and endings.

These are examples of two-measure turnarounds going to C. When playing four-measure turnarounds, the duration of the chords would simply be doubled. Memorize and transpose these and keep your ears open to those other players use.

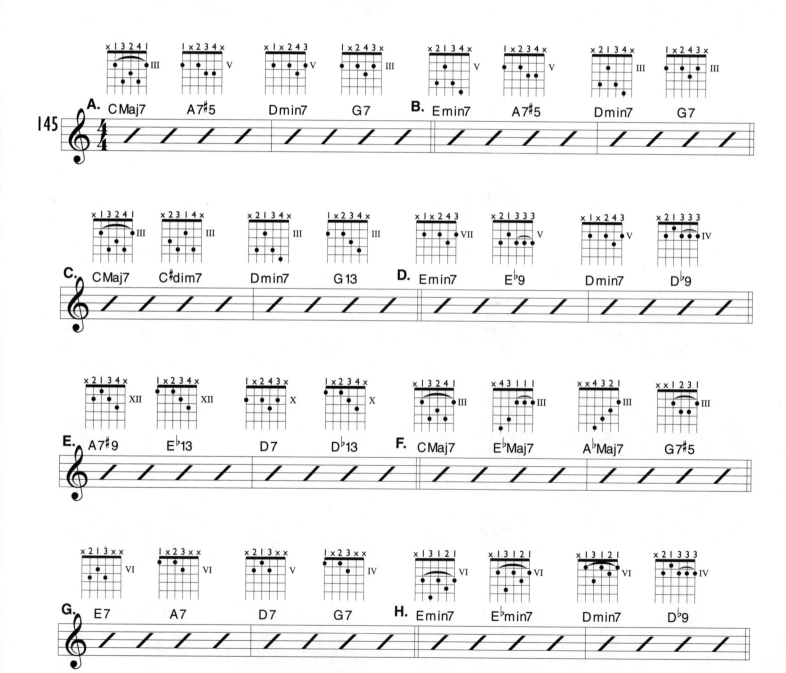

Lesson 1B: Soloing Over Turnarounds

Obviously, if turnarounds are common, you will need to know how to improvise your way through them. Create licks that you know will work over various turnarounds. This will help you make melodically smoother transitions back to the beginnings of your tunes. Study the following turnarounds going to C. Memorize and transpose the ones you like.

CHAPTER 8

Lesson 1A: Chord Solo

Here is a chord solo loosely based on the changes of the song *Misty*. This arrangement incorporates many of the concepts that have been covered in the "A" lessons of this book. Use it to reinforce your understanding of what you have learned. Have fun, and see you in *Mastering Jazz Guitar Chord/Melody!*

FOGGY

Track 48

Lesson 1B: Single-Note Solo

Here is a single note solo also loosely based on the chord changes of *Misty*. This solo incorporates many of the concepts that have been covered in the "B" lessons of this book. Use it to solidify what you have learned. Enjoy this and see you in *Mastering Jazz Guitar Improvisation*!

SINGLE NOTES IN THE MIST

Track 49

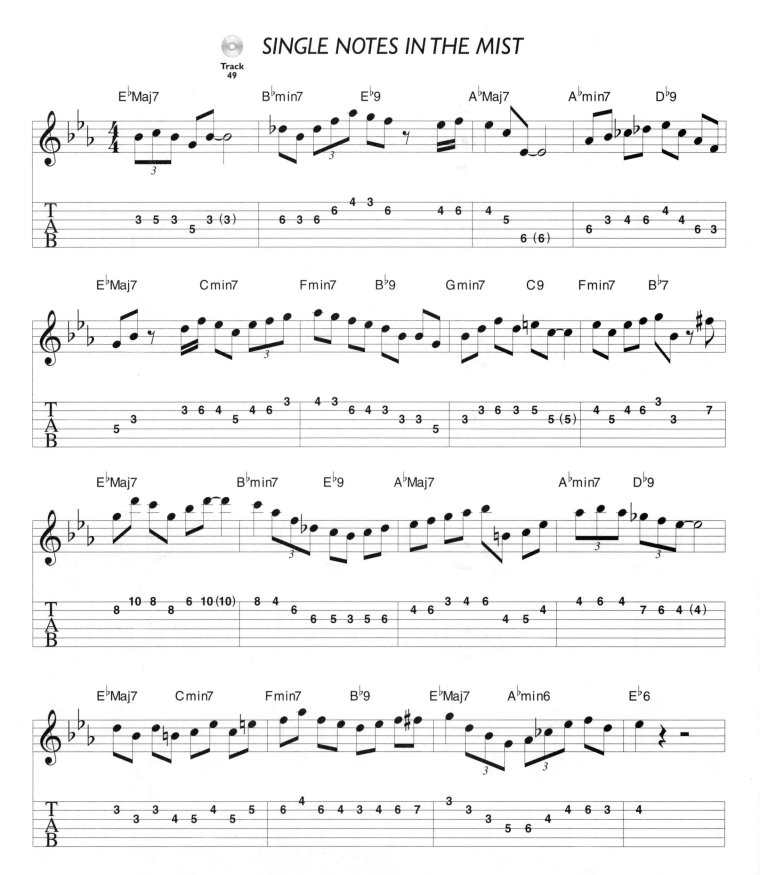

B

CODA

A Medley of Suggestions and Musical Concepts

PLAYING WITH GOOD TONE

Whether you play an electric or acoustic guitar, it is very important to always play with good tone. Being comfortable with your tone may be the single most important factor in giving a satisfying performance.

The environment you are playing in at any given time is one of the central issues of your tone. Are you playing outdoors? In a small club with "dead" acoustics? In a large gymnasium with lots of ambience? A recording studio? A cathedral? Each of these environments will affect your overall sound differently. Chances are the "perfect" amp and guitar settings for practicing at home will not do at all for a live performance. Expect this and show up to gigs early to allow lots of tweaking time. Also, various effects processors can make a difference. Spend time learning how your effects work so you have complete control over the sound. Perfect tone, like perfect nights, are rare commodities. Twiddling knobs is a fact of life.

In spite of all the external factors, your hands control the tone of your instrument more than any other factor. It pays to learn and maintain good technique. More than any room or effects processor, it will give you greater control of nuance. This is as true for electric guitarists as it is for acoustic players. Don't rely on rooms and electronics for your sound. Count on your own technique to ensure a consistently good sound. A great tone will make your performances more fulfilling. Work on it.

MORE ABOUT PRACTICING

In *Beginning Jazz Guitar* you learned that you need to practice slowly. You also need to identify exactly what you need to practice. You are probably asking yourself how anyone can practice all of the concepts, all of these chords and arpeggios, and all of these scales and melodic techniques introduced in this series of books. The answer is that you can't always practice everything. It is generally best to focus on a few aspects of your playing, but work on them very hard. With a little luck, you will live a long life and there will be plenty of time to practice all the things you want to work on. It would be unrealistic to expect to be able to work on everything every day. Some players maintain the same practice schedule for only a couple of weeks. They find that regularly changing their practice routines keeps things interesting, and they accomplish more.

The most important areas for practice are:

Reading (or sight-reading)   Learning Tunes
Harmony and Chord Studies   Ear-Training
Improvisation   Composition (for those so inclined)
Right-Hand Technique   Practicing for the Gig
Left-Hand Technique

This list is not in order of importance. What is important to you will change as time goes on. Practicing things you find easy is a waste of time. Practice those things that are most difficult for you. Try to cover two or three of these areas daily, and maintain the same routine for just a couple of weeks. Then, when you are ready, change it. Remember, jazz guitar is an art—and you can't force it along.

By far, practicing for the gig is the most important thing. This is where you are being heard. This gig, hopefully, will lead you to the next gig, and the next and so on. Many times, the kind of gigs you get determine what will become your strongest skills. For instance, I never really intended to study solo guitar techniques as much as I have, but for years I kept landing solo gigs. I practiced for the gig every day and through the years it has become a specialty of mine. Most of the areas of study I have become proficient in are the result of practicing for the gig I was playing at the time.

There will be times when structured practice is called for, but there will also be times when you will just have to follow your intuition. If you wake up in the morning thinking about last night's gig and realize that you didn't have enough dominant 7$^\flat$9 licks, you had better learn some more dominant 7$^\flat$9 licks that day.

There is not one right way to practice. Your practice life is a living, breathing and constantly changing force. Be honest about what you need to work on and let your intuition guide your course.

THE VALUE OF PRACTICING ALONG A SINGLE STRING

In *Beginning Jazz Guitar* there is a section about why we learn and play things in locked positions—fingerings that we can slide around the fingerboard. You can't beat this concept for getting mileage out of your ideas. One fingering can be moved around to many different octaves and keys. The trouble with playing that way is that sometimes it can lock us into thinking the same way all the time. Our solos become predictable. Sometimes, a change in perspective is in order. I suggest that you start learning all of your scales, modes and arpeggios up and down single strings. In fact, you could even practice reading music this way. After a while, try working on sets of two adjacent strings, then try it on sets of three strings.

The advantage to this is that, although the notes you are playing are the same as those in locked positions, your vantage point is much different. The easiest way to discover this for yourself is to record a progression and improvise using only one string. At first, your lack of familiarity will be evident, but after a while you may find that your ideas are radically different than usual. You may not want to play this way all the time, but it could be a refreshing change.

SINGING ALONG WITH IMPROVISED LINES

When you improvise, the ideal is to first hear an idea in your head, and then execute it. Many players don't really do this. They just play a lick and then say to themselves, "*Hmmm*, that worked," or "*Oops*, that didn't." Developing the ability to "hear first" is a lifetime pursuit. There will be times you can do this very well and times you just can't. Many factors contribute to this: mood, distractions, music being played, the level of musicianship in the band and how you are feeling that day, to name a few.

Singing along with what you are playing is a good way to begin training yourself to hear first. Sing or hum along as you play, trying to duplicate all the pitches and rhythms. Eventually you will find that your singing initiates your solo ideas. This is how you will begin to bridge the gap between your brain and your fingers.

It is in your best interests to take the time to develop this skill. For most players, this is just a practice technique. But some others, like George Benson, have made it part of their style. Try it for awhile and your solos will become more lyrical.

LISTENING TO THE GREATS

Listening is another important part of becoming a good jazz musician. You have to listen all the time. Listen to current artists, and listen to the greats of the past. Listen analytically, and listen for the influences you want in your own playing. Listen to all styles of music, and listen to all instruments. Listen to Jimi Hendrix and listen to Ravi Shankar. Listen to Purcell and Mozart and listen to James Taylor. Listening is how we communicate with all musicians: past, present and future. If you listen to Bach or Ellington, they are communicating with you; you are hearing music they both heard in their heads. Read through lots of printed music as well listening to recordings.

It is very important to study the history of music—all music. Learn about the music of other cultures as well. Having this perspective will improve your playing and give you a realistic view of where you stand as an artist.

It is a good idea for more advanced students to study one artist exclusively for a while. During this time read as much about the artist's life as you can find, learn several of their compositions, transcribe a few of their solos, and listen to their recordings constantly. Then move on to another artist. This is a fascinating way to study and improve your own playing and comprehension.

Practice listening. By this I mean that you should listen to a new piece of music the following way:

1. Listen to the tune and the whole band at once.
2. Listen again, focusing on only the drummer.
3. Next time, listen only to the bass part.
4. Now listen for the rhythm guitar and/or piano part(s).
5. Finally, focus on only the melody.

Now listen to the whole song again as you did at first. Did you learn anything? Did you get ideas for your own playing? If so, isolate them, learn them and incorporate them into your own playing.

Jazz Artists

The artists listed below are just some of the people who have made an indelible mark in jazz history. Their influence cannot be over estimated. Listen!

Guitar

Kenny Burrell	Scott Henderson
Larry Carlton	Alan Holdsworth
Charlie Christian	Barney Kessel
John Collins	Steve Khan
Larry Coryell	Pat Martino
Al Dimeola	John McLaughlin
Joe Diorio	Wes Montgomery
Herb Ellis	Oscar Moore
George Van Eps	Joe Pass
Ron Eschete	Django Reinhardt
Tal Farlow	Emily Remler
Bruce Foreman	Lee Ritenour
Frank Gambale	Howard Robert
Mick Goodrick	John Scofield
Ted Greene	Mike Stern
Jim Hall	

Trumpet / Trombone

Trumpet	Trombone
Nat Adderly (cornet)	Tommy Dorsey
Chet Baker	Al Grey
Clifford Brown	J.J. Johnson
Miles Davis	Jack Teagarden
Dizzy Gillespie	Bill Watrous
Benny Golson	Kai Winding
Freddie Hubbard	
Louis Armstrong	
Wynton Marsalis	

Vibes / Clarinet

Vibes	Clarinet
Gary Burton	Eddie Daniels
Lionel Hampton	Benny Goodman
Bobby Hutchinson	
Milt Jackson	

Violin / Flute

Violin	Flute
Michael Urbania	Yusef Latif
Stephan Grappelli	Hubert Laws
Stuff Smith	James Moddy
Jean Luc Ponty	Dave Valentin

Saxes

Cannonball Adderly	Lee Konitz
Anthony Braxton	Yusef Latiff
Michael Brecker	Charles Lloyd
Ritchie Cole	Gerry Mulligan
Ornette Coleman	Charlie Parker
John Coltrane	Sonny Rollins
Paul Desmond	Pharoah Sanders
Stan Getz	Wayne Shorter
Coleman Hawkins	Phil Woods
Joe Henderson	Lester Young

Keyboard

Chick Corea	Thelonius Monk
George Duke	Oscar Peterson
Bill Evans	Bud Powell
Russell Ferrante	George Shearing
Erroll Garner	Horace Silver
Dave Grusin	Martial Solal
Herbie Hancock	Art Tatum
Earl Hines	Billy Taylor
Keith Jarrett	McCoy Tyner
Cecil Johnson	Joe Zawinul

Bass

Steve Bailey	Jimmy Johnson
Tim Bogert	Bob Magnusson
Ray Brown	Michael Manring
Ron Carter	Charles Mingus
Paul Chambers	Jaco Pastorius
Stanley Clarke	John Patitucci
Nathan East	Chuck Rainey
Mark Egan	Lee Sklar
Charlie Haden	Steve Swallow
Luther Hughs	Buster Williams
James Jamerson	Victor Wooten
Alphonso Johnson	

Singers

Ella Fitzgerald	Carmen McCray
Billy Holiday	Bobby McFerrin
Eddir Jefferson	Sarah Vaughn
Kevin Letau	Casandra Wilson
	Nancy Wilson

MASTERING
CHORD/MELODY

JAZZ GUITAR

TABLE OF CONTENTS

Chapter 5—Simultaneous Chords and Walking Bass Lines

Chapter 6—Searching Out New Voicings

Coda—A Medley of Suggestions and Musical Concepts

Track 01

Companion online audio is included with this book to make learning easier and more enjoyable. The symbol shown on the left appears next to every example in the book that features an MP3 track. Use the MP3s to ensure you're capturing the feel of the examples and interpreting the rhythms correctly. The track number below the symbol corresponds directly to the example you want to hear (example numbers are above the icon). All the track numbers are unique to each "book" within this volume, meaning every book has its own Track 1, Track 2, and so on. (For example, *Beginning Jazz Guitar* starts with Track 1, as does *Intermediate jazz Guitar, Mastering Jazz Guitar: Chord/Melody* and *Mastering Jazz Guitar: Improvisation*.) Track 1 for each book will help you tune your guitar.

See page 1 for instructions on how to access the online audio.

INTRODUCTION

In this section, you will learn how to play in a style we call *Chord/Melody*. In this style, songs are arranged so the harmony, melody, rhythm and sometimes the bass parts are played simultaneously. These arrangements can be played alone or, if desired, make it possible for the guitarist to lead his or her own group. Players who study this style know that it can be one of the deepest forms of musical self-expression. Also, there are enough concepts to learn and apply to keep one intrigued for a lifetime.

It has always amazed me that many guitarists just stand there not knowing what to do when asked to play a song alone. The whole idea behind playing a musical instrument is to play music —play songs. It seems that most guitarists know the parts of songs they would play in a band, but if they had to play something as a solo, well, most players would be stuck.

This section is not for complete beginners. The material found here is for the student who has been studying the information in the first two sections of this book, *Beginning Jazz Guitar* and *Intermediate Jazz Guitar*, or the equivalent. You should be familiar with major scales, chord construction, major chord scales and altered chords. In the first two sections of this book, each lesson had two separate sections. The "A" section dealt with chords and harmony while the "B" section covered the topic of single-line improvisation. This section focuses completely on chord/melody and harmonic concepts. It starts right where the "A" sections of the *Intermediate* section left off. (*Mastering Jazz Guitar: Improvisation* starts where the "B" sections in the *Intermediate* part of this book left off.)

While I personally prefer reading musical notation, it is not necessary in order to obtain maximum results from this book. Examples are written in both standard notation and tablature. While TAB is effective, it is not nearly as expressive as musical notation. Non-readers are missing out on an overwhelming amount of musical and instructional material. You don't have to be a super sight reader, but the ability to decipher musical notation is very important. Of course, the better you read music, the better your comprehension and musicality will be. This will increase your enjoyment.

You may be surprised by the added benefits of becoming proficient in chord/melody playing. Some of these are: a much greater awareness of harmony, better visualization of arpeggio shapes, a more sophisticated sense of melody while improvising, and a dramatic improvement in technique and strength. Also, keep in mind that you may be able to find employment as a solo guitarist if band gigs aren't available.

After completing this section, you will be able to arrange your own chord/melody tunes and you will have a deep understanding of chord progressions and harmony. This will allow you to communicate with other musicians more effectively.

Take your time, practice slowly and have fun!

CHAPTER 1

Right-Hand Options

Most guitar students place about ninety percent of their attention and efforts on their left hand. Limitations in their playing are usually blamed on some fault of the left hand only. The real situation is that, with the exception of hammer-ons, pull-offs, trills and other decorative devices, it takes two hands to produce one note. Therefore, equal attention should be paid to both hands at all times.

In single-note playing, most guitarists have faster left hands than right hands. When both hands are fully developed, the right hand actually "powers" the left. Several different right hand techniques lend themselves to chord/melody playing. Pick style, fingerstyle, and combining the two all have their distinct sounds and advantages.

PICK STYLE

In the early days of solo jazz guitar, pick style was the preferred method. Strumming chords with a pick gives you the opportunity to enjoy many different attacks and timbres. Single note lines are played with alternating down and up strokes. Many players use this method when they first start studying chord/melody playing because it allows them the use of a good picking technique they have already developed in their previous studies. The only real disadvantage is that there are many chord voicings that will be impossible to play because of skipped strings in the fingering.

FINGERSTYLE CHORDS

There are actually many styles of fingerstyle playing. In the traditional method the thumb and first three fingers are used. In some folk styles, the thumb and two fingers work pretty well. I use all four fingers and the thumb. This chart shows the right hand finger designations:

> thumb = *p*
> first finger = *i*
> middle finger = *m*
> third finger = *a*
> pinky = *c*

Generally, *p* controls the sixth and fifth strings, while *i* is on the fourth, *m* is on the third, *a* is on the second and *c* is on the first. If *p* is playing on the fifth or fourth strings, *i* plays the third, *m* plays the second and *a* plays the first. Different songs and exercises will require some shifting of hand placement. It pays to be flexible.

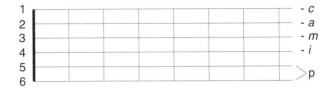
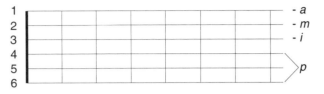

One real advantage of playing chords in this manner is that you don't have to worry about muting strings or barring over a note that is unwanted in the chord. You pluck only the tones you want to hear. Playing fingerstyle also allows you to lower or raise the volume of individual notes in a chord. One other consideration is that it is the only way to sound the voices simultaneously. When strumming with a pick or your thumb the notes will always appear one after the other. With fingerstyle techniques you sound harmonies like a keyboard instrument—all the notes of a chord at the same moment. There are many great chords that are impossible to play with a pick. Spend time working on right hand techniques. It will pay off in terms of greater flexibility and versatility and allow you to play many more styles of music.

To play single-note lines fingerstyle, most jazz players either alternate their first two fingers (*i,m*) or alternate their thumb and second fingers (*p,m*). There are many good classical guitar books available that should be investigated by anyone wishing to pursue this style of picking.

PICK AND FINGERS TECHNIQUE

In addition to using a pick and developing fingerstyle technique, it is also a good idea to practice using a pick along with your three remaining fingers. Most players occasionally do this and, for many, it is their primary way of playing.

Usually the pick is held between the *p* and *i* fingers and takes care of the sixth, fifth and fourth strings while *m* covers the third, *a* covers the second and *c* handles the first. The advantage to this technique is that it allows you to switch from fingerstyle to using a pick with very little effort. When playing strictly fingerstyle, you either have to palm the pick, which can interfere with your right hand technique, or put it somewhere else (like in your mouth). The constant switching can be a hindrance. The major disadvantage is that you are limited to playing four-note chords, since two of your fingers are occupied with holding the pick.

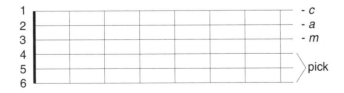

Like almost everything else with guitar it is best to learn every technique instead of relying on just one or two. This way you will be prepared for any musical situation that comes your way.

CHAPTER 2

Combining Melody and Harmony

LESSON 1: RECOGNIZING CHORD TONES

A chord/melody arrangement allows you to play the melody with chords. Usually the melody will be the highest note in the chord, and the tones underneath produce the harmony. Not every note in an arrangement needs to be harmonized. Some players lean toward heavy harmonization, and others prefer a more sparse approach. Ultimately, it is a matter of personal taste.

One of the first skills that needs to be developed is the ability to recognize chord tones in a melody. In Examples 1, 2 and 3, the melody notes that are also part of the accompanying chord are highlighted.

 = chord tone

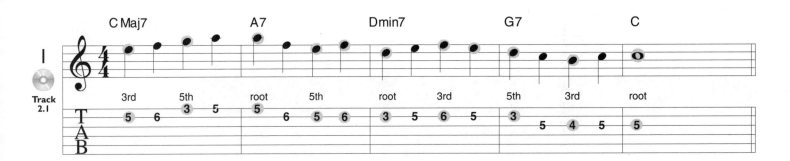

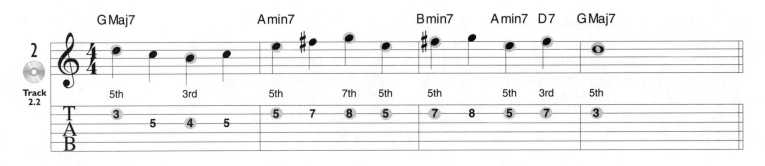

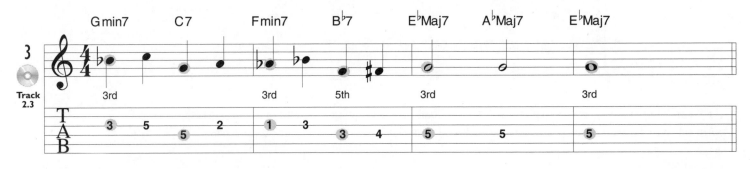

Obviously, the better you know your chord formulas and arpeggios, the easier it will be to recognize chord tones. The next step is to find chord voicings that have the melody notes on top. Here are some possible harmonizations for Examples 1, 2 and 3.

Harmonizations for Example 1

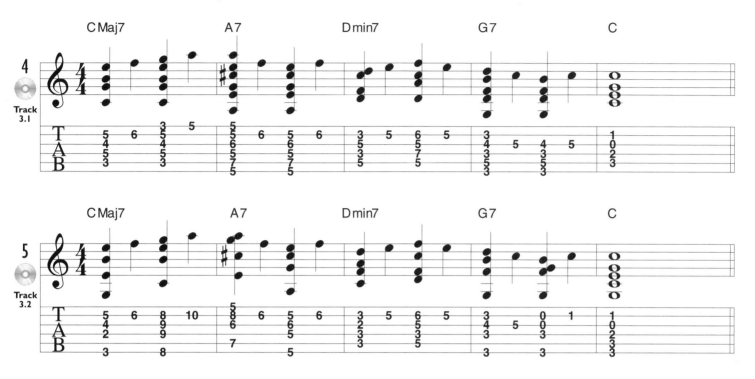

Harmonizations for Example 2

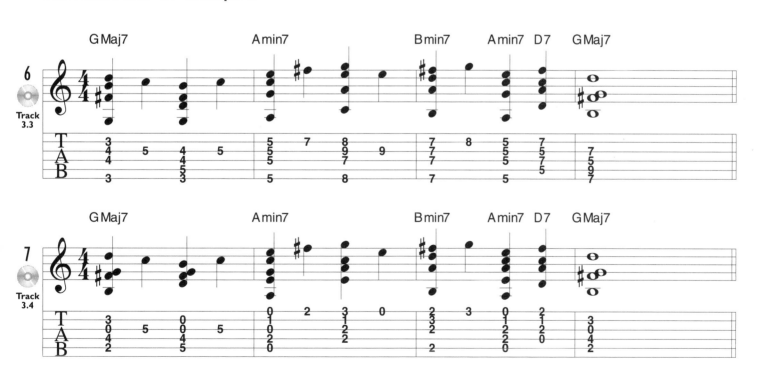

It is often necessary to raise the melody one octave in order to use larger chord voicings.

Harmonizations for Example 3

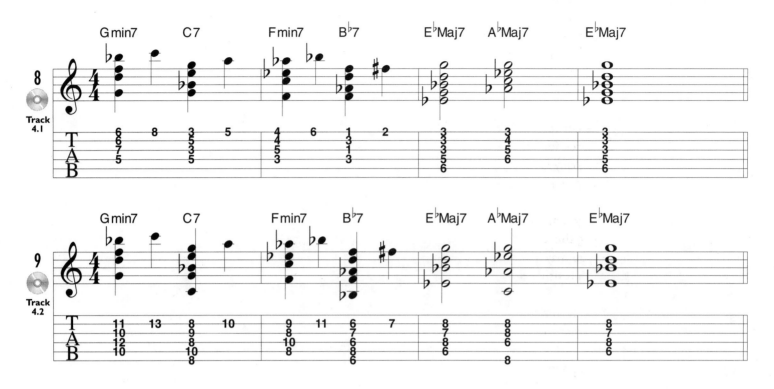

For practice, harmonize the following melodies in as many ways as you can.

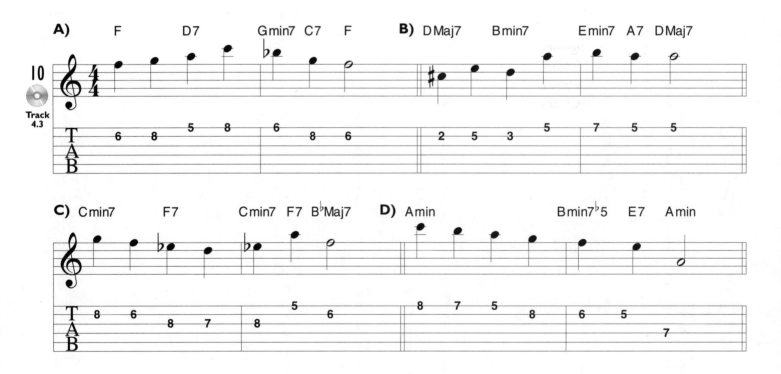

LESSON 2: GUIDELINES FOR ARRANGING

As simple as some of the last examples were, they represent the basic process of harmonizing a melody on the guitar. From here on we will be embellishing this process. There will always be some new harmonizing technique you will want to try. Just keep adding to your collection of harmonic devices and you will gradually develop your own style. Before we investigate some of these techniques, it is important for you to become familiar with some guidelines. They will make your arranging more complete and efficient.

1. When using a lead-sheet (a sketch of a song that shows words, melody and chord symbols only) as a source for your basic melody and chord changes, it is generally helpful to raise the melody an octave. Check the highest and lowest notes in the song to see if an octave change would make the tune easier to harmonize.

2. Consider the possibility that the song might lie on the fingerboard better in a different key. Changing the key can often change the basic character of the tune itself. For instance, you may want to try keys that allow the use of open strings. The extra investigation is usually well worth the effort.

3. Learn to play the melody in single notes first. Explore it in every octave to make sure you understand what the melody is about.

4. Memorize chord changes and be able to play them in various areas of the fingerboard.

5. Arrange your song with the basic chords first. When you have a handle on the basic arrangement, then dress up the harmonies with passing chords, substitutions and harmonizations.

6. Don't carve your arrangements or chord changes in stone. Basically, you want skeletal arrangements from which you can improvise melodically, harmonically and rhythmically. Once you gain confidence with this approach, it is a lot more fun, which, never forget, is the whole idea.

LESSON 3: CHORD ENHANCEMENT

Generally, sheet music will provide the lyrics, the melody and some very basic chord changes for a song. After you know the basic changes you will, no doubt, want to *enhance* the harmonies. Any chord can be *enhanced* as long as it doesn't interfere with the melody. To *enhance* means to simply add extensions or alterations to the basic chord. To most jazz musicians, all the chords within a given quality, or family, (major, minor, dominant, etc.) are interchangeable. In other words, a Major 6th chord can be thought of in the same light as a Major 9th chord or a Major 7th chord. Functionally, they are all the same.

In the chart below, all the chords are interchangeable with any other chord in the same column. At first you will hunt and peck to find really good sounding chord enhancements, but with experience it gets easier and more fun. Context is everything. Taste should be your primary concern. Not everything needs to be enriched.

Major Chords	**Minor Chords**	**Dominant Chords**
Major Triad	minor triad	dom7
Maj6	min6	dom9
Maj7	min7	dom11
Maj9	min9	dom13
Maj13	min11	dom7/6
Maj add9	min13	dom7/11
Maj7/6	minadd9	dom7sus
Maj6/9	min7/11	dom9sus
	min6/9	dom7$^\flat$5
		dom7$^\sharp$5
		dom7$^\flat$9
		dom7$^\sharp$9
		dom7$^\sharp$5$^\sharp$9
		dom7$^\flat$5$^\flat$9
		dom7$^\flat$5$^\sharp$9
		dom7$^\sharp$5$^\flat$9
		dom13$^\flat$9

There are others, but this list is a good start!

It should be noted that chord enhancement is not the same as chord substitution. Chord substitution implies replacing a chord with another chord that has a different root. We'll be getting into this extensively very soon.

In Example 11, a melody is given with basic chord changes. It is then harmonized a few times using the principles of chord enhancement. Make sure you understand each enhancement before moving on.

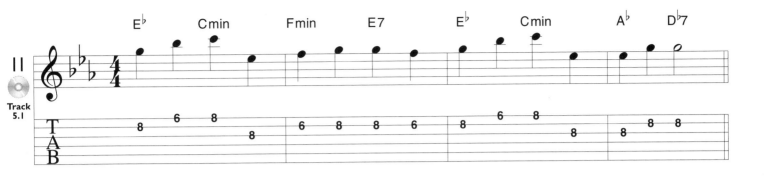

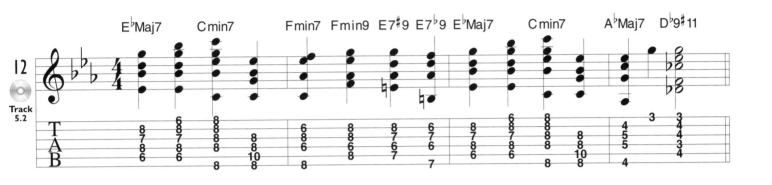

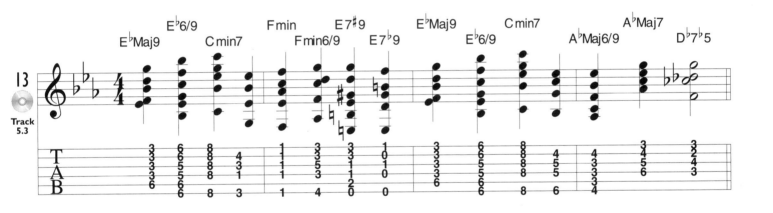

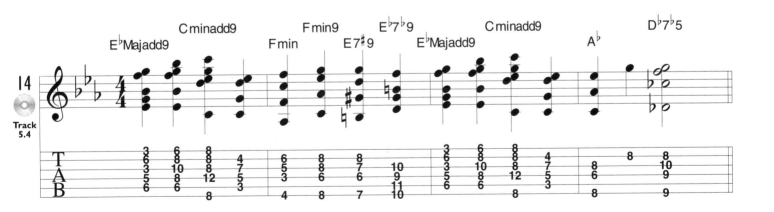

Here is melody (Example 15) and three different harmonizations (Examples 16-18).

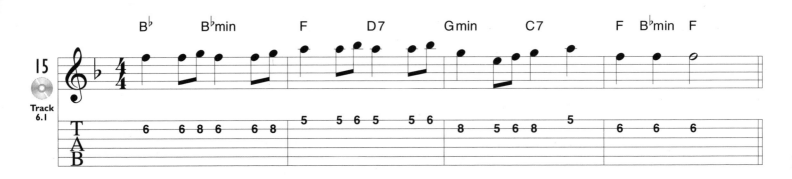

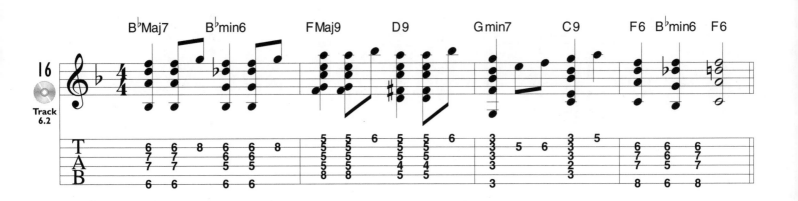

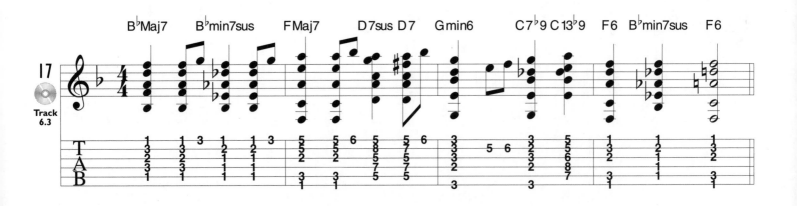

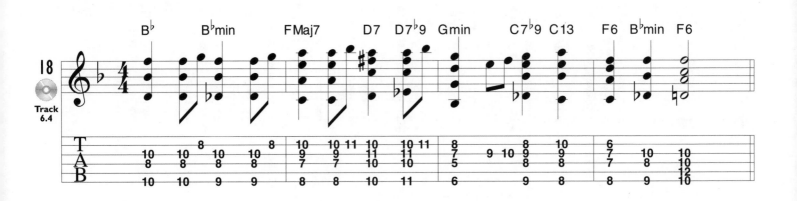

Check out this melody and three possible harmonizations.

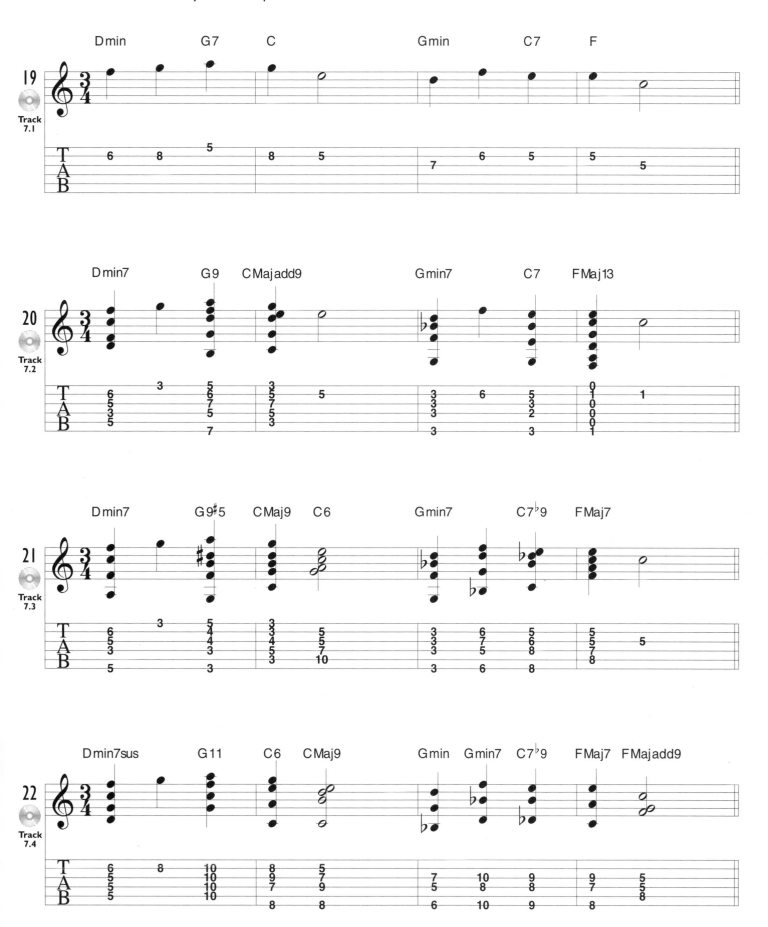

Here is a melody you are sure to know in a chord melody arrangement using chord enhancements.

HOME ON THE RANGE

Track
8

Traditional

08   Mastering Jazz Guitar: Chord/Melody

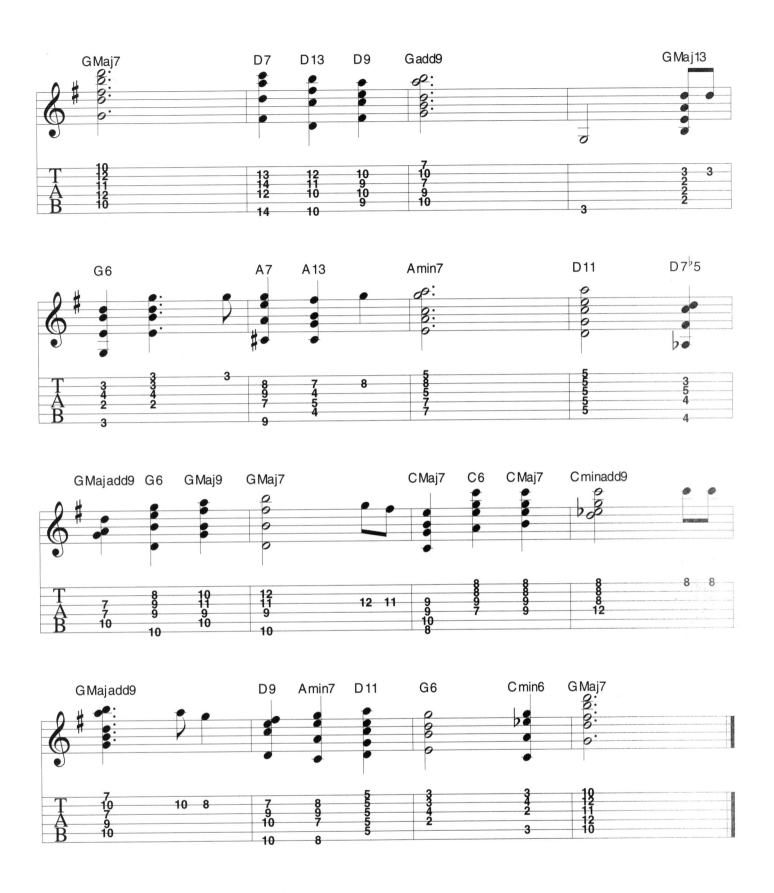

CHAPTER 3

Techniques for Harmonizing
Non-Chord Tones

It is fairly easy to harmonize melodies when the notes happen to be chord tones. Melodies that contain non-chord tones present us with a different kind of challenge. The lessons in this chapter illustrate some ways to handle these situations.

LESSON I: DIADS

Diads, also known as double-stops, are two-note harmonizations. They work very well for chord tones and non-chord tones. Any interval is possible, but 3rds and 6ths are the most common. Experiment and use your good taste. The diads are highlighted in these examples.

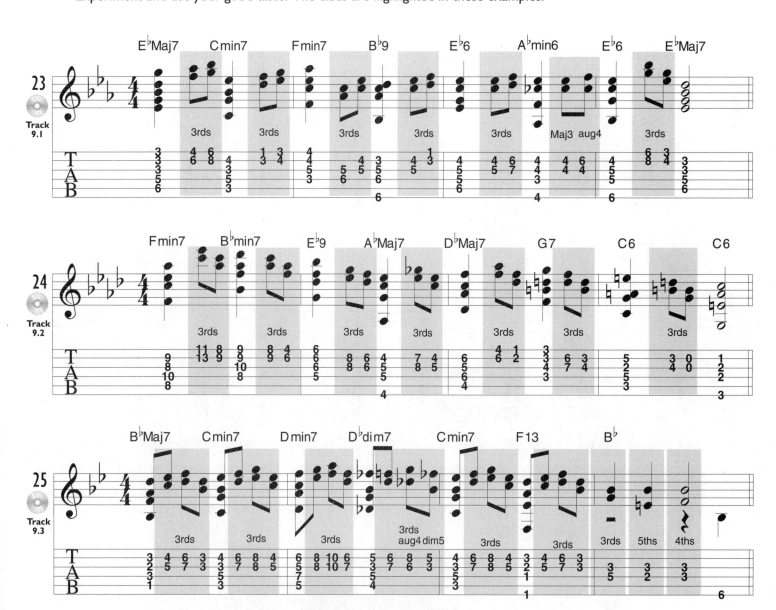

Here is a traditional melody harmonized with diads and chord enhancements.

THE BLUE BELL OF SCOTLAND

Track 10

Traditional

LESSON 2: ADDING THE NON-CHORD TONE

Very often we add a non-chord tone that is in the melody to the chord. This will change the name of the chord, as you will be adding higher extensions and altered tones. This is a common way to come up with enhancements. If it sounds good, use it. If not, harmonize it some other way. Here are three melodies and harmonizations using this technique.

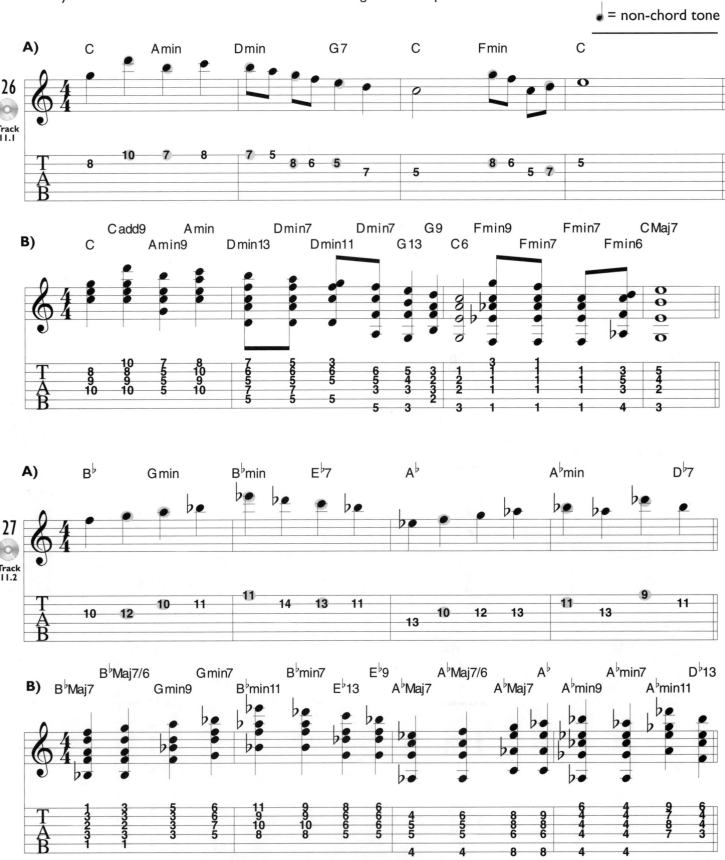

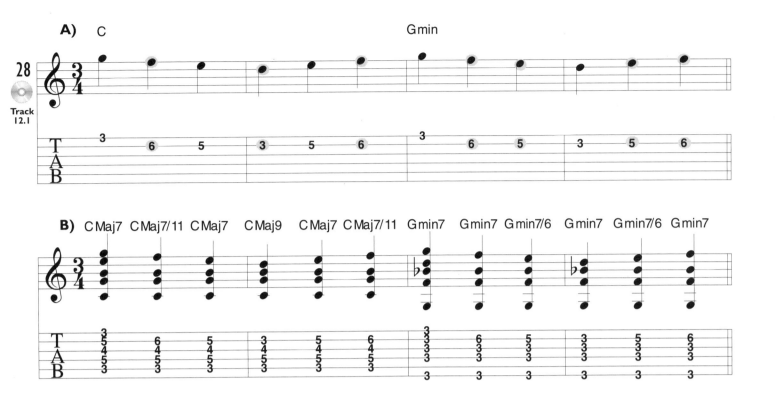

Here is a Stephen Foster song harmonized using this technique.

BEUTIFUL DREAMER

Track 12.2

by Stephen Foster

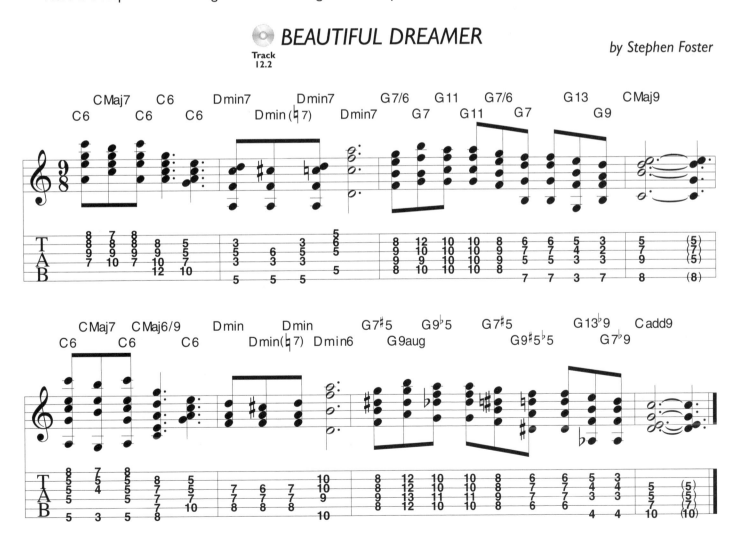

LESSON 3: VOICE LEADING

Voice leading is the term we use to describe the movement of individual voices from one chord to another. This is very important when choosing voicings for a chord melody arrangement. Also, we must decide which of the many enhancement and substitution possibilities to use. Many times trying random voicings will work just fine. Other times, you may want smoother, less abrupt chord changes. Good voice-leading often means arranging your chords so that the voices actually travel in whole and half steps. Look at Examples 29 and 30.

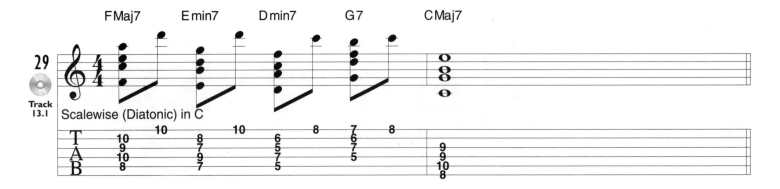

The notes of the chords in Example 30 move scalewise (by whole and half steps of a specific scale) through several different major scales.

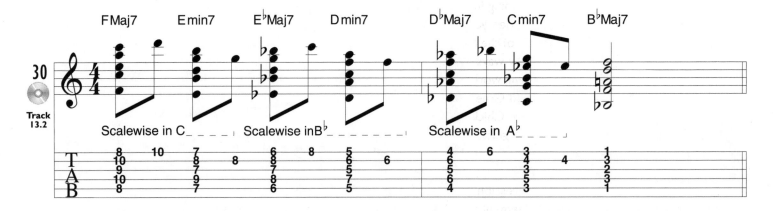

There are other times when only certain voices move in this step-wise manner. Usually, it is the 3rd and the 7th degrees of the chords. This is because chords are defined by their 3rds and 7ths which differentiate major, minor and dominant chords.

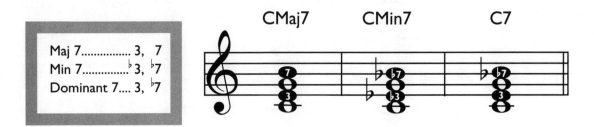

In a ii-V7-I progression, the ♭3 and the ♭7 of the ii chord resolve to the ♭7 and 3 of the V7 chord respectively. The ♭7 and the 3rd of the V7 chord then resolve to the 3rd and the 7th of the I chord respectively. If this is arranged well, the other voices in the chords are free to travel in more creative directions. Experience will be your best teacher.

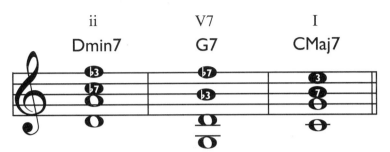

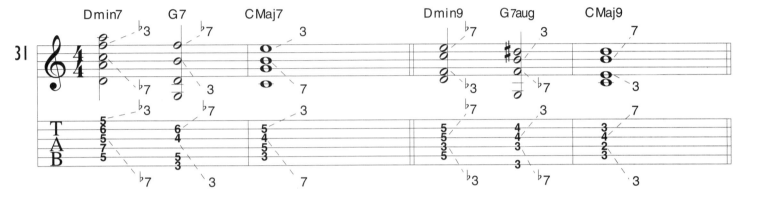

Coming up with interesting voice leading in your arrangements is one of the most enjoyable aspects of chord/melody playing. When you play through the examples in this book, try to listen to each voice separately. Most of the time, whole- and half-step motion is used, although there are exceptions. There are many ways to treat chord progressions, so the bottom line is that whatever sounds good to you will work. Listen to the voice-leading ideas of great chord/ melody players, like Johnny Smith, Ted Greene, George Van Eps and Lenny Breau. Also listen to keyboard players like Keith Jarrett, Chick Corea, Oscar Peterson and especially Bill Evans. Much of this material adapts well to guitar. Orchestral or big band music can also be great sources of voice-leading ideas.

Here are four common chord progressions that demonstrate good voice leading. Listen to them carefully, analyze the voice movement and make the ones you like part of your vocabulary. Read across from left to right.

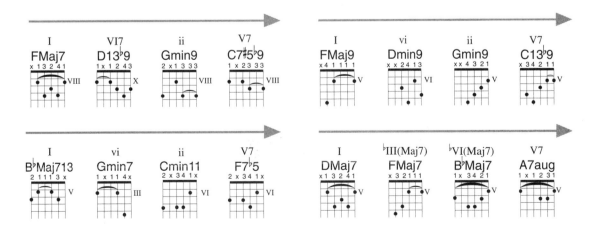

LESSON 4: PASSING CHORDS

A *passing chord* is a chord added between two others to create a smoother transition. Very often you can harmonize both chord and non-chord tones as passing chords.

One common application of passing chords is the use of a dominant chord (altered or unaltered) with a root that is a half step higher, or lower, than the chord being approached. These chords can end up being non-diatonic, or from outside the key. This is OK. It provides an opportunity for good voice leading and adds an element of surprise to a progression. Example 36 "A" shows a basic harmonization. "B" shows how passing chords might be applied. The passing chords are highlighted.

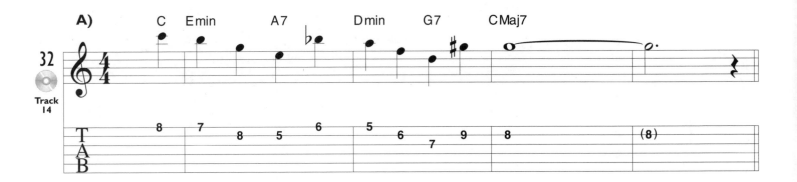

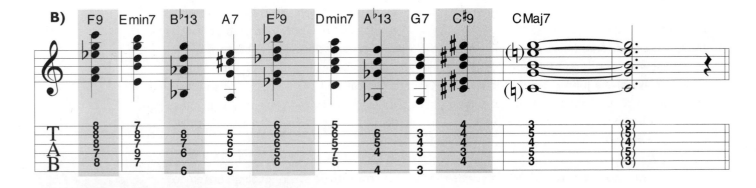

Kenny Burrell *(b. 1931) has performed and recorded with a wide range of jazz musicians. Grounded in bebop and blues, he has worked with such artists as John Coltrane, Coleman Hawkins, Jimmy Smith, Stanely Turrentine, Dizzy Gillespie and Sonny Rollins.*

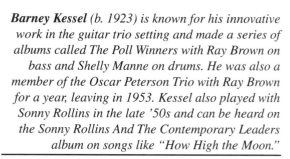

Barney Kessel (b. 1923) is known for his innovative work in the guitar trio setting and made a series of albums called The Poll Winners with Ray Brown on bass and Shelly Manne on drums. He was also a member of the Oscar Peterson Trio with Ray Brown for a year, leaving in 1953. Kessel also played with Sonny Rollins in the late '50s and can be heard on the Sonny Rollins And The Contemporary Leaders album on songs like "How High the Moon."

Here are a few more examples of this technique.

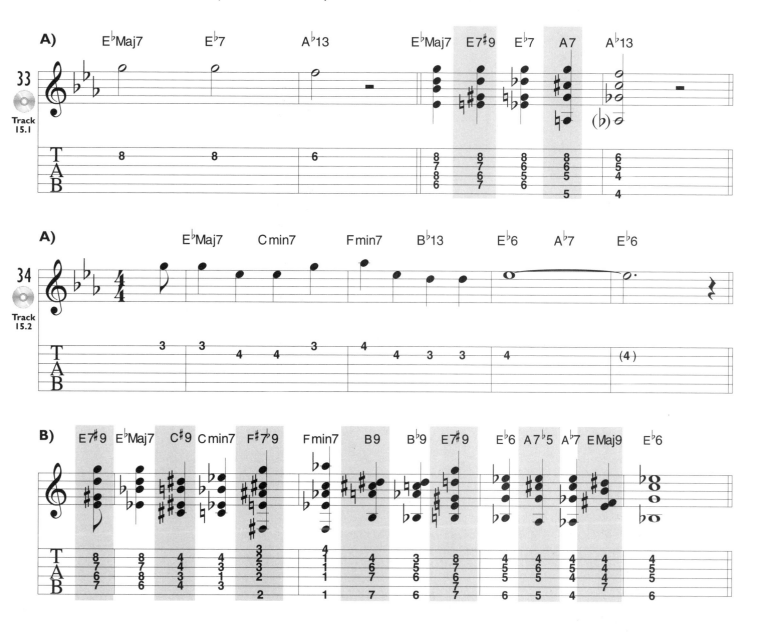

Here is a familiar tune in a chord/melody arrangement demonstrating the use of half-step dominant passing chords. These chords are highlighted.

VIRGINNY

Track 16

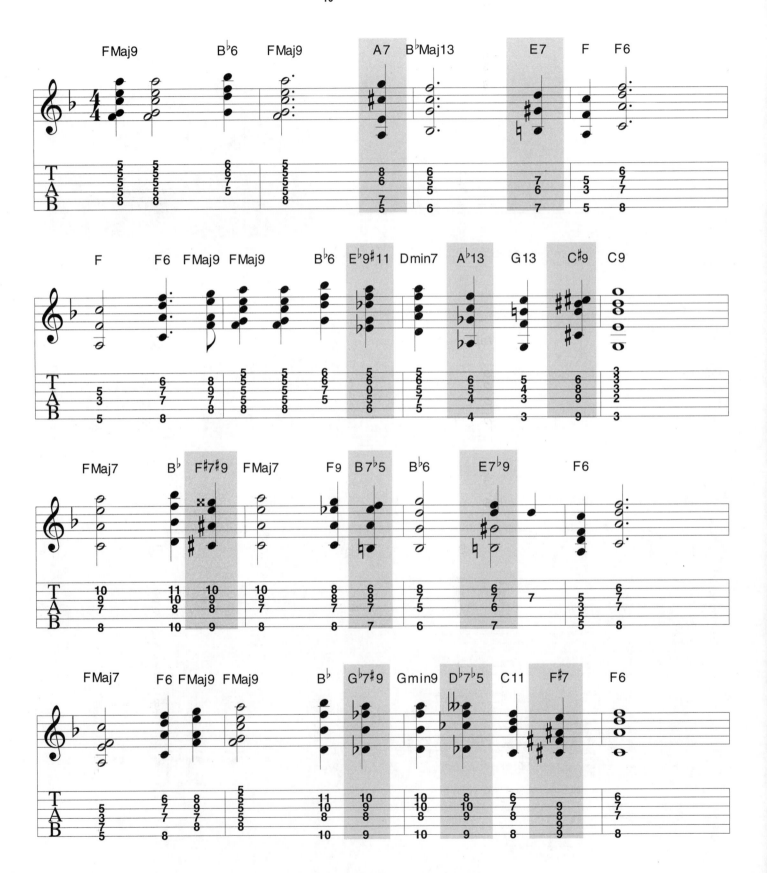

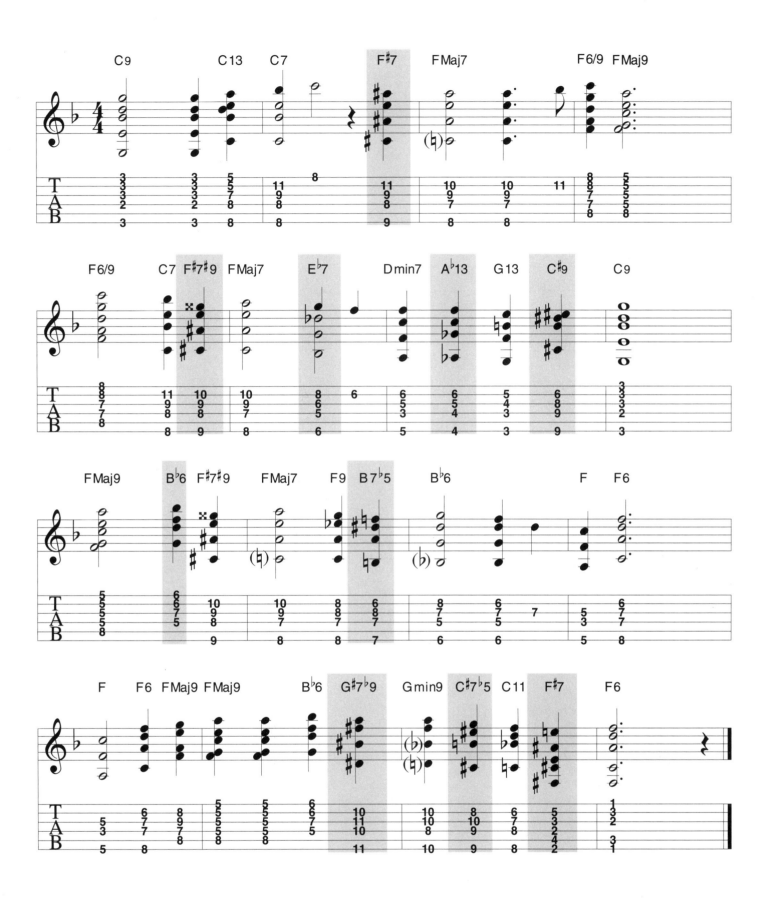

Approaching chords with dominant passing chords works well with just about any progression. When you stop and think about all the possible voicings available, it becomes obvious that you will never have to play a song the same way twice (unless you want to). *Blues in G* shows what happens to a twelve-bar blues when you use this approach. Passing chords are highlighted.

BLUES IN G

Track 17

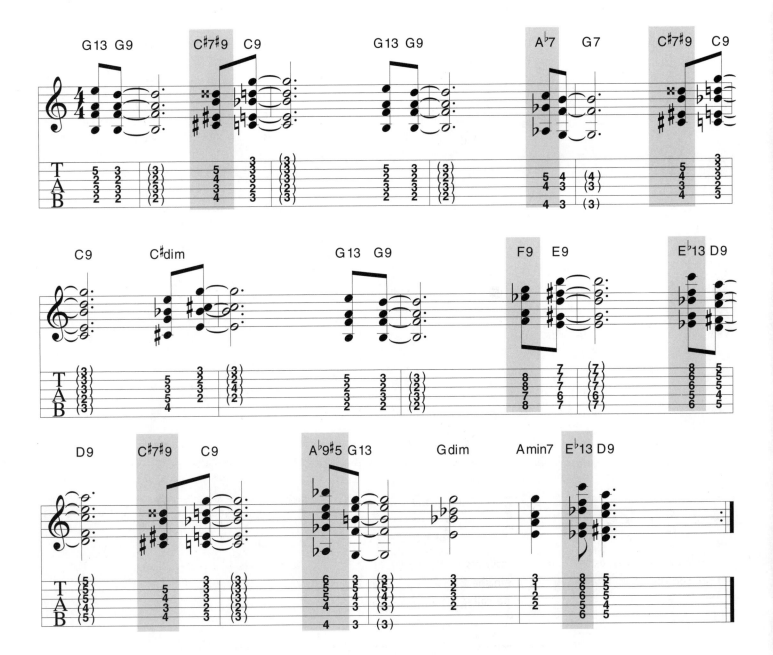

DIMINISHED CHORDS

Diminished chords make nice passing chords and are extremely easy to use. You can place them between any two chords as long as the diminished chord moves to a chord that has a root one half step higher than its own. This will provide a smooth transition because the diminished chord always sounds as if it wants to *resolve* upwards. As the diagrams below illustrate, diminished chords repeat themselves every three frets, so you can choose from among many possible locations on the fingerboard.

G Diminished

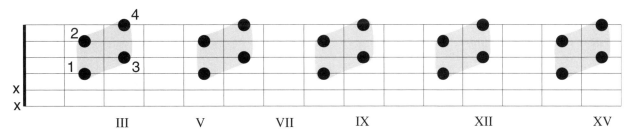

C Diminished

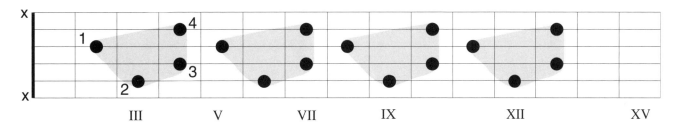

G♭ Diminished

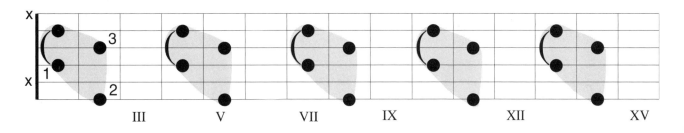

Since all the notes can be *enharmonically respelled*, any note in a diminished chord can be considered the root. For instance, E diminished is spelled E-G-B♭-D♭. If we enharmonically respell the D♭ and call it C♯, that chord can be called C♯dim (C♯-E-G-B♭).

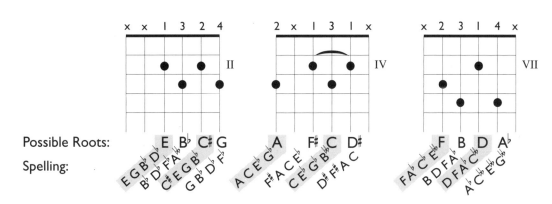

Chapter 3—Techniques for Harmonizing Non-Chord Tones   **221**

The tendency of a diminished 7th chord is to resolve to a chord one half step higher than its root. After centuries of cultural conditioning, our ears like to hear dissonant intervals resolve to consonant intervals. This is evident when analyzing chord progressions found in pop, rock and country music as well as jazz. The diminished 7th chord contains a *tritone* (a root with a ♭5), which is considered very dissonant but is also responsible for much of the "spiciness" found in jazz harmonies. In moving from a Bdim7 to a CMaj7 the root (B) is attracted upward to the root (C) while the ♭5 (F) is attracted downward to the 3rd (E) which changes the tritone to a very consonant sounding major 3rd and produces a satisfying and "expected" resolution.

Diminished 7th chords resolving upward one half step. In Example 35, the same diminished 7th chord is spelled four different ways so that it can resolve to four different chords.

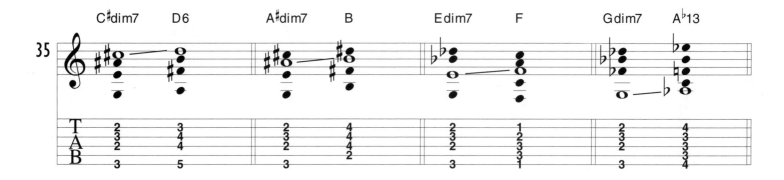

When using diminished chords as passing chords, make sure that one of the notes in the chord is one half step away from the root of the chord you are approaching.

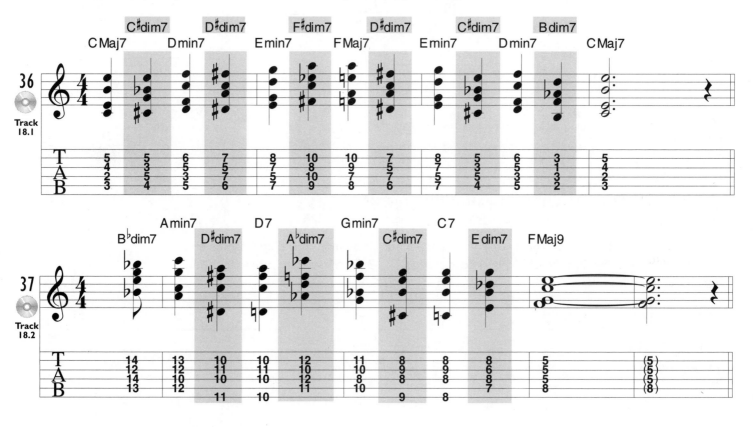

Approaching the I chord with a diminished chord from one half step below the root is a common substitute for the V7. The reason this works is that the two chords have three notes in common and both resolve nicely to I. This example in the key of C illustrates how the tones of a V7 (G7) and a vii (Bdim7) of the final I chord (CMaj7) are similar. It also shows how these tones tend to resolve. The ♭7 (F) of the V7 chord, which is also the ♭3 of the vii chord, tends to resolve downward to the 3 (E) of the I chord. The 3 (B) of the V7, also the root of the vii, becomes the 7 (B) of the I chord. The 5 (D) of the V7 (B) chord, also the ♭3 of vii, resolves down to the root of I (C).

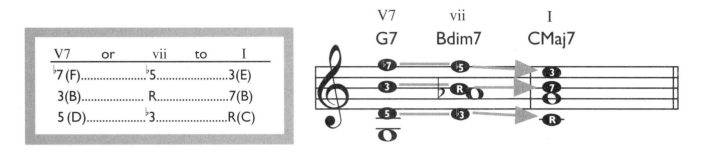

The reason these tones resolve this way is a matter of what we are used to hearing. As you play through the examples that follow, notice how satisfying the resolutions are. Also, pay close attention to the similarities between the substituted diminished chords and the V7 chords. They are all shown in the context of a ii-V7-I progression, since this is the most common situation.

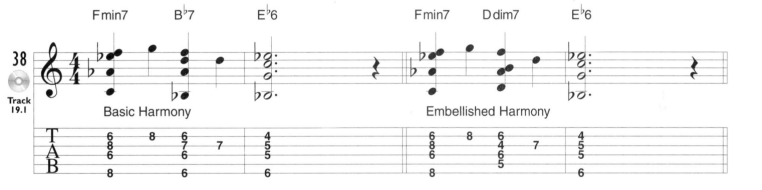

You can also play diminished chords that share the same root as the chord you are approaching.

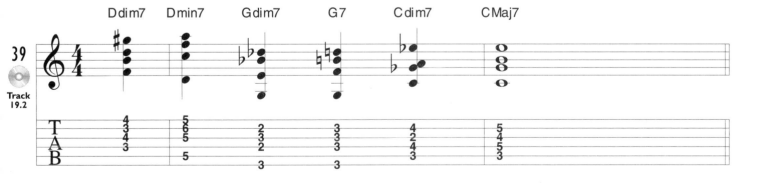

MIN7♭5 (HALF-DIMINISHED) CHORDS

You can use min7♭5 chords in place of min7 chords with the same root as long as the melody note is not the natural 5th of the chord. For instance, if the chord is Dmin7, and the melody note over that chord is an A, substituting with a Dmin7♭5 wouldn't work because the A♭ (♭5) in the chord would create the interval of a minor 2nd against the melody. This would pretty much demolish the harmony and the melody of the tune (you can probably kiss the gig good-bye, too).

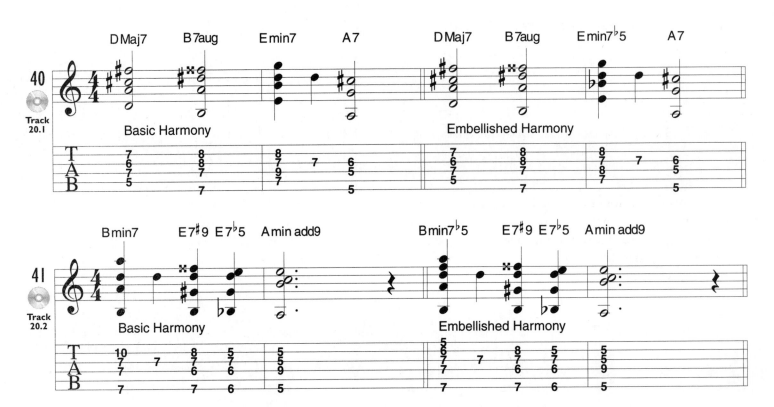

Sometimes you can use min7♭5 chords to replace the V7 chord. The root of the min7♭5 chord should be a major 3rd above the root of the V7 chord. Once again, the reason this works is that the two chords have three notes in common and sound quite similar.

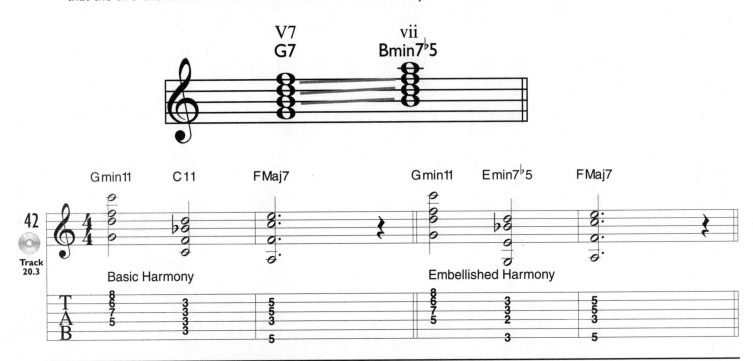

Here's another blues progression to help you review some of the things you have learned so far. Practice this slowly and gradually pick up the tempo. The half-step approach dominant chords are highlighted. Also notice the use of repeated diminished chord voicings in measure six.

BLUES IN F

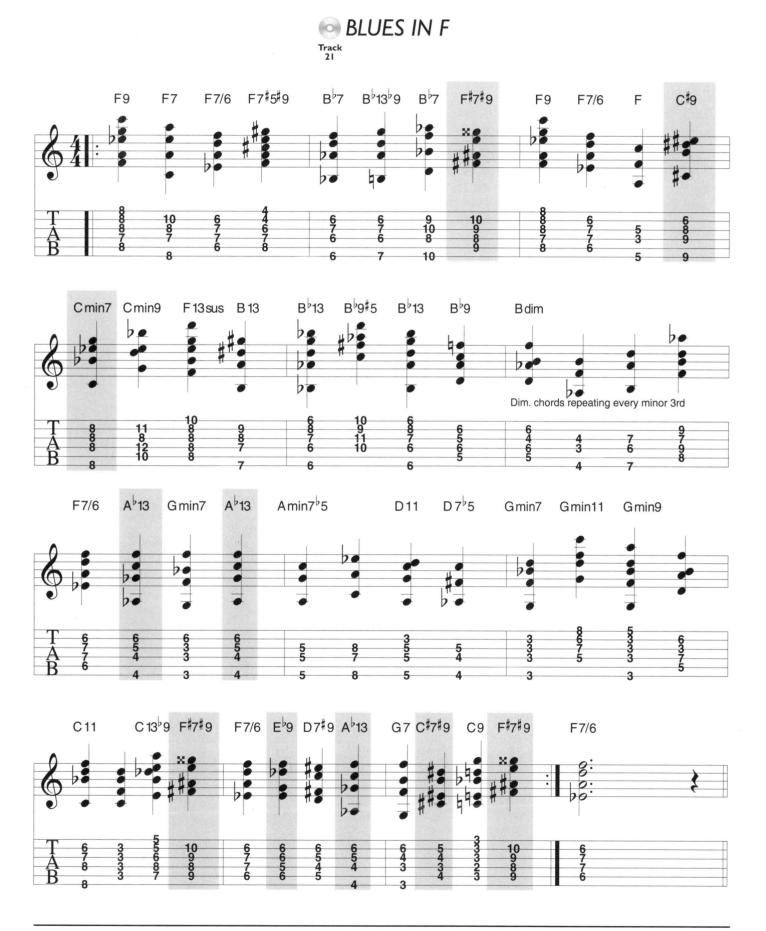

Dim. chords repeating every minor 3rd

In conventional harmony, we use chords that are constructed primarily from stacking 3rds. In quartal harmony, chords are constructed by stacking 4ths.

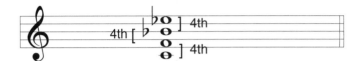

Chords built with 4ths have a sort of rootless character, making them rather ambiguous in regard to key centers. They have no standardized names so we will name them with the lowest note of the chord. If the bass is F, and there are a total of three notes a 4th apart, we will call the chord "F quartal 3." If there are four notes in the stack, we will call it "F quartal 4," and so on. Quartal chords can be used to harmonize melodies which would ordinarily be harmonized with a minor chord.

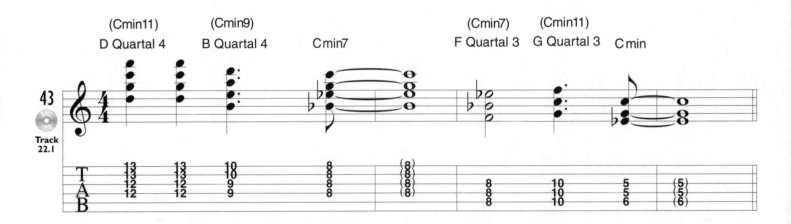

Quartal chords can also be used to create tension in a progression.

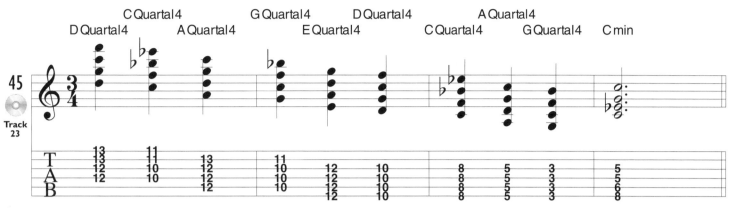

The previous examples used *pure (perfect) 4ths*. It is possible to employ what we call *diatonic 4ths* as well. When harmonizing a major scale in 4ths we need to make adjustments to the chords to stay within the bounds of the diatonic key. In the example below we are building quartal 3 chords in C. Notice that when we come to the seventh degree of the scale we use a B♮ to make an augmented 4th instead of a B♭, which would make a "pure" perfect 4th. We make this adjustment to stay in key since there is no B♭ in the C scale. At times you might find it preferable to use chords built from "diatonic" 4ths. It's really a matter of taste, so experiment.

The following chart shows the chord shapes for the quartal chords in C, and what happens when we invert these shapes.

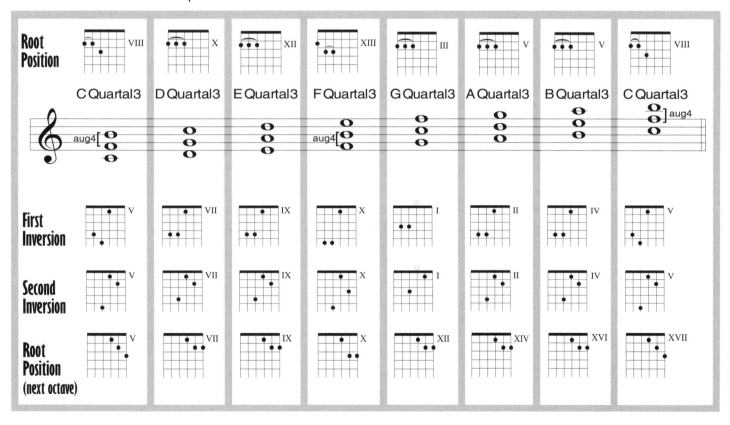

SINGLE NOTES

Some players prefer a chord/melody style with fewer chords. They will play mostly single notes and add chords only when the chord changes. Sometimes this is the best way to deal with chord tones and non-chord tones alike.

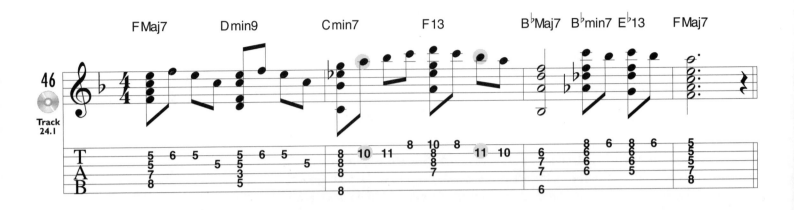

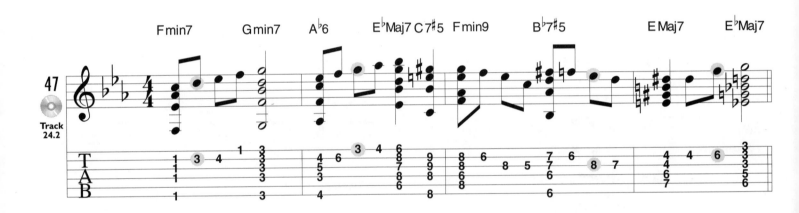

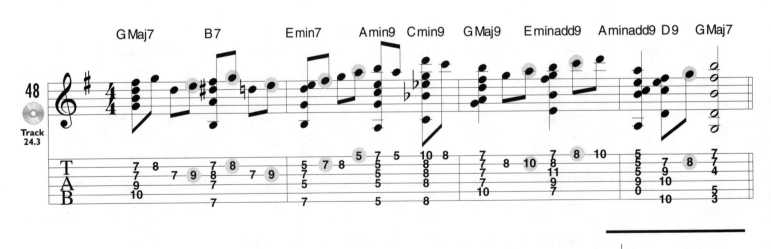

♩ = non-chord tone

Doubling melody notes in octaves will create a stronger effect than single notes, and sometimes you might find this kind of emphasis desirable. Listen to Wes Montgomery and George Benson to hear great examples of this kind of playing. These diagrams illustrate some octave shapes on the fingerboard.

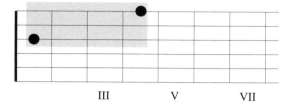

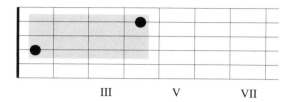

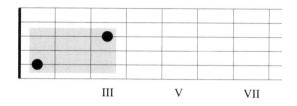

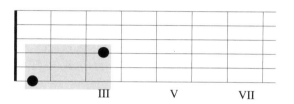

Practice these examples to get an idea of how this concept can be applied.

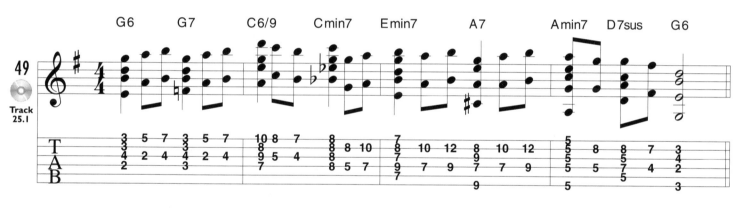

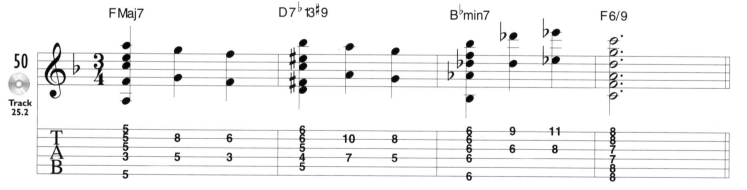

At this point, you should begin composing two- to four-bar melodies with fairly standard chord changes. Two or three per day would be good. Start applying all of these concepts until your ear gets accustomed to the sounds. After a while you should try your hand at simple but complete songs followed by standards and jazz tunes. Constantly listen to the great players. Listen to arranging techniques in television and movie scores. Listen to small instrumental groups and big bands. You'll be surprised how much of this material transfers over to arranging for the guitar.

CHAPTER 4

Enhancing Chord Progressions

One of the most satisfying aspects of playing chord/melody style guitar is manipulating chord progressions to create more interesting harmonies. The following lessons show many of the ways this can be done. The goal is to be aware of all these techniques and be flexible with them so that you can utilize them "on the spot." This is why you should learn your songs in a skeletal form so that you can actually start to improvise harmonies as you play.

It will take awhile to become comfortable with this material. Take your time and, most of all, enjoy the sounds. There are lots of exciting and surprising harmonies to be discovered. Remember that not every technique sounds great in every context. There really are no hard and fast rules in this study. The process of experimentation is a large part of the enjoyment.

Along with these studies, you should be learning lots of songs. Buy a copy of one of the many jazz "fake" books that are available. Apply these techniques where you can. You will make these harmonization techniques second nature by using this information in actual playing situations.

LESSON 1: PASSING-CHORD APPROACHES

The concept of using "like qualities" is similar to the material in Lesson 4 of Chapter 2, but instead of using only dominant chords as passing chords, use the same quality as the chord you are approaching from either a half step above or below. For instance, precede a GMaj7 with either an F#Maj7 or a G#Maj7.

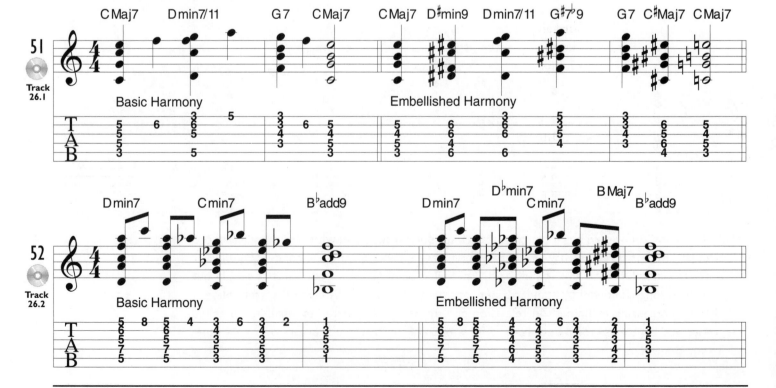

LESSON 2: THE IV-I APPROACH

When approaching a major I chord you may precede it with a IV chord (a major chord whose root is a perfect 4th higher). You can use this technique to handle non-chord tones or as harmonization of a chord tone. In Examples 53 and 54, the IV chords are highlighted.

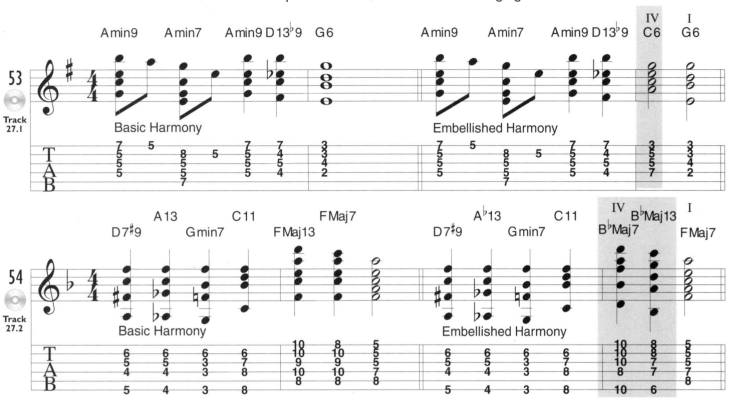

LESSON 3: THE V7-I APPROACH

Many jazz chord progressions utilize root movements (from one chord to another) of 4ths. As you already know, V7-I is the most common chord progression. In this technique, you may consider any chord a I chord and precede it by its own V7 chord, which can be enhanced or altered. These chords are known as "secondary dominants" because they are dominant chords other than the diatonic V7 chord. Here are some examples:

Basic Harmony:

Embellished Harmony:

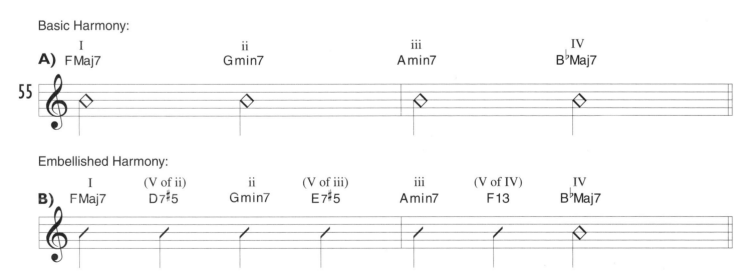

Examples 56 and 57 use the secondary V7 chords to harmonize chord tones. The secondary V7 chords are highlighted.

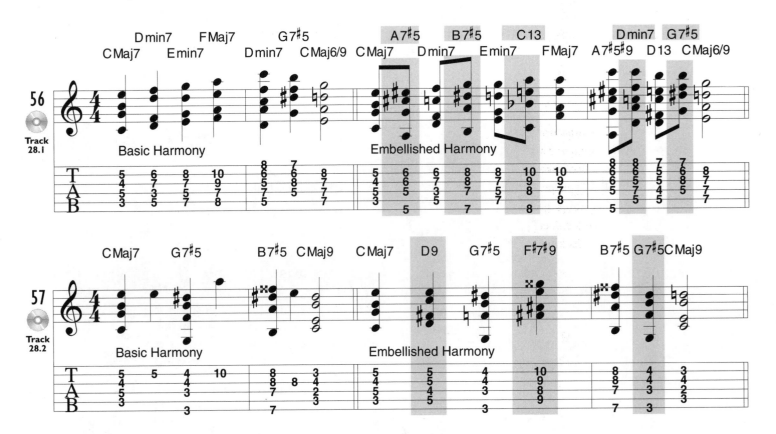

In this example, the secondary V7 chords harmonize two non-chord tones and one chord tone.

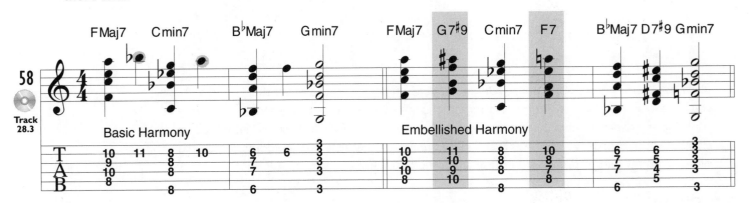

♪ = non-chord tone

This technique builds on the one introduced in the last lesson. The I chord is often preceded by a V7 chord, and V7 chords are very often preceded by ii chords. The ii-V7-I progression defines or establishes a key because of the way the roots, 3rds and 7ths of these chords move (see page 215). When you do this, you are actually traveling through the cycle of 4ths (see page 17, if you need to review the cycle of 4ths).

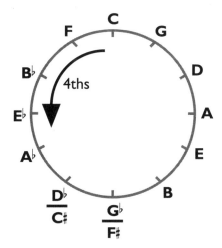

Traveling counter clockwise through the cycle of 4ths, any three consecutive notes represent the movement of a ii-V7-I progression. For instance, Cmin7-F7-B♭Maj7 is a ii-V7-I in B♭; Fmin7-B♭7-E♭Maj7 is a ii-V7-I in E♭, and so on.

Since any chord in a progression can be considered a I chord, you should experiment with "two-fiving" your way into any chord. In other words, play the ii and the V7 of the chord you are approaching. For example, if you are approaching an E♭Maj9 (I) chord, insert Fmin7 (ii) and B♭13 (V7) right before it. This is a good way to temporarily suspend the original harmony for a measure or two. It also provides smooth voice-leading into any chord. For variety, try making the ii chord dominant once in a while, or try changing the ii chord to a min7♭5. You can use this technique as a way to handle non-chord tones, or for further harmonization of a chord tone.

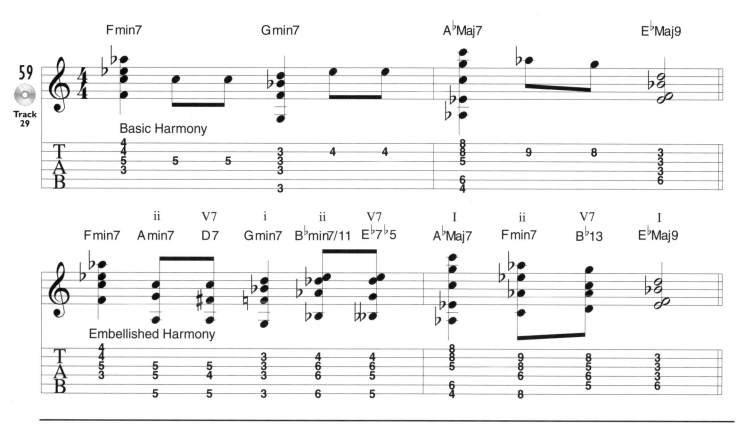

Based on the song "*Scotch and Soda*," by Guard, the following example shows the basic chords in boxes and the chord embellishments. Each embellishment has been labeled ① through ⑥. Check the legend on the bottom of page 235 to know what each number means.

💿 RUM AND COKE

Track 30

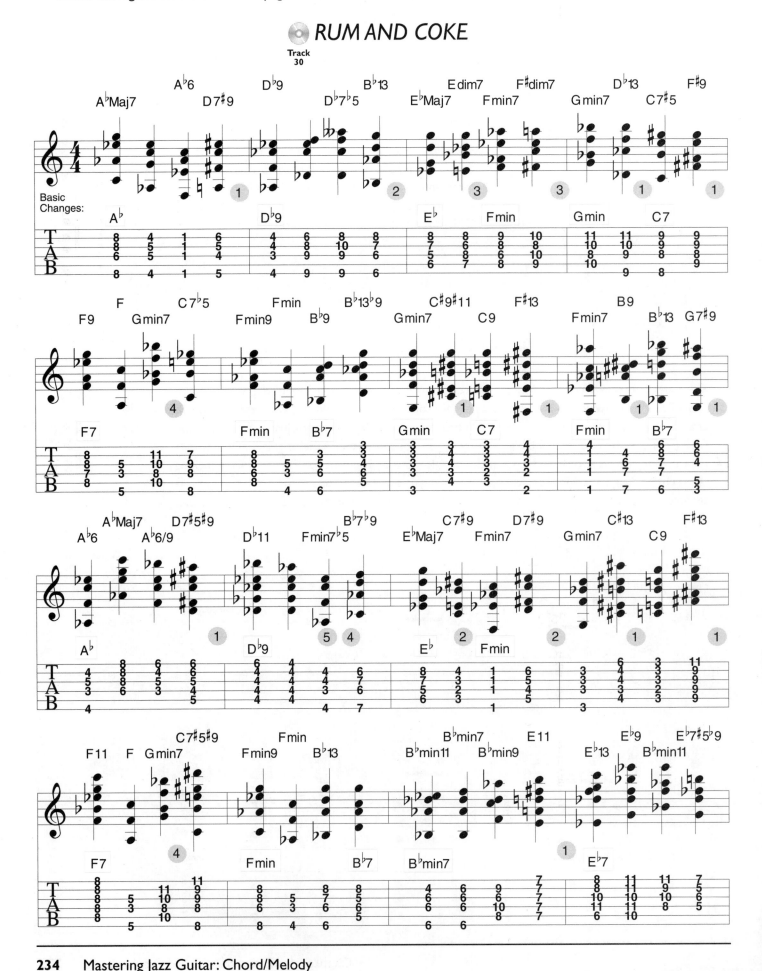

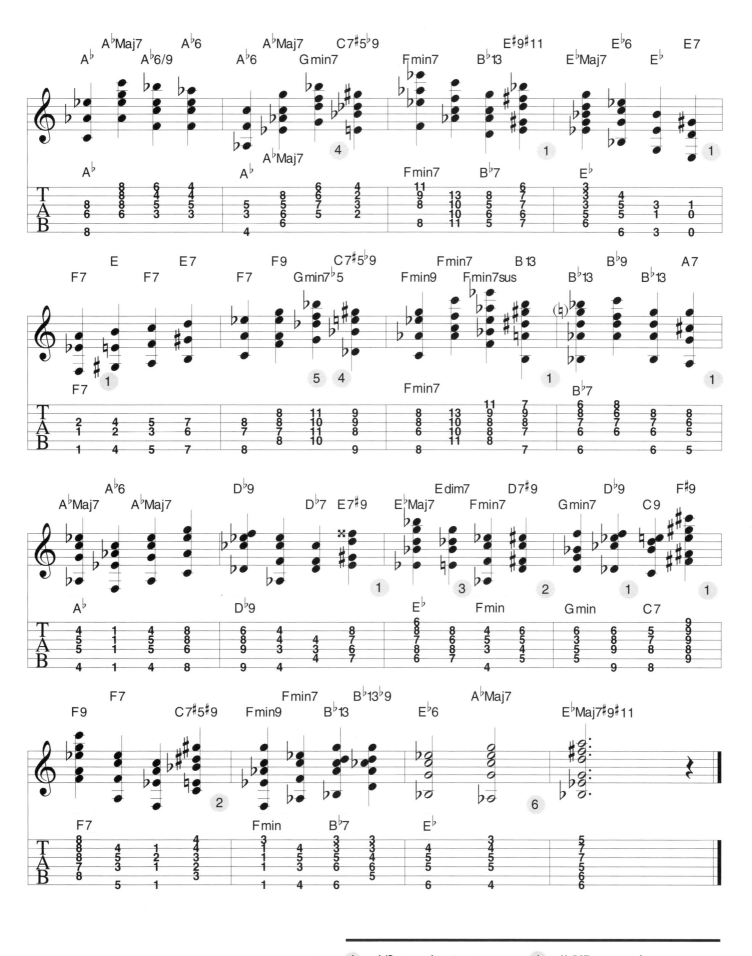

①	= 1/2 step dominant	④	= ii-V7 approach
②	= V7-I	⑤	= half diminished substitution
③	= Diminished approach	⑥	= IV - I

LESSON 5: BACKCYCLING APPROACHES

Backcycling is a way to extend the ii-V7-I approach covered in Lesson 4. When you precede a destination chord with V7, that is a root movement of a 4th. If you precede the V7 with the ii, that is also a root movement of a 4th. *Backcycling* means that you can keep working your way *back* through the *cycle* of 4ths, preceding each chord with the previous chord in the cycle. You keep moving through the cycle of 4ths until you reach the destination chord. For instance, if you are playing an E chord and the destination chord has F as the root, precede the F chord with a C chord, which is a 4th below. Then precede the C chord with a G chord, precede the G chord with a D chord, precede that with an A chord, and the root movement of the progression is now E-A-D-G-C-F, a perfect backcycle. This means the chords that are traveling through the cycle will often be substituting for the basic chords. Experiment with alternating minor and dominant chords as you move along. Then try various altered and unaltered dominant chords on each root.

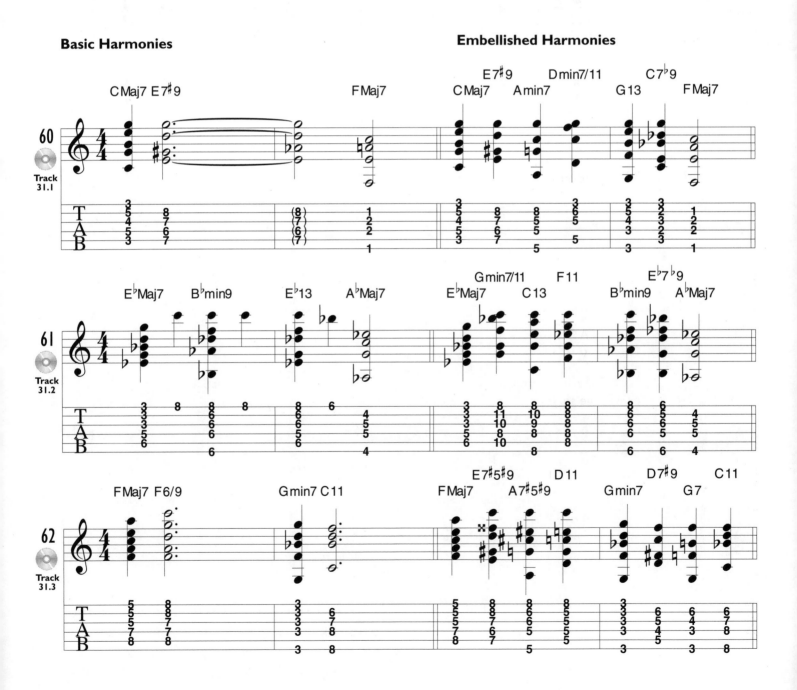

Basic Harmonies   **Embellished Harmonies**

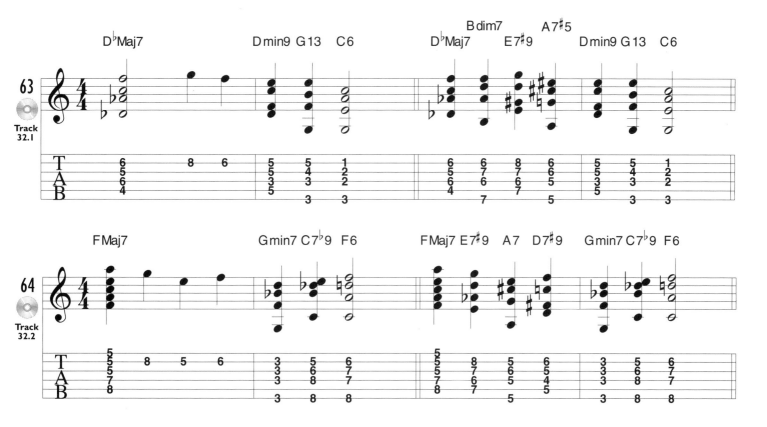

The fingerboard is laid out very conveniently for backcycle thinking.

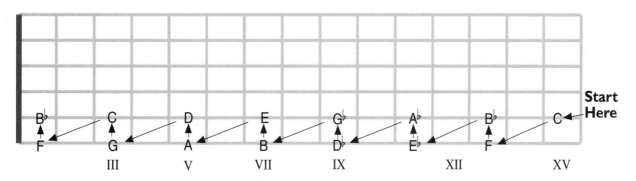

If you haven't already done so, you should memorize the cycle of 4ths.

When a progression travels from V7 to I, we often replace the V7 chord with a dominant chord whose root is a diminished 5th (or augmented 4th) away. We call this interval a *tritone* because it is equal to the distance of *three* whole steps. The technique of substituting a chord a tritone away also works with secondary dominant chords.

Here is an example that shows why this works: D♭7 is the tritone substitute for G7. When you compare the spelling of both chords, a D♭7 looks and sounds like a G7♭5♭9 without a root. Basically, you have added altered tones to the original chord and dropped the root. Also, you have enharmonically respelled the 3rd of the G7♭5♭9 (B), so that it appears as C♭. This principle is used extensively in jazz harmony.

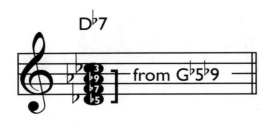

Once again, here is our cycle diagram. This time notice how each dotted line connects two roots that are a ♭5 apart. This is known as the alternate cycle.

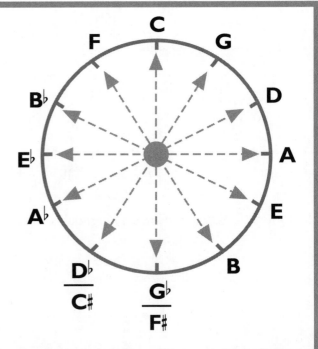

Basic Harmonies

Embellished Harmonies

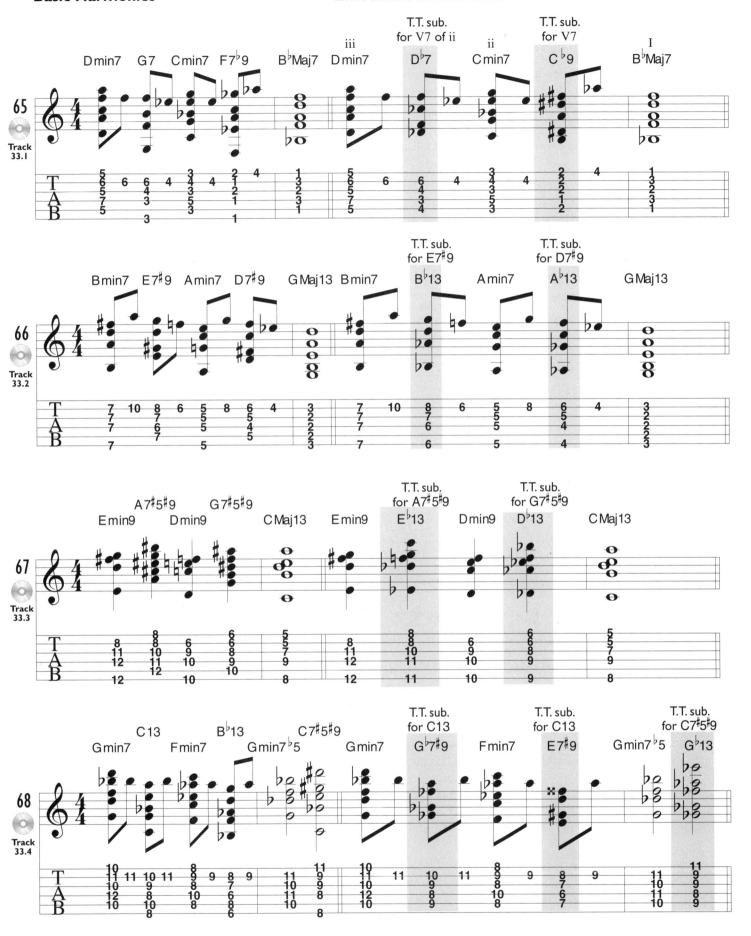

T.T. sub. = Tri-Tone substitution

LESSON 7: THE ♭V7-I APPROACH

We can approach any chord from another chord whose root is a tritone away. This is different from the tritone substitution approach where the new chord is deduced from the root of the V7 chord. In this approach, we deduce the new chord from the root of the destination chord. For instance, if Emin7 is the destination chord, it can be approached with a B♭13, which is a tritone away. Any chord can be approached this way.

Basic Harmonies　　　　　　　　　　　　　　　**Embellished Harmonies**

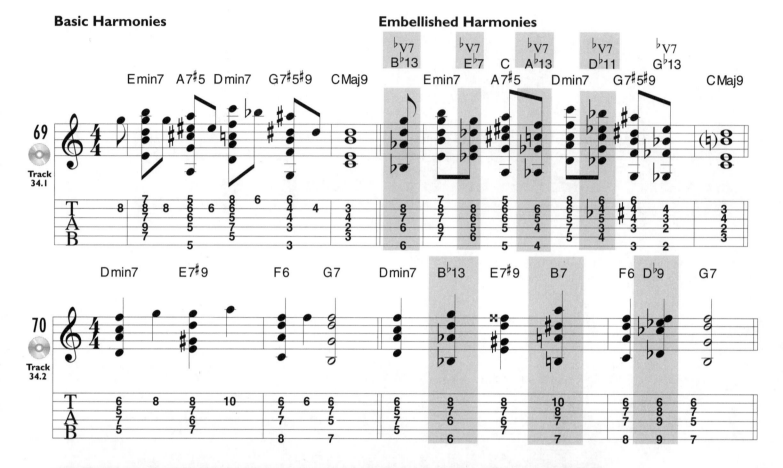

LESSON 8: THE ii-V7-I AND ALTERNATE CYCLES

This way of approaching the destination chord combines the dominant and alternate cycles together. In Example 71, if we consider F6 to be the I chord, we can precede it with Gmin7(ii), C13(V7) and G♭7♯9 (the tritone substitution for C dominant). All you are really doing is inserting a tritone substitution before or after the V7 in a ii-V7-I progression. This is fairly easy to do and adds a lot of movement to the progression. Once again, experiment occasionally with making the ii chord a dominant chord (altered or not).

Basic Harmonies　　　　　　　　　　　　　　　**Embellished Harmonies**

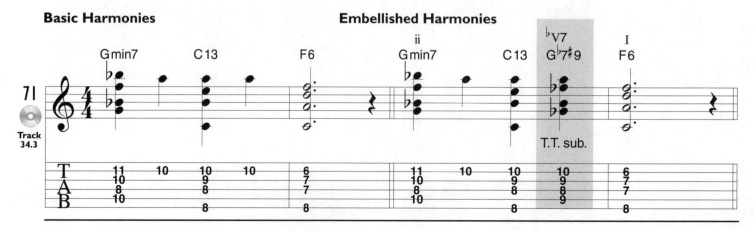

Basic Harmonies · **Embellished Harmonies**

Track 72 (Track 35.1) — music notation: Cmin9, F11, B♭add9 | Cmin9, F11, B7 (T.T. sub.), B♭add9

LESSON 9: SURPRISE CHORDS

Here are some things you can do to find some surprise chords that will liven-up your chord/melody arrangements. Start with the melody note and look around for various other ways to harmonize it. Ask yourself: "What other chords and voicings do I know with this note as the highest note?" If the note is written as a sharp, try thinking of its enharmonic equivalent (written with a flat). This will give you new ideas. Look for voice-leading opportunities. Move the previous chord's voices around in whole and half steps to see where they lead. If you come up with something you like, make sure the voice-leading to the chord that follows makes sense as well. Sometimes you'll find a great surprise chord quite by accident. Consider it a gift — accept graciously, then use it.

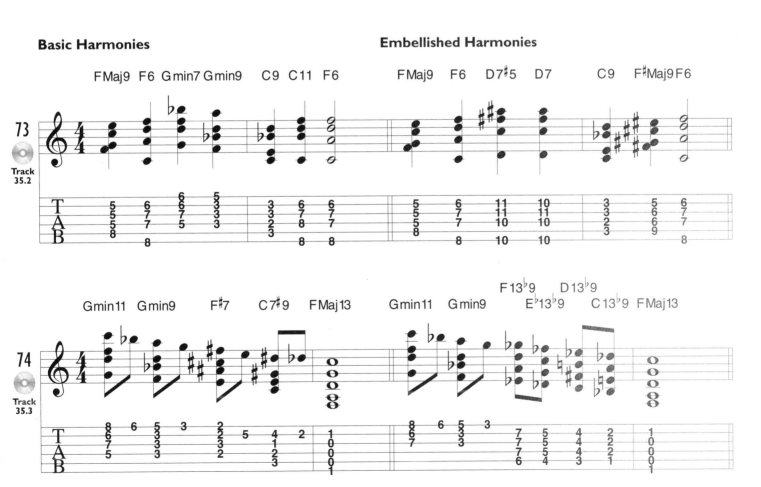

CHAPTER 5

Simultaneous Chords and
Walking Bass Lines

This technique can give the illusion of two instruments playing at once. While this will take some practice, the sound is well worth the effort. You will also acquire greater mastery of the fingerboard, a better working knowledge of chord theory and a much more powerful pair of hands. This chapter will cover the basic technique for accompaniment-style playing. Many thanks to Ted Greene for my first exposure to this style of playing. His influence has been profound.

The first thing you must learn is quite a few voicings for major, minor (with and without flatted 5ths), and dominant triads (three note chords) on the *lower* strings. Much of this style has to do with connecting these chords with bass notes in between.

LESSON 1: THE BASIC VOICINGS

These examples will give you the ingredients for ii-V7-I progressions in the key of C. Transpose them to other keys too. There are many to develop so take your time.

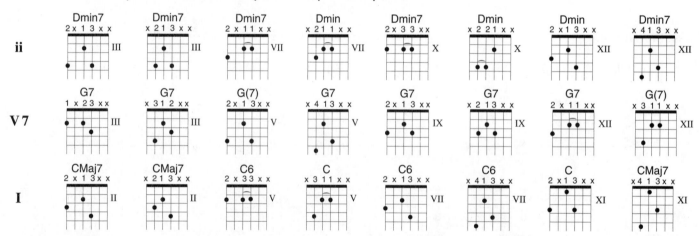

Suggestions:

1. Notice that the triads are organized according to chord quality. You might want to work on one quality at a time while learning the approaches to bass lines that follow.
   Some students seem to learn them faster that way.
2. Finger these chords with as few fingers as possible. Two fingers should be adequate for many of them. This is important because you will eventually want to keep as many fingers free as possible for playing melodies and improvising.
3. Learn the voicings in all twelve keys first. Then put them through all the bass line approaches you will learn in this book in all twelve keys. This may seem like a lot of work, and it is, but it will really pay off in the long run.

Other considerations:

1. Remember that the idea is to sound like two instruments. The chords and the bassline are two distinct parts. Your right thumb *p* should handle the bass notes while *i* and *m* should take care of the other two notes in the triad. Later, you'll use your *a* and *c* fingers to cover any remaining notes in the chord. (See page 198 for a review of the names of the right hand fingers.)
2. Put a bass note on every beat and have the chords appear as "punches" (accents). Keep the volume balance between the bass notes and chords realistic like a guitar (or keyboard) player and a bass player together. Listen to a lot of guitar and piano trios to capture the "vibe." Imagine the two instruments as one.
3. Your second finger of your left hand will probably end up doing the most of the sliding around from bass note to bass note.

LESSON 2: BASS LINES—SCALEWISE APPROACH

In this approach you use the tones of the scale that the chord is built from to connect the various triad voicings of the chord. Example 75 is a C Major scale on the sixth string starting on E.

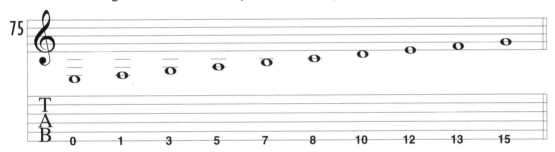

Now play this scale again, but every time you come to a bass note that belongs in a Dmin7 triad, strike the chord instead of just the note by itself.

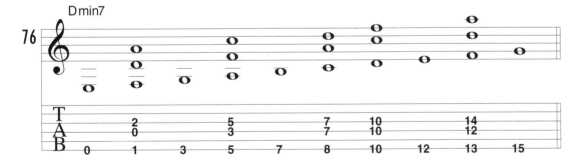

Example 77 shows the same approach along the fifth string.

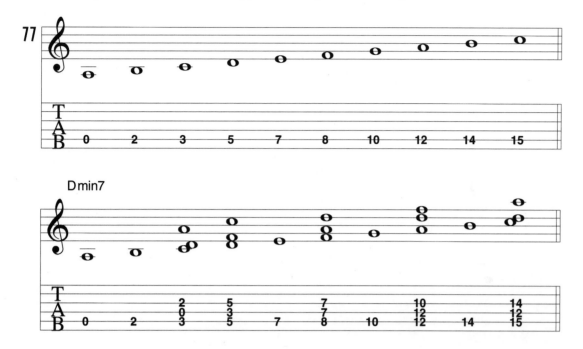

The extent of the possibilities becomes evident when you start combining the scales and chords along both strings. Study this example in the key of C where the ii chords are Dmin.

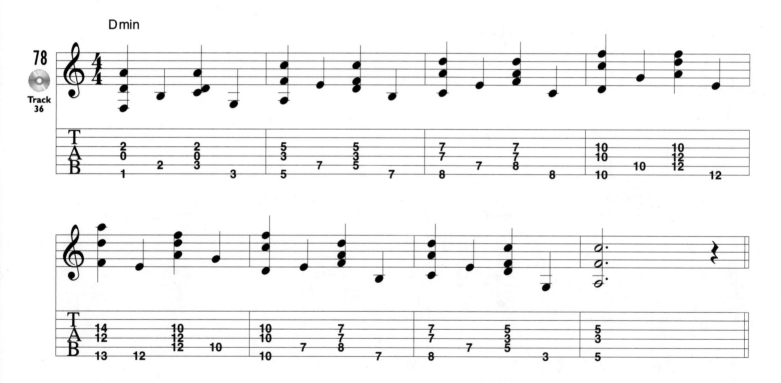

Example 79 shows the V7 chord in the key of C (G7) played every time a chord tone appears in the bass.

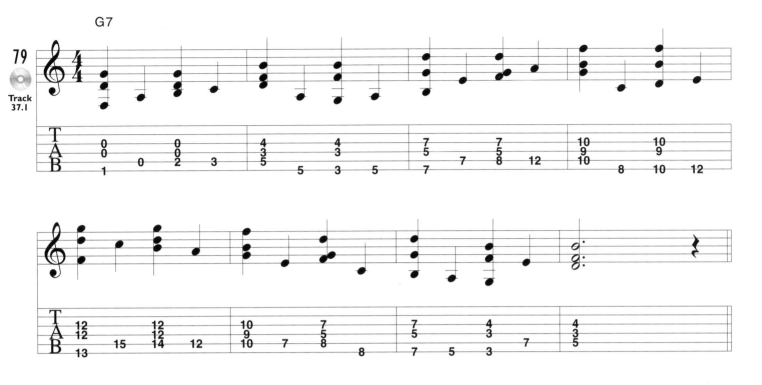

Example 80 shows the same idea with I chords in the key of C (C, CMaj7, C6).

By now, you have noticed that some major, minor and dominant triad shapes are identical. Once you get a handle on this, it becomes a real benefit and adds to the variety in your music.

LESSON 3: BASS LINES—HALF-STEP APPROACHES

Chords can usually be approached from the note a half step above or below the lowest voice in the triad. This is a common feature of walking bass-lines.

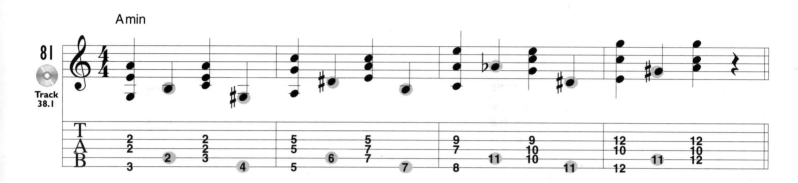

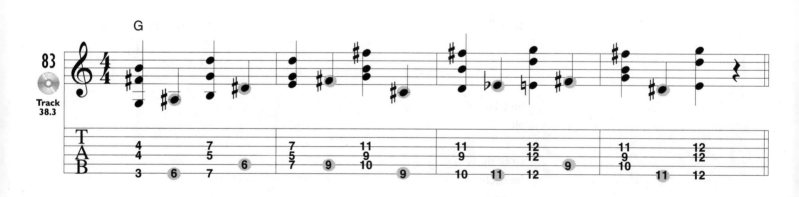

♩ = half-step approach

It takes more than triads and creative bass lines to create a realistic sound. By now you should be tired of plodding along in quarter notes. Here are some other ideas to spice up your rhythmic feel.

Try delaying the chord by playing the bass note on the downbeat and the chord slightly after (but within the same beat)—a dotted eighth-note-sixteenth feel.

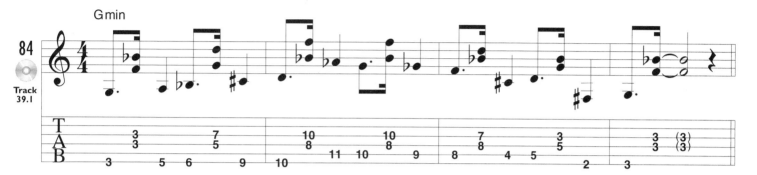

Try delaying the bass-note by playing the chord on the downbeat and the bass-note slightly after (but within the same beat).

Whenever possible, let two notes of the triad ring as you hit the next bass note. Practice slowly to learn the mechanics of this idea well.

A real playing situation would include all of these ideas (including playing straight quarter notes). You need to learn these so well that the technique becomes intuitive. Just keep practicing. You should be able to vamp (to vamp is to repeat a small section, or in this case, one harmony) with creative bass lines on all qualities of chords in all keys before going on. Carry on!

After becoming familiar with the triads, bass line approaches and rhythmic alterations, it is time to start using this information in actual chord progressions from songs that you know. Since the chord progressions for many songs are really just a series of ii-V7-I progressions, it makes sense to organize your triads and bassline approaches into ii-V7-I patterns. The possibilities are endless and you should experiment with this extensively. The following examples will help get you started.

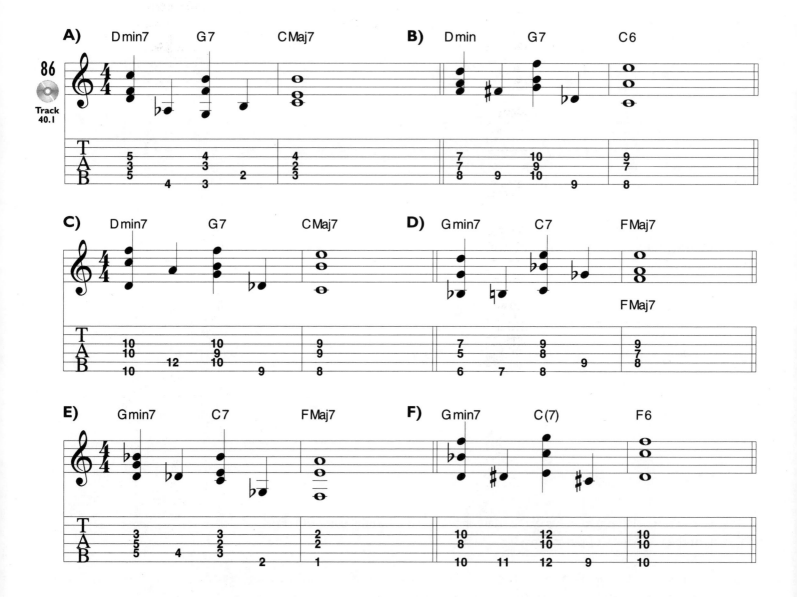

Here is a sample progression, based on the chord progression of *All the Things You Are*, by Hammerstein and Kern, using lots of the techniques you have been learning.

EVERYTHING YOU'RE NOT

Track 41

LESSON 6: BASS LINES—COMBINING TECHNIQUES

When you combine basslines with enhanced chord progressions you have an accompaniment arrangement like this one, based on an *Everything You're Not (All the Things You Are)* comping pattern.

ACCOMPANIMENT FOR EVERYTHING YOU'RE NOT

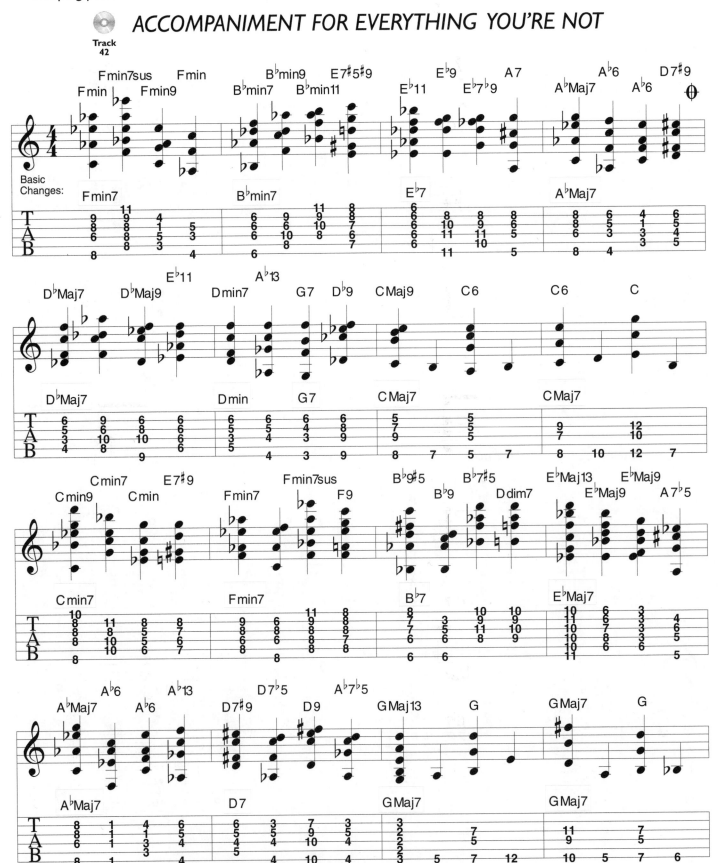

CHAPTER 6

Searching Out New Voicings

Most of us start out learning "garden variety" chords and eventually move on to using more exotic sounds. There are numerous ways to discover new chords to add to your vocabulary. The following lessons will deal with a few of these. It is very important to write down new discoveries immediately, and start using them in songs right away. This is how you will accumulate and remember a vast vocabulary of chords.

LESSON 1: MOVING VOICES

This technique is rather obvious, but it is a great way to quickly expand your choice of voicings. Start with a chord form you already know and experiment with moving the different voices around to higher and lower octaves. Some of these changes will be dramatic, others not so, but there are many sounds waiting to be discovered within the shapes you already know. Check out these examples and look around further for yourself.

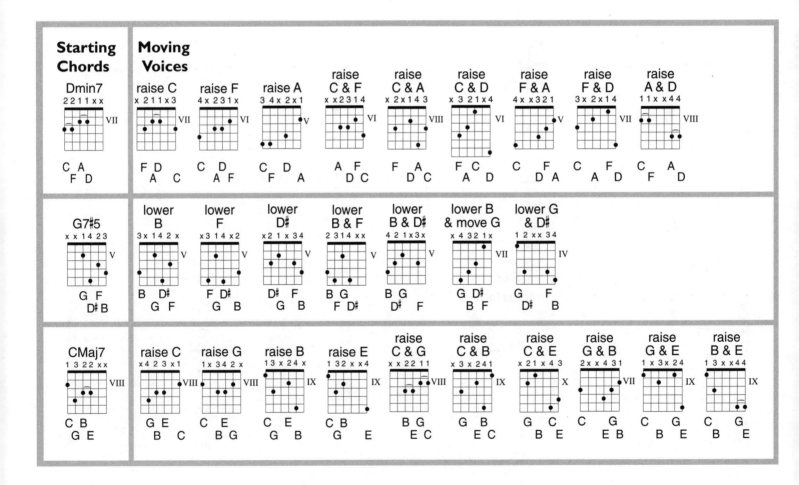

LESSON 2: SYMMETRICAL CHORD MOVEMENT

Many chords shapes retain their function (dominant chords stay dominant, etc.) when moved around in certain symmetrical intervals, even if the name changes (for instance, C7♭5 becomes C9#5♭5). Learning to see (and use!) this information can take awhile, but once you do, it will open up a world of new sounds. This area of harmonic information is huge. The three different situations covered here will help you to investigate further.

CHORDS WITH 9THS AND ALTERED 5THS

Chords with 9ths and altered 5ths may be moved around in whole steps and still retain their function. They usually don't remain exactly the same chord, like the diminished 7th and #5 chords do, but their basic dominant quality is retained. These are a little more difficult to manipulate, and they don't all sound great in every situation, but after some experimenting you will discover a whole new way of thinking about altered dominant sounds. Here are three examples. Try this with other voicings you already know. Take your time and read from left to right.

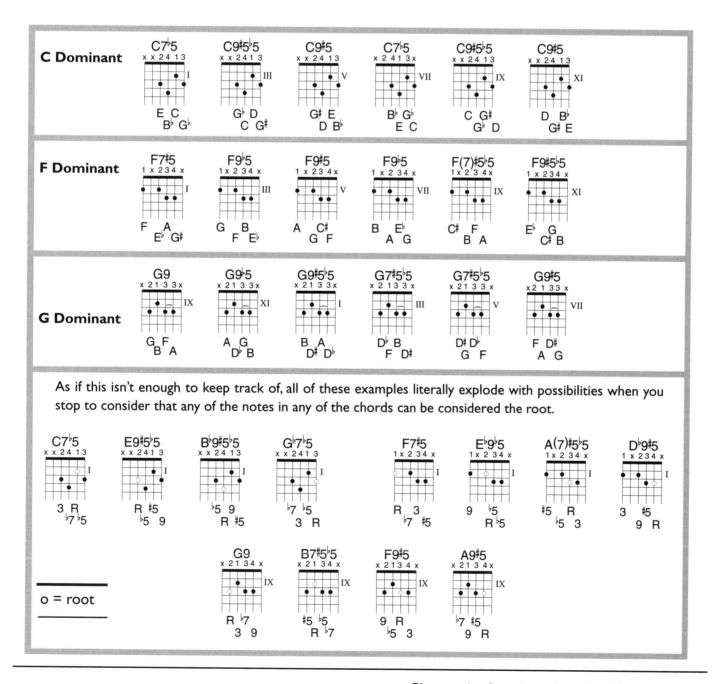

CODA
A Medley of Suggestions and Musical Concepts

CREATING ARRANGEMENTS

Harmonizing melodies with great chords and running dazzling bass lines through them is still only part of the picture of chord/melody playing. Presenting a song is an event that has an opening, a body, and a conclusion. This is an important part of creating an arrangement. Once you know the melody and the chord changes, and have a pretty good handle on some enhancement techniques, it is time to think about how to use what you know to make the song interesting.

Here are some areas to consider:

1. Harmonize each time through the progression in a different way.
2. Start the song in single notes and gradually add more harmony as the tune progresses.
3. Play the song in different time feels.
4. Modulate to different keys.
5. Create medleys (link several songs together in one arrangement).
6. Put the melody in the bass voice or in a middle voice.
7. Arrange the tune as if you were an entire band. Play the head. Take a solo. Take a bass solo. Do a shout chorus (which you can think of as a chordal solo with a big band feel). Improvise with single notes for four bars, followed by a chordal improvisation for four bars, followed by a bass solo for four bars. Continue doing this for the entire length of the chord progression. This is called "trading fours."
8. Reharmonize sections of the tune by composing a new bassline and letting that guide your harmonizations.
9. Compose your introductions last. You might have something in the body of the song that would sound nice in the intro. This will help tie the different parts of the song together.
10. Learn lots of special techniques such as of artificial harmonics.
11. Study classical guitar exercises for the right hand. This will give you many ideas for song interpretation.
12. Practice a lot.
13. Listen a lot.

LISTENING TO THE GREATS

No list can be exhaustive, but these players have contributed profoundly to chord/melody style playing. Listen to:

Lenny Breau	Ron Eschete	Jim Hall	Joe Pass
Joe Diorio	Mick Goodrick	Carl Kress	George M. Smith
George Van Eps	Ted Greene	Wes Montgomery	Johnny Smith

REALITY CHECK

The intention of this book has been to expose you to some new sounds and ideas. These examples only scratch the surface. It will be necessary to apply these concepts to many songs to fully understand their implications. For most players it should take years to exhaust all the material in this book. Knowing hundreds of chord voicings and techniques is not as important as finding your artistic voice and then expressing it. Great knowledge brings great flexibility, but it is how you *use* what you know, rather than how *much* you know that counts. Music history is full of performances with great artistic and emotional merit by musicians without a wealth of theoretical ammunition. Remember this if you feel overwhelmed by the amount of information there is to learn. Keep studying, compete only with yourself and be true to your art. What you play will then have validity.

BYESVILLE

Track 43

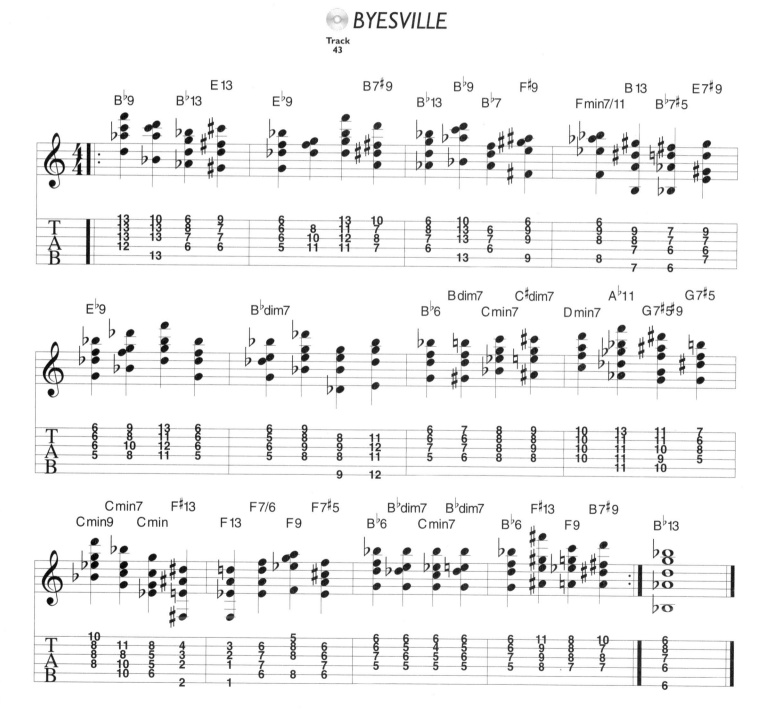

MASTERING IMPROVISATION

JAZZ GUITAR

TABLE OF CONTENTS

Chapter 5—Connecting Your Ideas

CODA—*A Medley of Suggestions and Musical Concepts*

Track
01

Companion online audio is included with this book to make learning easier and more enjoyable. The symbol shown on the left appears next to every example in the book that features an MP3 track. Use the MP3s to ensure you're capturing the feel of the examples and interpreting the rhythms correctly. The track number below the symbol corresponds directly to the example you want to hear (example numbers are above the icon). All the track numbers are unique to each "book" within this volume, meaning every book has its own Track 1, Track 2, and so on. (For example, *Beginning Jazz Guitar* starts with Track 1, as does *Intermediate jazz Guitar, Mastering Jazz Guitar: Chord/Melody* and *Mastering Jazz Guitar: Improvisation*.) Track 1 for each book will help you tune your guitar.

See page 1 for instructions on how to access the online audio.

INTRODUCTION

Welcome to the fourth and final section of this book. Guitar students typically spend a lot of time looking around for information that will take them to a higher level. When I was growing up, it was very difficult to learn how to play jazz. There were no instructional videos, and the books that were available were just not very helpful. There were no guitar schools. Most students were self-taught and some took lessons, but really good teachers were very hard to find. I was lucky—I've had some great teachers.

Today, there are videos, books, guitar schools, tapes, CDs and very talented teachers all over the place. But there is still something missing: books that give a complete overview of what you need to know to become a proficient jazz guitarist. Hopefully, this book fills that gap. Any student who starts with the *Beginning* section of this book and proceeds through to the end will be exposed to most of what they need to know to play jazz guitar.

You will find some complex subjects in this section, as well as some very simple ideas that you can start to use immediately. Chapter 1 begins with a discussion of improvising over altered dominant chords.

This section is not for beginners. It is for guitarists that have worked through the first two sections of this book: *Beginning Jazz Guitar* and *Intermediate Jazz Guitar*, or have received the same sort of information elsewhere. To get the most out of this section, you should be proficient with the pentatonic scales, blues scales, the major scale, diatonic harmony and chord scales, transposition, diatonic arpeggios, neighbor tones, triads, licks and formulas for extended and altered chords.

In the first two sections of this book, each lesson had two separate sections. The "A" sections dealt with harmonic principles and chord work while the "B" sections handled the topic of single-line improvisation. This entire section concerns itself with single-line improvisation. It starts right where the "B" sections in the *Intermediate* book left off. *Mastering Jazz Guitar: Chord/Melody* starts where the "A" sections of the *Intermediate* book left off. You may want to go through this section in order, or you may want to use it as a sourcebook of concepts and techniques to investigate in your own way.

The concepts and exercises in this book are intended to inspire you for a lifetime of study and enjoyment. Since jazz improvisation is an ever expanding field of information, one never really finishes doing this work. Enjoy the journey.

CHAPTER 1

Improvising Over Altered Dominant Chords

Altered dominant chords are some of the most distinctive sounds in jazz. Much of the challenge and enjoyment of playing jazz comes from learning how to improvise using the altered tones from these chords. At times, this may seem like a formidable task, and in some respects, it is. The key is to digest this material a little at a time.

Devices and Ideas

Before we move much further, let's define some vocabulary. You will see the term *device* quite often. For our purposes, a *device* is any tool that we use for improvising. Scales, licks, arpeggios and melodic patterns are all considered devices. Another term that will be used often is *idea*. An *idea* is simply any melodic inclination you may have at any particular time.

If you have been improvising exclusively over unaltered diatonic chords, you are probably wondering how to start adding the altered tones. There are many ways, but we will begin by using scales. A chord with altered tones is a chord that contains a ♭5 (or ♯11), ♯5, ♭9, ♯9 or any combination of these. Many students believe that you simply add these tones to existing scales and arpeggios that you already know. This is part of the picture, but there are many easier and more organized ways to accomplish the same end. There are different scales that contain these altered tones. Part of the task at hand is to learn which altered tones are found in what scales, then organize these scales in your mind and practice applying them over the appropriate chord changes. The first of these scales we'll be talking about is the diminished scale.

LESSON 1: THE DIMINISHED SCALE

The formula (in half steps and whole steps) for the diminished scale is W-H-W-H-W-H-W-H.

H = Half step
W = Whole step

Here it is in G, diagramed along each individual string where the formula is easy to see.

THE G DIMINISHED SCALE

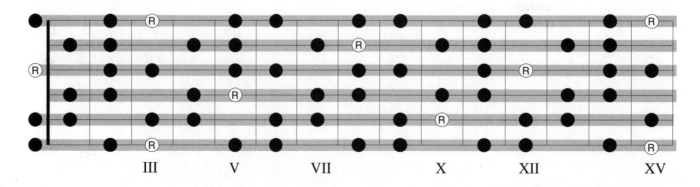

There are really only three separate diminished scales possible. Because of the formula, a diminished scale beginning a minor 3rd higher than the original root will contain exactly the same notes, although they are sometimes spelled enharmonically (for instance, G♭ may be spelled as F♯). Think of the scale as repeating itself every time you play it a minor 3rd higher.

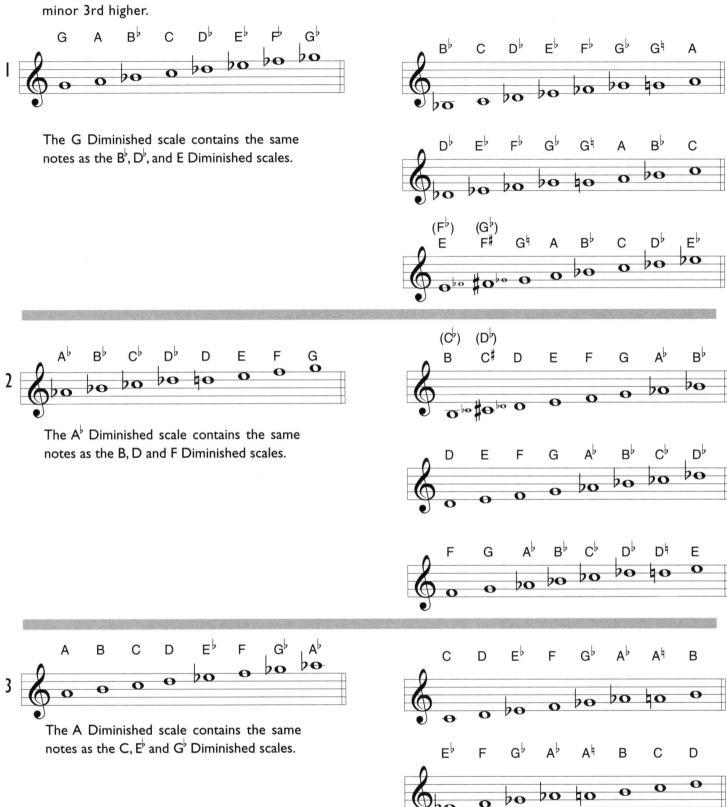

The G Diminished scale contains the same notes as the B♭, D♭, and E Diminished scales.

The A♭ Diminished scale contains the same notes as the B, D and F Diminished scales.

The A Diminished scale contains the same notes as the C, E♭ and G♭ Diminished scales.

The diminished scale is especially important in jazz improvisation because it has multiple uses. Obviously, it works well over diminished triads and diminished 7th chords. When you start this scale on the root of a diminished chord, the scale contains all of the chord tones of all four possible enharmonic spellings of that diminished chord.

A little less obvious is the diminished scale's use over altered dominant chords. When we apply the diminished scale to altered dominant chords (excluding the ♯5, since the diminished scale has a ♭5), we play the scale whose root is one half step higher than the root of the chord. For instance, play an A♭ Diminished scale over an altered G Dominant chord. Example 5 shows how the ♭5 (or ♯11), ♭9, and ♯9 are included in the scale.

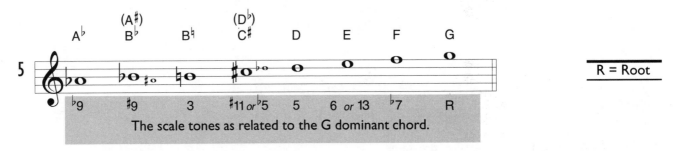

R = Root

The scale tones as related to the G dominant chord.

Example 6 shows the chords this scale can be used over.

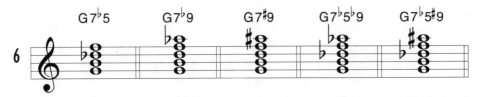

Part of your training as a jazz musician is to learn to recognize the sound of altered tones in chords. This will help you know which scales to use and what notes to emphasize. Ear-training is beyond the scope of this book, but it is well worth your time to investigate this subject thoroughly.

Here are four fingerings for the diminished scale in G. Memorize and practice them with melodic patterns that you know. Also, just spend some time noodling around with them. This will help you get acquainted with the sound.

THE G DIMINISHED SCALE

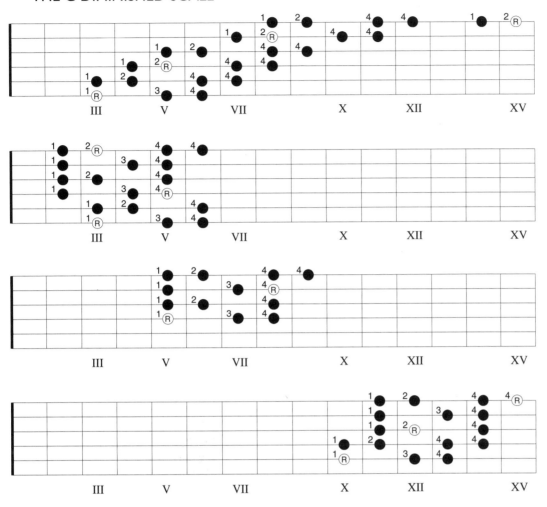

These fingerings require quite a few shifts from one position to another. When practicing shifts, try to make it sound like there was no shift at all. Do not slide into position or lessen the time value of any note to get to the next note in time. If you are shifting from your fourth finger to your first finger on the same string, listen to how it sounds when you play the first note with your first finger and the second note with your third finger. Then try to duplicate that sound with the correct fingering. Your listener should not be able to hear the shift.

Some players prefer to look at this scale as the "half-whole" scale when it is used over altered dominant chords. The scale still alternates whole steps and half steps, it's just that you start with a half step instead of a whole step, as in the diminished scale. If you prefer this way of thinking, then the scale would begin on the root of the altered dominant chord instead of a half-step above. It's a matter of personal preference. Experiment.

Here is a sampling of licks based on the diminished scale. Memorize the ones you like and start using them over diminished and altered dominant chords in your solos. The tablature provided shows only one of the possible fingerings for these licks. Experiment playing them in all possible fingerings. Try making up licks of your own, too.

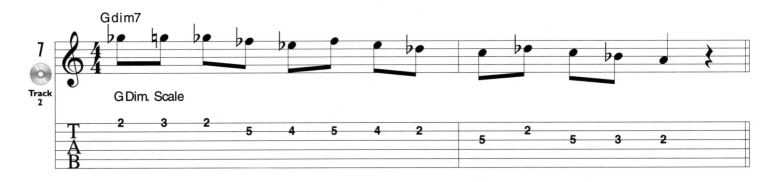

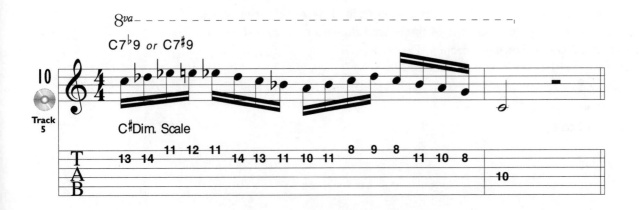

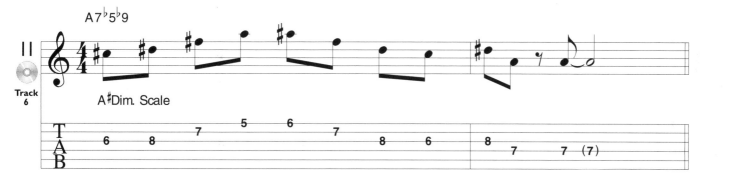

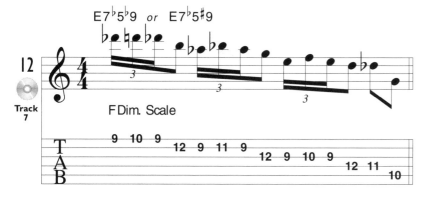

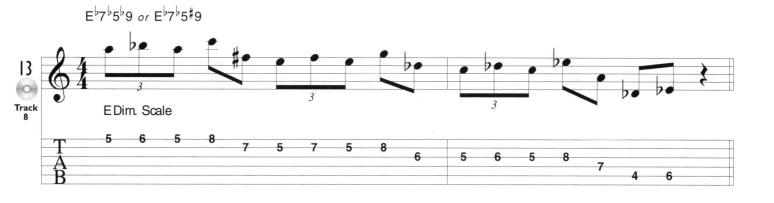

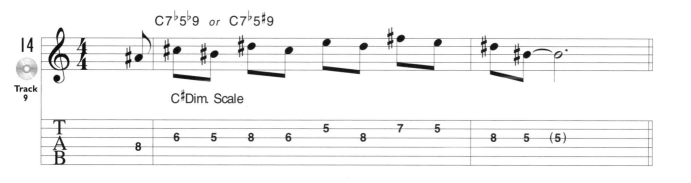

Here is an example of the diminished scale used in the chord progression from the first sixteen bars of Duke Ellington's "Take the "A" Train." Listen to Joe Pass and Wes Montgomery for their frequent use of the diminished scale.

LESSON 2: THE WHOLE TONE SCALE

This scale is very useful for soloing over altered dominant chords. Here is the formula for the whole tone scale: W-W-W-W-W-W.

W = Whole step

The following diagram shows the C Whole Tone scale along single strings.

THE C WHOLE TONE SCALE

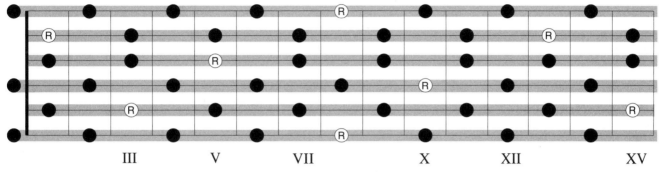

There are really only two whole tone scales. Because of the arrangement of whole steps, whole tone scales beginning from every other note on the chromatic scale contain identical tones (remember that we can enharmonically respell any note). Or, you can think of the whole tone scale as repeating itself every major 2nd.

Look at the last note of the C Whole Tone scale in Example 15. On paper, the last note, C, looks like a diminished 3rd (A♯ to C) instead of a major 2nd (A♯ to B♯), which are both whole step intervals. This makes the last interval in the scale look unlike a whole step on paper. The enharmonic spelling, C, is used because the B♯ is more difficult to read.

The C Whole Tone scale contains the same notes as the D, E, F♯, G♯ (A♭) and A♯ (B♭) Whole Tone scales.

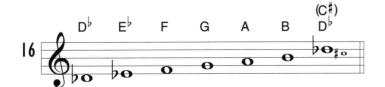

16

The D♭ Whole Tone scale contains the same notes as the E♭, F, G, A and B Whole Tone scales.

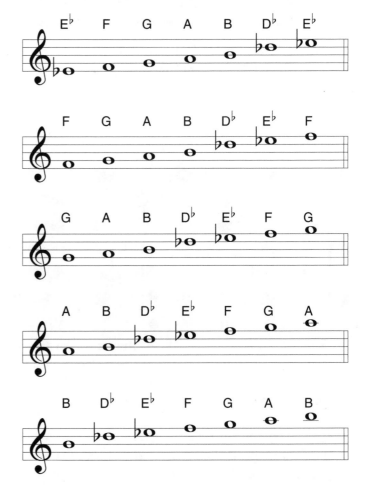

The whole tone scale contains both the #5 and ♭5 of dominant chords. You may start this scale from any tone in a dominant 7#5 or dominant 7♭5 chord. Example 17 shows the G Whole Tone scale and the chord tones it contains. Example 18 shows some chords the scale will work over.

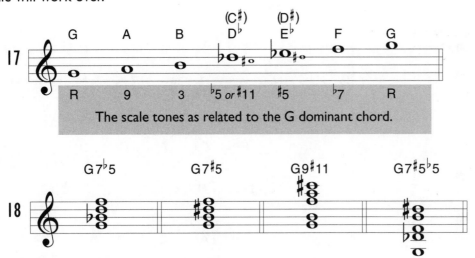

17

| R | 9 | 3 | ♭5 or #11 | #5 | ♭7 | R |

The scale tones as related to the G dominant chord.

18

G7♭5   G7#5   G9#11   G7#5♭5

Here are five fingerings for the C Whole Tone scale. Memorize and practice them from all roots. Be sure to apply your melodic patterns too.

THE C WHOLE TONE SCALE

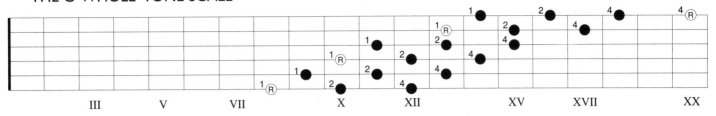

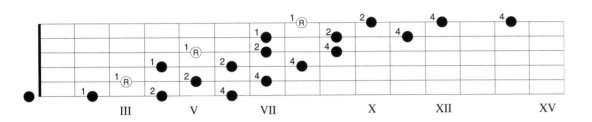

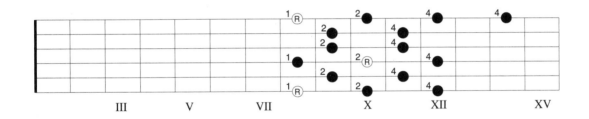

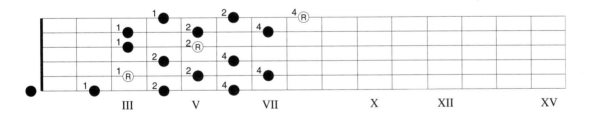

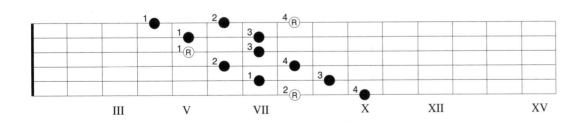

Here are some licks based on the whole tone scale. Learn the ones you enjoy and start using them over dominant chords with a #5 or ♭5. Making up licks of your own is something you should be doing all the time. It's a good way to get to know the scales you are learning. The licks you learn should always be practiced in all fingerings and octaves. The tablature is only here to give you a quick start.

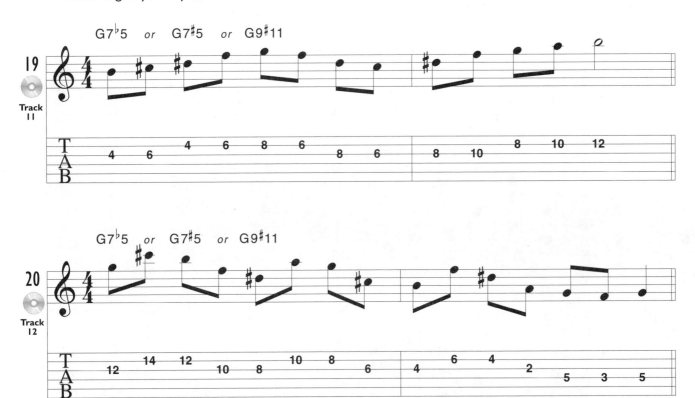

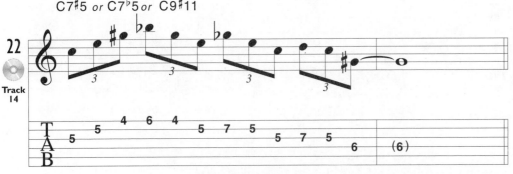

This solo is based on the chord progression from the first sixteen bars of *Once I Loved*, by Antonio Carlos Jobim, and utilizes the whole tone scale on 7♯5 chords. It also uses the diminished scale over both diminished chords and altered dominants.

ONCE
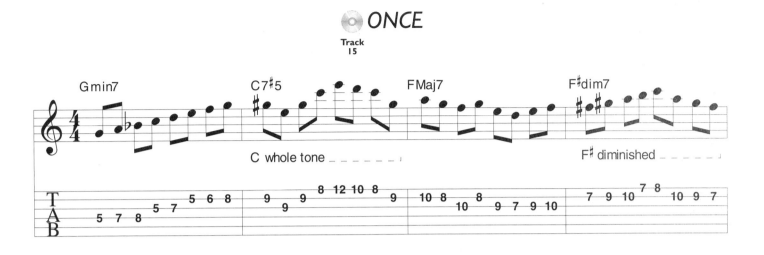

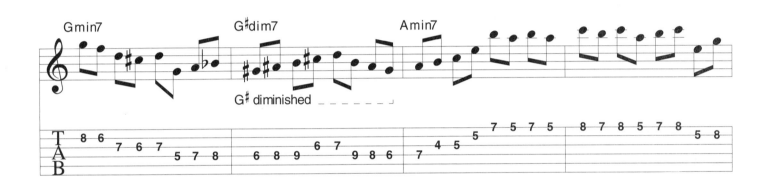

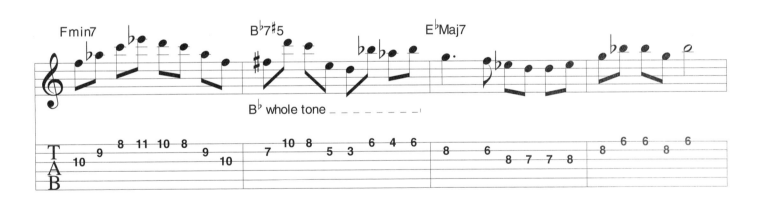

LESSON 3: THE SUPER LOCRIAN MODE (DIMINISHED WHOLE TONE SCALE)

The formula for the super locrian scale is: H-W-H-W-W-W-W. It is actually the seventh mode of the melodic minor scale. By starting on the seventh degree of the melodic minor scale and proceeding to the same note one octave higher, you create a super locrian mode. This scale is a weaving together of the diminished and whole tone scales. The first half of the scale is diminished and the second moves in whole tones. Learn the scale along individual strings. Here it is in E.

THE E SUPER LOCRIAN SCALE

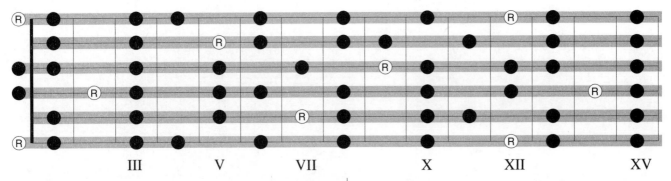

This scale has multiple uses. It works well over min7♭5 (half-diminished) chords since it corresponds to the vii chord in the harmonized melodic minor scale. We will discuss this harmony in greater detail later in this book.

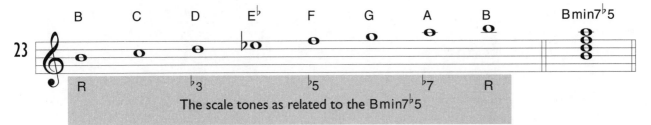

The scale tones as related to the Bmin7♭5

By far the most common use of this scale is over altered dominant chords. It contains the ♭5(♯11), ♯5, ♭9 and ♯9—every possible alteration! Begin this scale on the root of the altered dominant chord you wish to improvise over. Some players prefer to think of this as starting on the root of the melodic minor scale one half step above the root of the altered dominant chord. In other words, when improvising over an altered G7 chord you could think in terms of playing an A♭ Melodic Minor scale, instead of a G Super Locrian scale. It all leads to the same place and is a matter of personal preference.

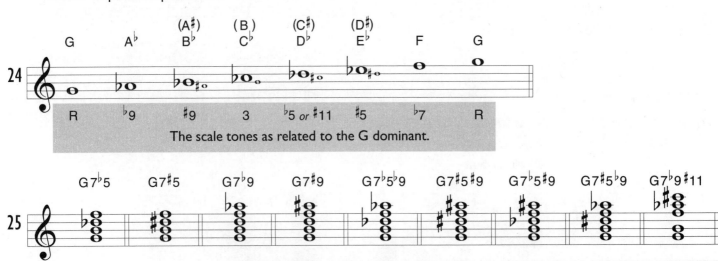

The scale tones as related to the G dominant.

Here are six fingerings of the super locrian scale. As usual, memorize one or two at first and start working with them.

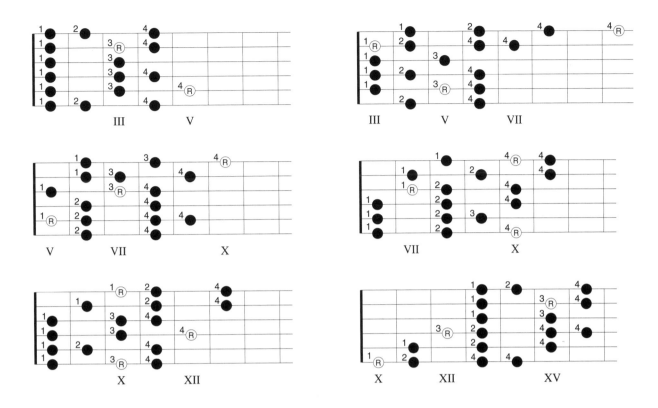

Here are several licks based on the super locrian scale. Transpose them to all possible keys and start using them in your solos. Experiment with different fingerings, too.

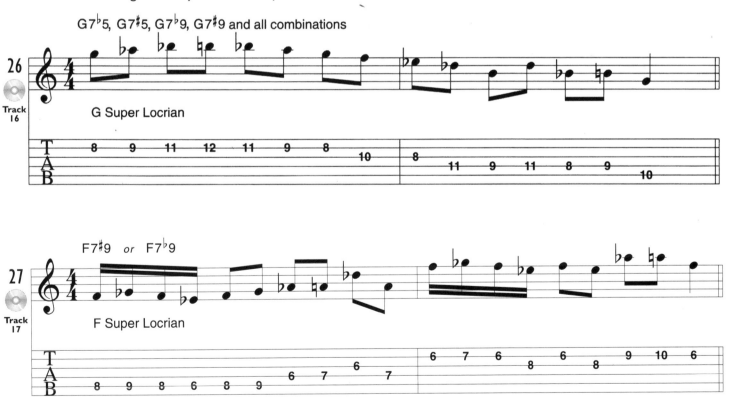

C7#5, C7#9, C7♭9 and all combinations

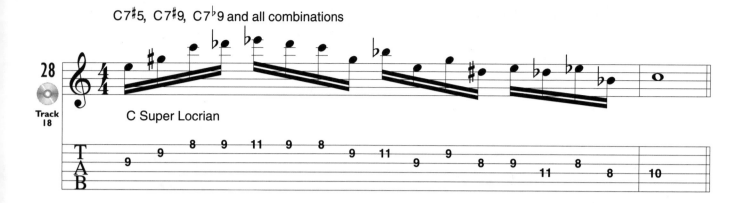

28 Track 18

C Super Locrian

B♭7♭9 *or* B♭7#5 *or* B♭7♭5

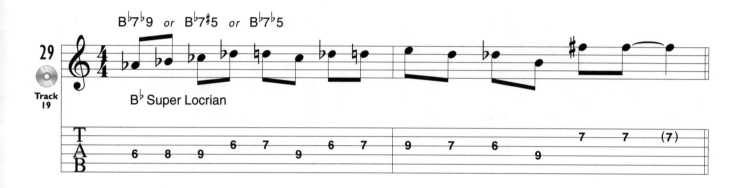

29 Track 19

B♭ Super Locrian

D7♭9 *or* D7#9

30 Track 20

D Super Locrian

There are many ways to solo over altered dominant chords, and we will cover many of them in this book. The diminished, whole tone and super locrian scales should be considered basic. Learn these well and you will find them useful in almost every situation where altered chords are present. Veteran jazzers Tal Farlow, Wes Montgomery, John Scofield and Pat Metheny all use these sounds. Listen to alot of jazz played on all instruments and you will become familiar with these devices.

This is a sample solo based on the first sixteen bars of *How High the Moon*. It utilizes the diminished, whole tone and super locrian scales. Experiment with the fingerings!

MOON

Track
21

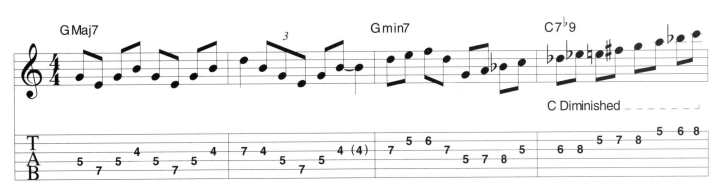

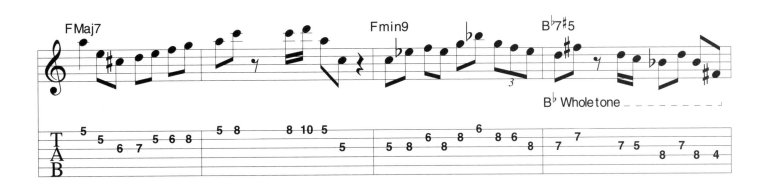

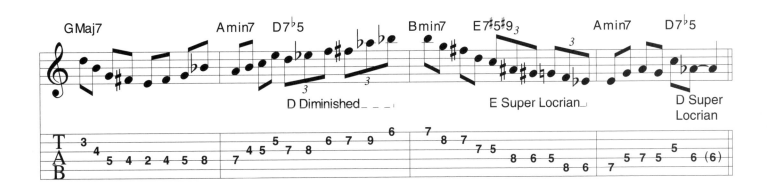

Chapter 1—Improvising Over Altered Dominant Chords   **277**

LESSON 4: USING THE ALTERED SCALE OVER A ii—V7—I PROGRESSION

Now that you have started experimenting with the altered tones found in the diminished, whole tone and super locrian scales, you may be wondering just where these sounds are most useful.

The answer is: any time you need to improvise over an altered dominant chord. Many times this will be in the context of ii-V7-I progressions, although altered chords are certainly found elsewhere as well. It is traditional to alter the V7 chord in ii-V7-I progressions. Just make sure that the altered tones don't clash with the melody or solo being played at the time. Good taste should dictate your choices.

You need to be able to recognize the altered sounds within the chords, and then choose the appropriate scale to solo with. One reason altered tone recognition is so important is that we need to *spell out* the chord changes in our solos by starting phrases on chord tones. *Spelling out* the changes refers to making sure we can actually hear the chord changes in the solo—even if there is no chordal accompaniment being played. If this concept is new for you check out the "B" sections in Chapter 2, Lessons 3 through 7 in *Intermediate Jazz Guitar*.

Many players like to start their phrases on the highest alteration in the chord. For example, when playing over a G7#5#9, starting a phrase on the #9 would really capture the flavor of the chord. You should feel free to start on any chord tone. You will have to experiment and let your ear be your guide.

Below, you will find many examples of the use of altered scales over ii-V7-I progressions. You will also find examples of neighbor-tone approaches to chord tones to help with spelling out the changes (neighbor-tone approaches are covered thoroughly in Chapter 2 of *Intermediate Jazz Guitar*). Once you have learned these examples, start making up your own. The task at hand is to learn to get from whatever device you are using to improvise over the ii chord to the altered scale of your choice for the V7, and finally to a device that works well over the I chord. Becoming proficient at this takes a while, so have patience. The good news is that as you pursue this study, you will gain more control over your solos than you could ever imagine. The options are numerous and so are the potential melodies. Have fun!

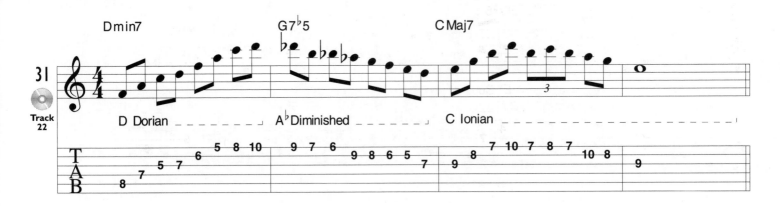

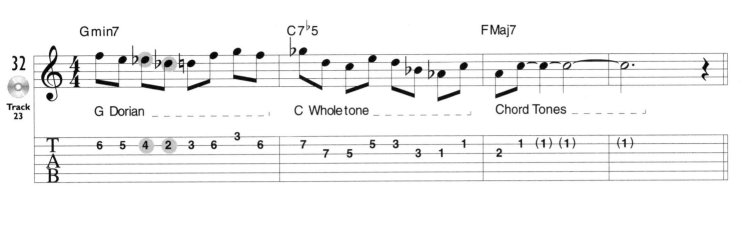

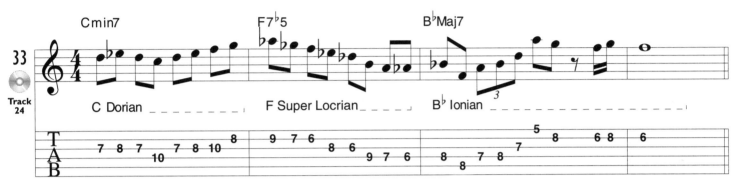

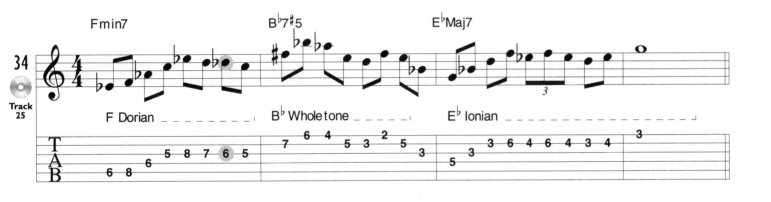

♩ = Neighbor tones

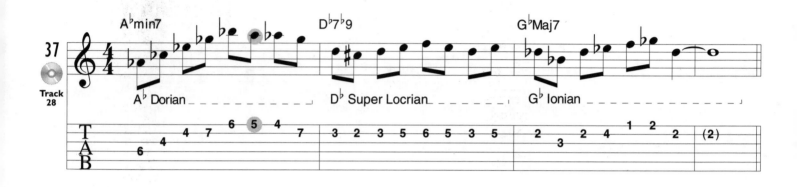

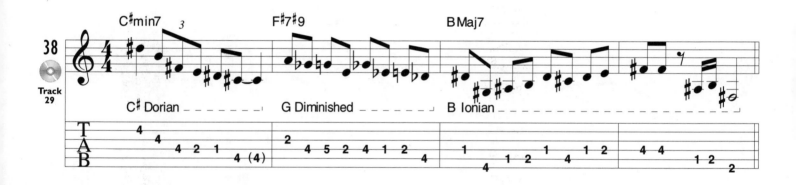

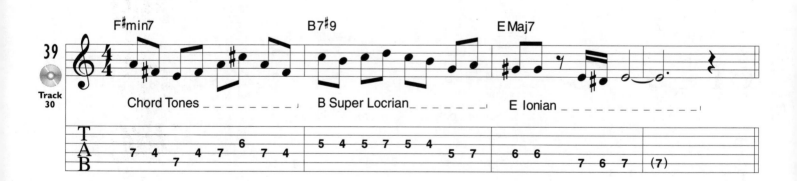

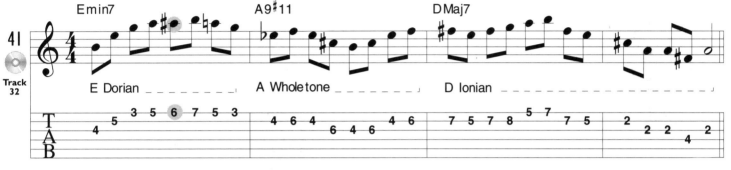

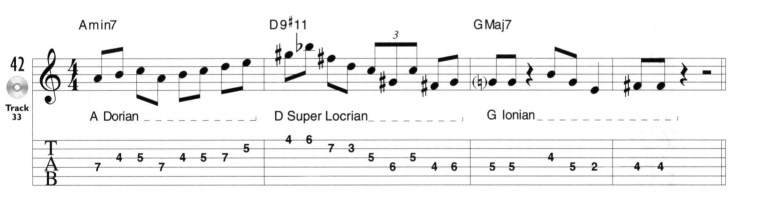

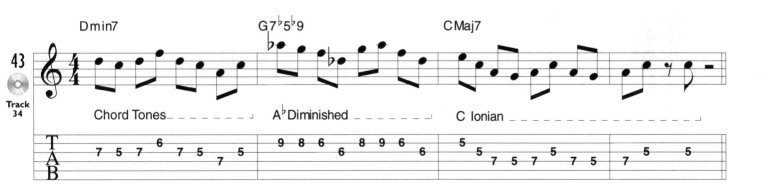

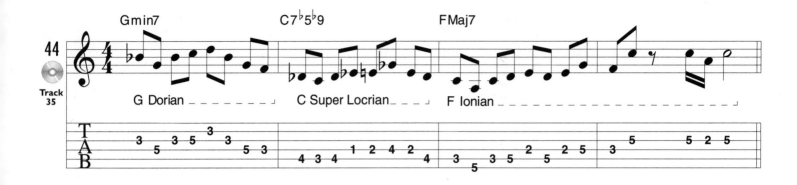

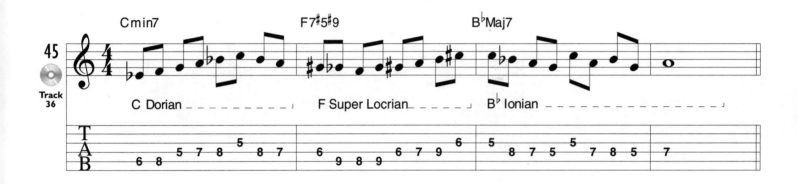

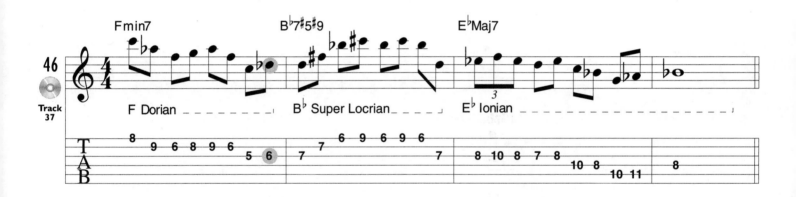

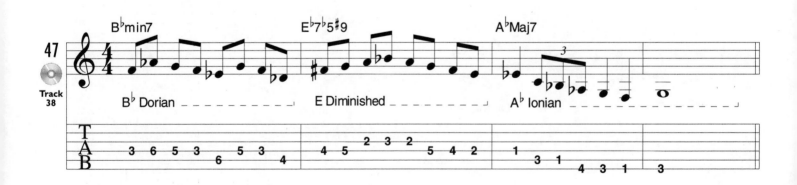

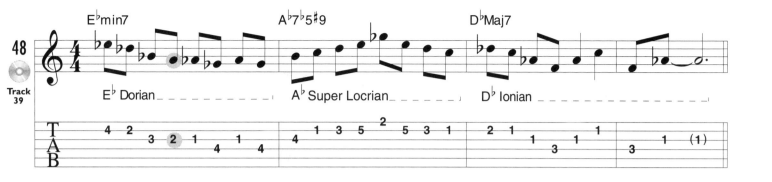

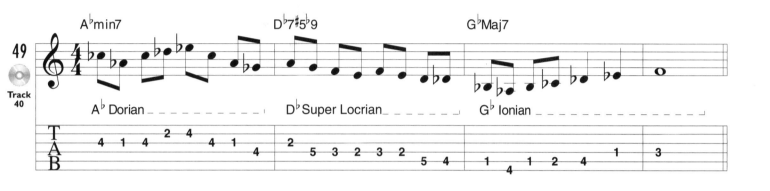

LESSON 5: TARGETING THE ALTERED CHORDS—THE ALTERED CLUSTERS

You should be getting comfortable using the diminished, whole tone and super locrian scales within the context of ii-V7-I progressions. Make sure you are training your ear to recognize the various altered tones when you hear them. While all of this training leads to some very powerful improvising skills, there is still another step that will help you locate your altered tones more easily.

In *Intermediate Jazz Guitar* you learned some fingerings for the diatonic arpeggios. At that point, you were learning how to start your phrases from chord tones and how to embellish them with neighbor tones. Now that you are playing over chords with altered tones, you need a system to quickly locate those tones not found in the diatonic scale. Don't panic! You don't need to learn a new set of arpeggios. The system that follows is a quick and easy way to memorize where all the altered tones are in relation to a chord's root. Think of these as small isolated clusters of altered tones—not scales, and not arpeggios. These clusters should be memorized. You will actually find them very easy to learn.

Here's how you use altered clusters: Your ear tells you that a C7♭5 chord is being played. You decide to start your phrase from a chord tone. You locate a 7♭5 cluster and begin a phrase with one of those tones and continue on with whatever device comes to mind. These clusters are particularly helpful when the chord changes are moving along quickly and there is no time to really develop a scale idea. Hitting one of the chord tones ensures that you will still be spelling out the changes. This is a more effective way to begin phrases and reinforce the altered sounds than only working with scales.

There are eight different kinds of altered clusters shown here (7♭5, 7♯5, 7♭9, 7♯9, 7♭5♭9, 7♯5♯9, 7♭5♯9 and 7♯5♭9) and there are five clusters shown over the fingerboard for each one. Each cluster has a root (R), a 3rd (3) and a 7th (♭7) in addition to whatever altered tone(s) there may be (♭5, ♯5, ♭9 or ♯9). The natural 5 is also added to those clusters in which there is no altered 5. Playing these clusters will help you hear the basic structure of the chords.

PHOTO • COURTESY MUSE RECORDS

*One of the most original of the jazz guitarists to emerge in the 1960s, **Pat Martino** (b. 1944) made a remarkable comeback after brain surgery in 1980 to correct an aneurysm, which caused him to lose his memory and completely forget how to play. He has recorded with such artists as Willis Jackson, Eric Kloss, Jack McDuff and Jimmy Smith.*

C7♭5

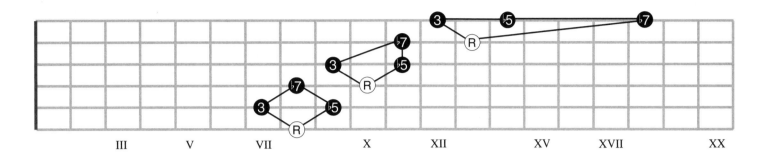

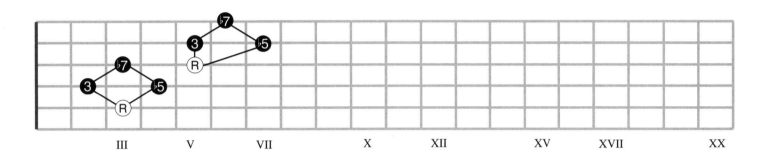

C7♯5

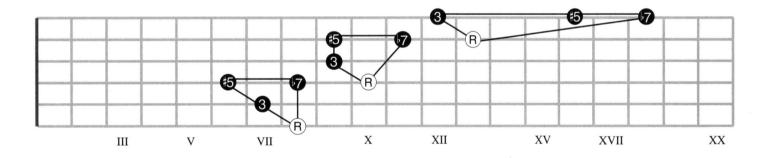

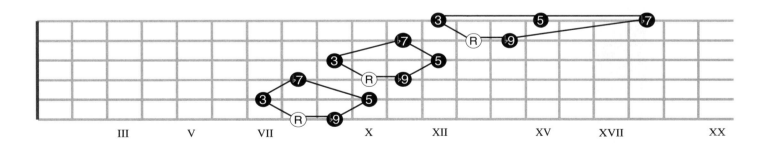

C7♭9

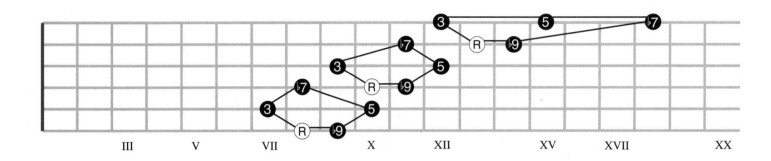

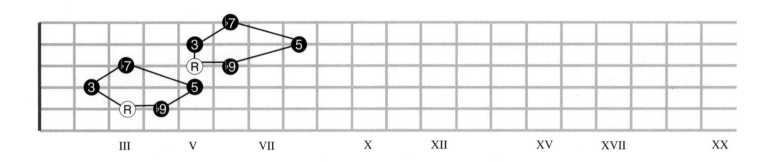

C7♯9

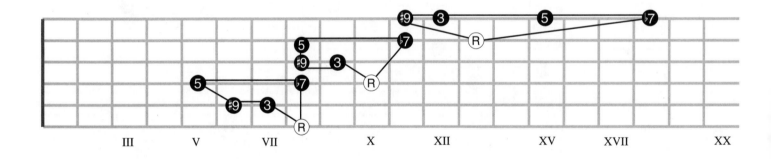

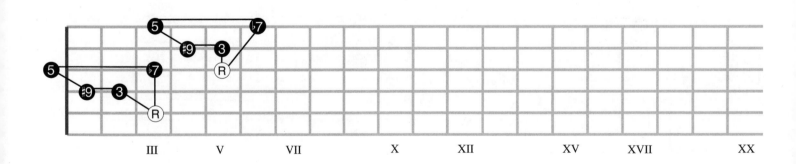

C7♭5♭9

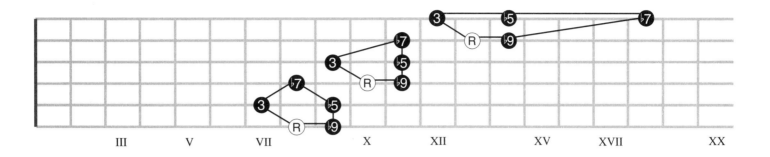

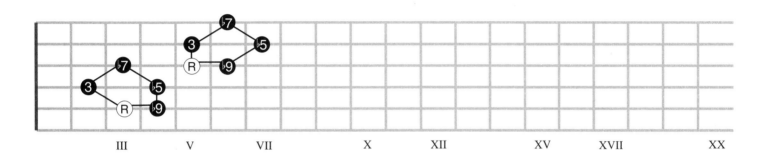

C7♯5♭9

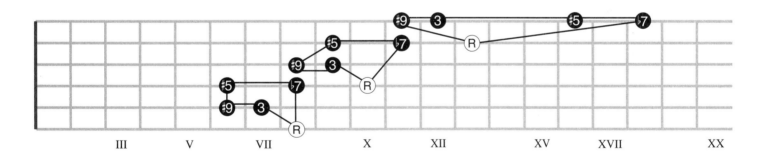

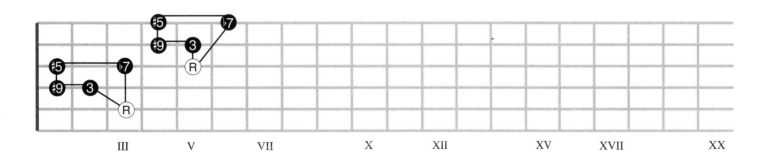

C7#5♭9

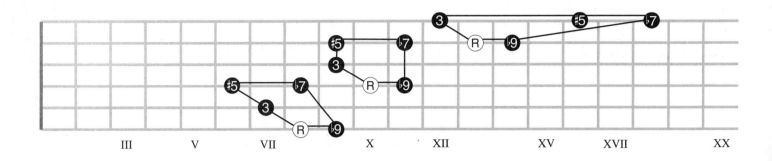

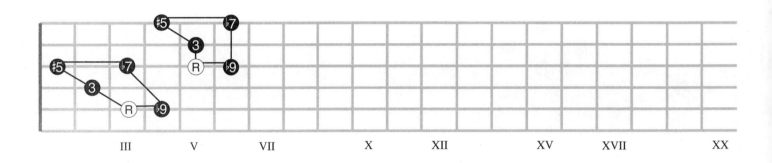

C7♭5#9

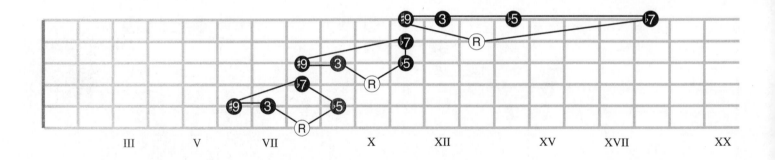

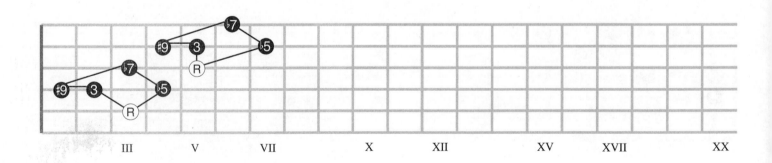

Here are some examples showing the use of altered clusters. Each example is shown in one position and octave. It is very important to play all of the examples in all possible fingerings and octaves. By this stage of your development, this process should be considered basic and routine with everything you learn.

You can alter a lick you already know by changing some of the notes to fit various different harmonic situations. Revamping your licks in this manner is a very good way of getting more mileage out of them. It will also guarantee that you always have enough ideas to use for all the various altered chords.

In Example 52, the original lick (A) is put through a number of alterations (B-L). Put some of your own licks through the same changes.

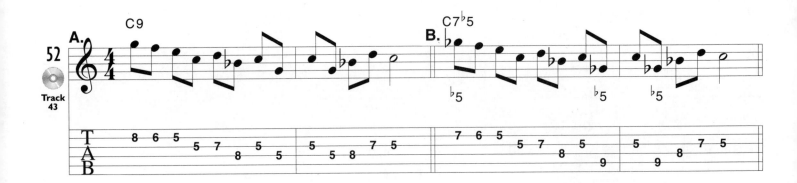

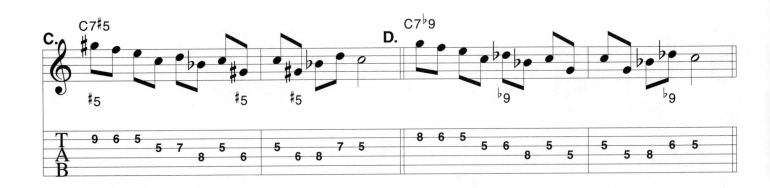

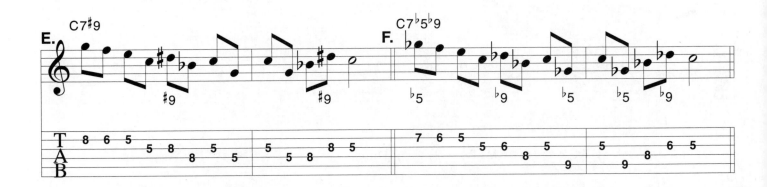

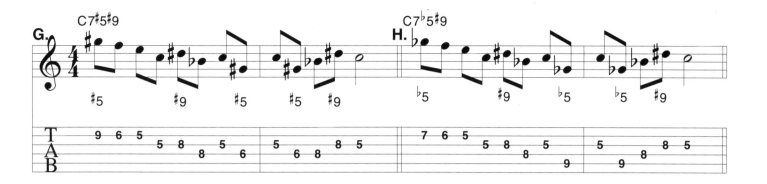

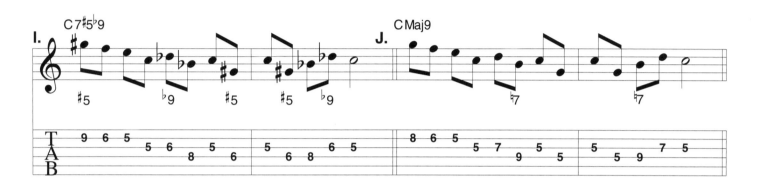

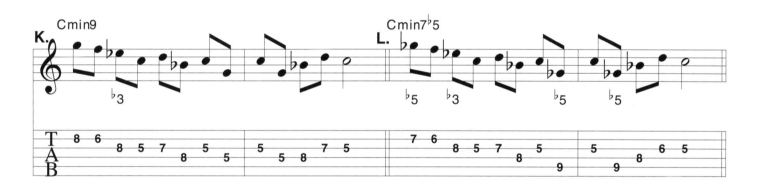

CHAPTER 2

The Minor Scales and
Their Modes

In this chapter you will be learning about the melodic and harmonic minor scales and their modes. Learning this material will give you more ways to handle altered dominant chords and other interesting harmonic situations you will encounter later in this book. Take your time with this. This chapter serves as a basic overview of the subject. For a complete study of each mode, I suggest you work through the *Guitar Mode Encyclopedia*, also published by Alfred Music Publishing and the National Guitar Workshop.

These sounds have been used for centuries in many different contexts. Listening to players such as Frank Gambale, Scott Henderson, Mike Stern and John Scofield will show you how these sounds work in the contemporary jazz style.

The three minor scales that are most commonly used in our culture are the natural minor, the melodic minor and the harmonic minor. The natural minor scale is the same as the Aeolian mode and was introduced in *Intermediate Jazz Guitar*.

LESSON I: THE MELODIC MINOR SCALE

Traditionally, the melodic minor scale is thought of as a natural minor scale with raised sixth and seventh degrees, but only in the ascending form. The descending form returns to the natural minor. The reasons for this have to do with melodic compositional devices used in classical music. In this book, and most others involving jazz studies, the term "melodic minor" refers to the ascending form only. Some jazz musicians call this scale the "jazz minor."

You should approach the study of the melodic minor scale the same way you worked with the major scale in the previous volumes of this series. The first step is to check out the fingerings. They are labeled based on the string and finger used to play the lowest root in the fingering. Fingering 6/1 means that the lowest root found in the fingering is on the sixth string and played with the first finger. 5/2 would indicate that the root is found on the fifth string and played with the second finger.

This system of labeling fingerings works well for the major and minor scales. Fingerings for the other scales we have studied thus far in this book do not fall so neatly into this system. In any case, most of the things you learn need to be explored in all fingerings—not just the ones used for examples in this book. In the subsequent lessons we'll take a look at the chords and modes generated by this scale and their applications. Following all that we'll investigate some arpeggios related to this scale.

The formula for the melodic minor scale is: W-H-W-W-W-W-H. Most players prefer to think of this scale as a major scale with a ♭3. The following diagram shows the scale in F along single strings.

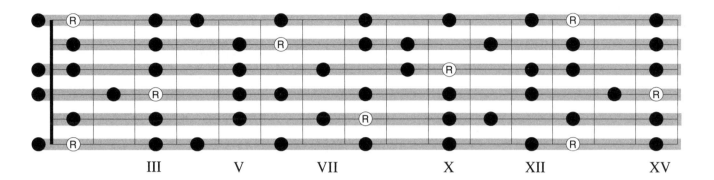

Here are six fingerings for the melodic minor scale in locked positions. They are shown here in the key of A Minor, but you should move these around the fingerboard to all the keys and practice them with a variety of melodic patterns.

A MELODIC MINOR

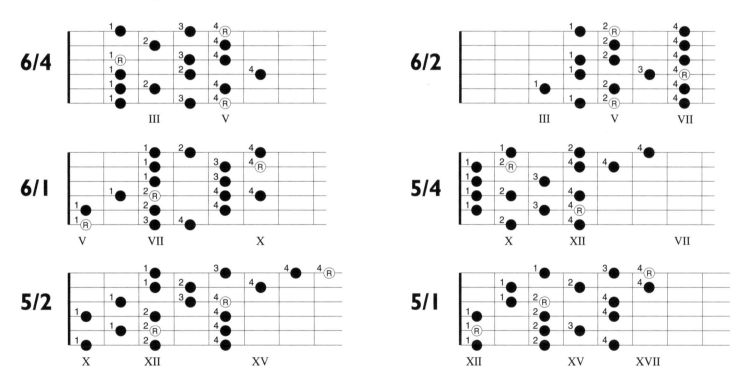

LESSON 2: THE MODES OF THE MELODIC MINOR SCALE

Just as artists need a wide variety of colors from which to choose, jazz musicians need many sounds at their disposal. Generating modes from the melodic minor scale creates seven new scales which we can then use over various types of chords. Example 52 shows the chords and then the modes generated from the melodic minor scale. Remember that each mode may be used over the corresponding chord with the same root. For instance, F Lydian ♭7 (the fourth mode of the C Melodic Minor scale) can be used over F7 (the IV chord of the same scale).

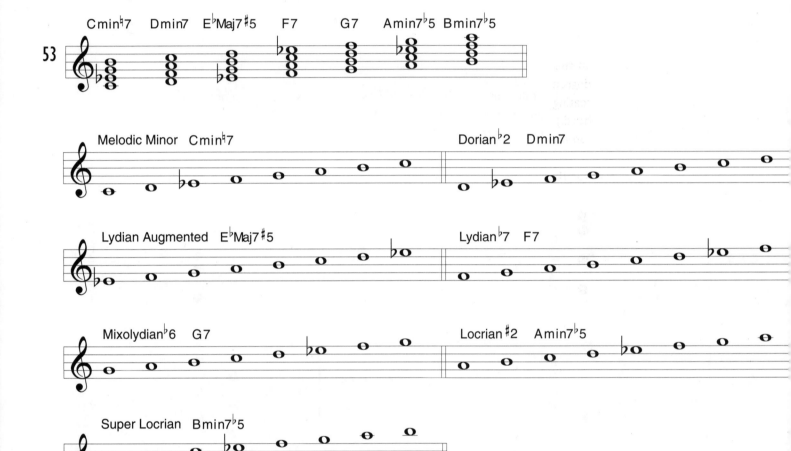

Exercise
Transpose this scale and its modes to all keys.

Here are applications for the modes of the melodic minor scale. All of these work because the altered tones of the chords listed in the applications are contained in the mode.

◼ MELODIC MINOR SCALE

Application:
1. As a progressional scale over any of the chords in the harmonized melodic minor scale.
2. Starting at the root of minor triads or minor sixth chords.
3. Starting 1/2 step above the roots of dominant $7^{\flat}5$, $7^{\sharp}5$, $7^{\flat}9$, $7^{\sharp}9$, $7^{\sharp}5^{\sharp}9$, $7^{\flat}5^{\flat}9$, $7^{\sharp}5^{\flat}9$ and $7^{\flat}5^{\sharp}9$.
4. Starting on the 5th of dominant chords with $^{\sharp}11$ or $^{\flat}5$.
5. Starting on the 6th of major chords with a $^{\sharp}5$, $^{\flat}5$ or $^{\sharp}11$.

(see page 293 for fingerings)

◼ DORIAN $^{\flat}2$

Application:
1. Starting at the root of min7 chords. (This is rarely used because the second degree of the mode is one half step away from the root of the chord creating the sound of a $^{\flat}2$ or $^{\flat}9$—not a very pleasing sound over a minor chord.)
2. Starting on the root of a $7^{\flat}9$sus chord.

Here are two fingerings for this mode in B, and two typical voicings of the chord it can be used over.

 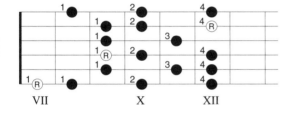   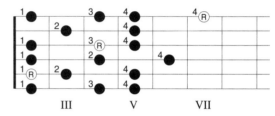

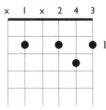 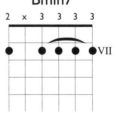

◼ LYDIAN AUGMENTED

Application: Starting from the root of major chords with $^{\sharp}5$, $^{\flat}5$ or $^{\sharp}11$.

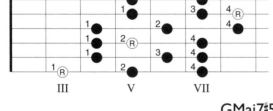   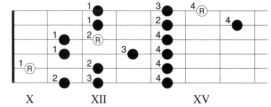

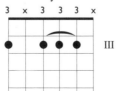 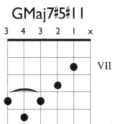

■ LYDIAN ♭7

Application: Starting at the root of dominant chords with or without a ♯11 or ♭5.

6/1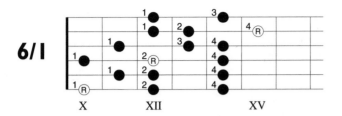

5/1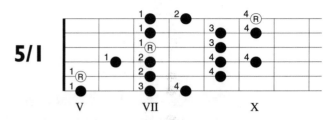

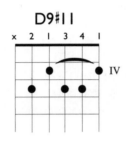

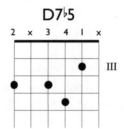

■ MIXOLYDIAN ♭6

Application: Starting at the root of dominant chords with a ♯5.

6/1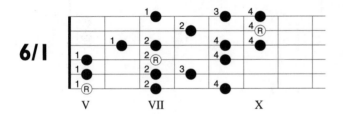

5/1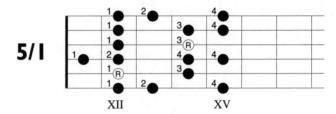

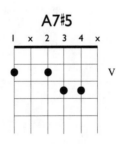

LOCRIAN ♯2

Application: Starting at the root of half diminished chords.

6/1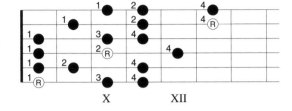

5/1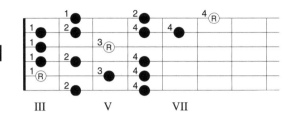

Cmin7♭5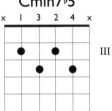

Cmin7♭5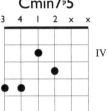

SUPER LOCRIAN

Application:
1. Starting at the root of half diminished chords.
2. Starting at the root of dominant chords with any combination of altered 5ths and 9ths.

6/2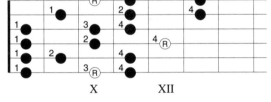

5/3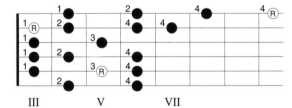

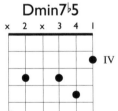

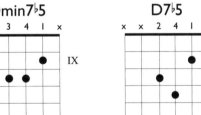

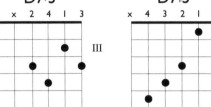

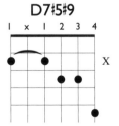

As you have learned, the melodic minor scale produces the following types of chords: min♮7, min7, Maj7♯5, dominant 7 and min7♭5. You should already have plenty of Maj7, min7 and dominant 7 arpeggios at your disposal from either you own studies or the previous book in this series, Intermediate Jazz Guitar. With that in mind, here are some arpeggio fingerings for the more unique chords found in this scale. Like the other, you should know these in all keys.

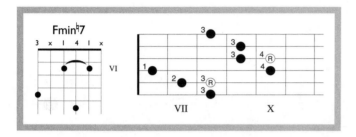

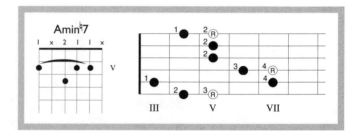

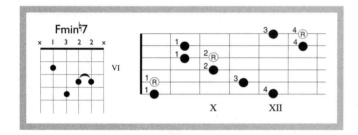

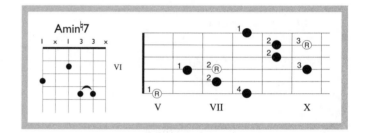

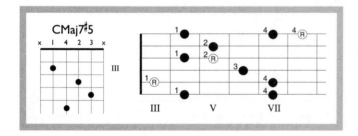

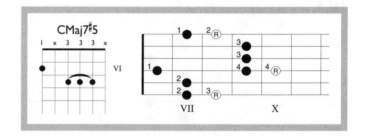

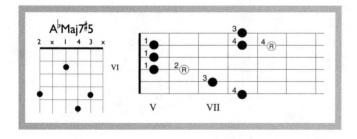

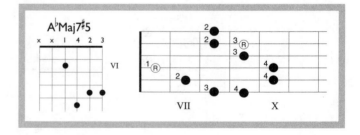

LESSON 4: THE HARMONIC MINOR SCALE

Just as the major and melodic minor scales provide us with many interesting sounds, the harmonic minor scale has many useful devices to offer.

The formula for the harmonic minor scale is W-H-W-W-H-W+H-H. Many players prefer to think of this scale as the natural minor scale with a raised seventh degree. Its distinctive feature is the augmented 2nd between the sixth and seventh degrees (W+H steps). Remember, the natural minor scale is the same as the Aeolian mode generated from the major scale.

The following diagram shows the E Harmonic Minor scale along single strings.

E HARMONIC MINOR

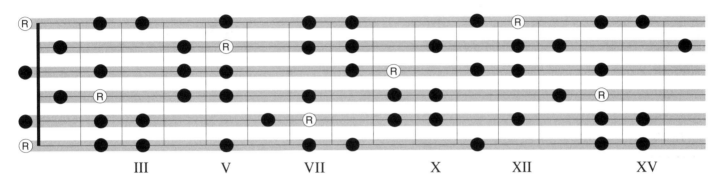

Here are six fingerings for the A Harmonic Minor scale.

A HARMONIC MINOR

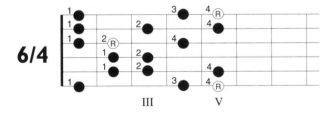

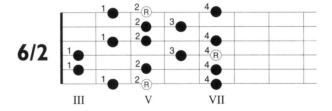

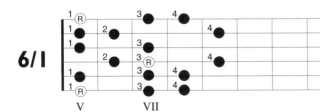

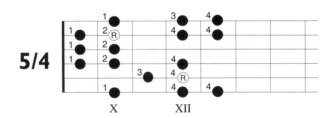

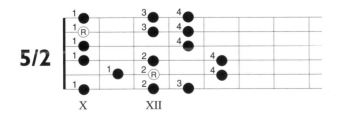

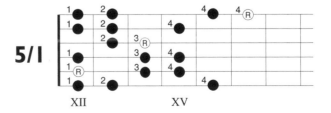

LESSON 5: THE MODES OF THE HARMONIC MINOR SCALE

As with the modes of the major and melodic minor scales, when we generate modes from the harmonic minor scale we create seven new scales to use over various types of chords. Example 54 shows the chords and then the modes generated from the harmonic minor scale. Remember that each mode may be used over the corresponding chord with the same root. For instance, the 3rd Mode (Ionian ♯5—the third mode of the A Harmonic Minor scale) can be used over CMaj7♯5 (the III chord of the same scale).

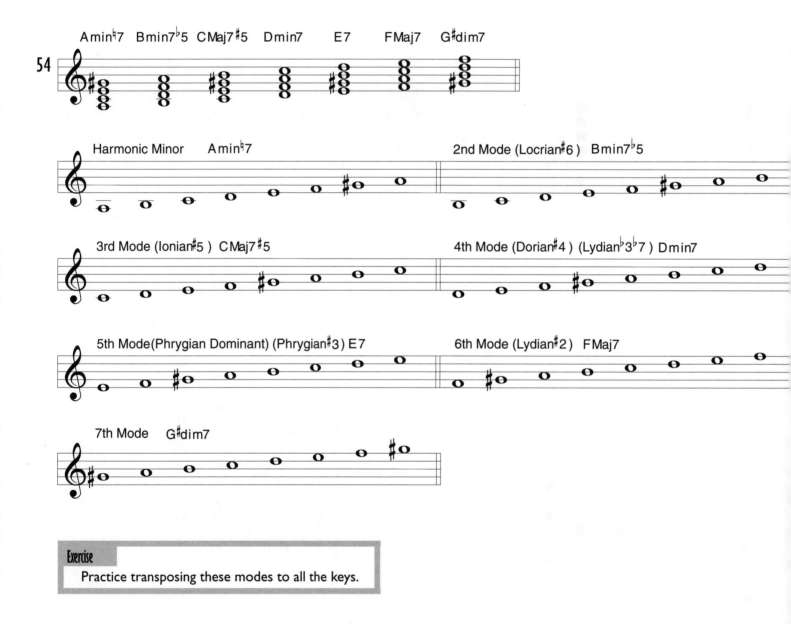

Exercise

Practice transposing these modes to all the keys.

Here are applications for the modes of the harmonic minor scale. All of these work because the altered tones of the chords listed in the applications are contained in the scale.

■ HARMONIC MINOR SCALE

Application: 1. As a progressional scale over any of the chords in the harmonic minor scale.
2. Starting at the root of minor triads or min$^\natural$7 chords
3. Starting at the 4th of dominant chords with a $^\sharp$5 and/or $^\flat$9
4. Starting at the 5th of dominant chords with $^\sharp$5, $^\flat$5 or $^\sharp$11.

■ 2ND MODE (LOCRIAN $^\sharp$6)

Application: Starting at the root of half-diminished chords

6/1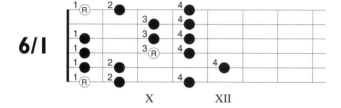

5/3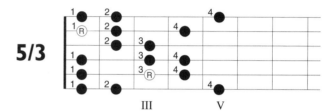

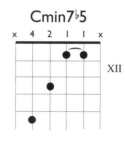
Cmin7$^\flat$5

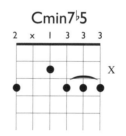
Cmin7$^\flat$5

■ 3RD MODE (IONIAN $^\sharp$5)

Application: Starting at the root of Maj7$^\sharp$5 chords.

6/4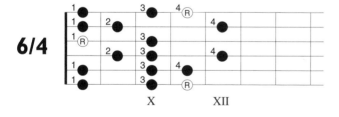

5/4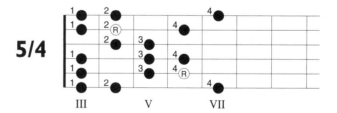

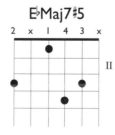
E$^\flat$Maj7$^\sharp$5

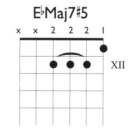
E$^\flat$Maj7$^\sharp$5

4TH MODE (DORIAN ♯4)

Application: Starting at the root of minor chords.

6/4
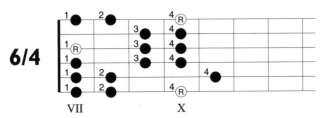

5/4
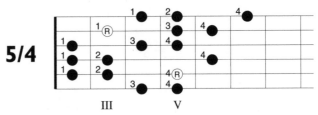

Dmin7
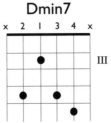

Dmin9
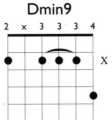

5TH MODE (PHRYGIAN DOMINANT)

Application: Starting at the root of dominant 7th chords with or without ♯5 and ♭9.

6/4
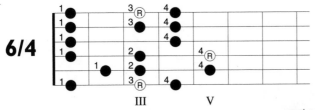

5/4
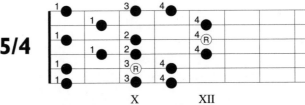

G7♭9
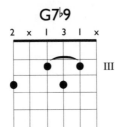

G7♯5
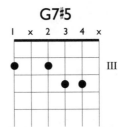

6TH MODE (LYDIAN ♯2)

Application: Starting at the root of Maj7 chords with or without a ♯11.

6/1
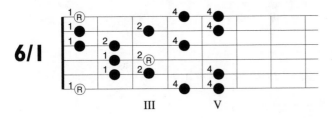

5/4
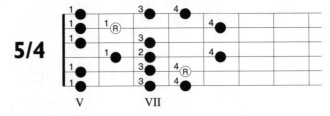

FMaj7
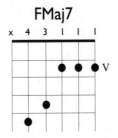

FMaj7♯11
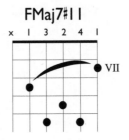

7TH MODE

Application: Starting at the root of Diminished 7 chords.

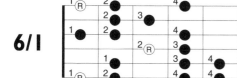

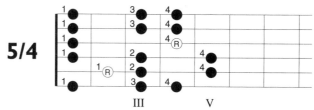

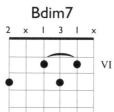

Bdim7

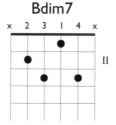

Bdim7

LESSON 6: ARPEGGIOS IN THE HARMONIC MINOR SCALE

The harmonic minor scale produces the following types of chords: min♭7, half diminished, Maj7♯5, min7, dom7, and dim7. The only one of these types of arpeggios we haven't already covered are those for the dim7—so here they are.

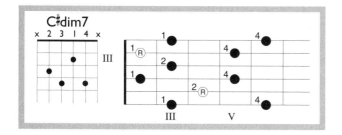

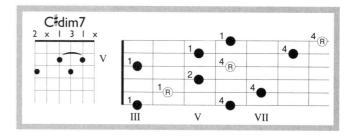

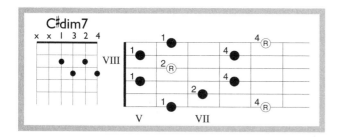

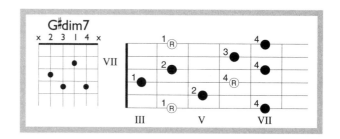

LESSON 7:
THE ii min7♭5—V7♭9—i min7 PROGRESSION

The ii min7♭5-V7♭9-i min7 progression is often referred to as the *minor ii-V7-I*. These harmonies can all be derived from the harmonic minor scale. One common way to improvise through these changes is to just use the harmonic minor scale whose root matches that of the I chord.

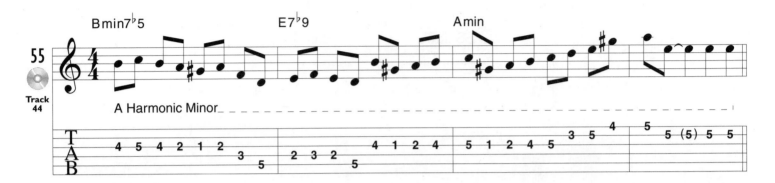

You can also treat each chord in the ii min7♭5-V7♭9-i min7 progression separately. For instance, for the ii min7♭5, you can use minor ideas that have a root a minor 3rd above the root. So, in the key of D Minor, G Minor ideas would work over Emin7♭5 (ii in D) because Gmin6 and Emin7♭5 contain the same notes (E-G-B♭-D). For the V7♭9 you can use a diminished scale. For instance, a B♭ Diminished scale would work over A7♭9 (V7 in D). You can think of this from two different perspectives:

1. As you learned on page 264, you can use a diminished scale one half step above the root of a dominant chord that contains a ♭9. B♭ Diminished scale is one half step above the root of the A7♭9 chord.

2. You can always use a diminished scale from the root of a diminished chord. As illustrated in the chart on the right, a rootless A7♭9 has the same notes as a B♭dim chord.

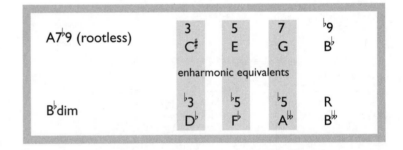

When you get to the i min7 chord, simply use any minor device you like.

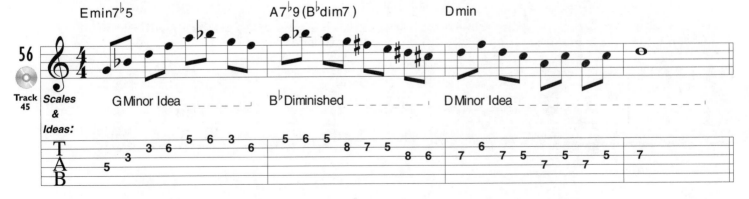

The ii min7♭5-V7♭9-i min7 progressions are extremely common so it really pays to practice them.

CHAPTER 3

Using Arpeggios

LESSON 1: CHORD SUPERIMPOSITION

By now, you have accumulated many different arpeggio fingerings and are becoming adept at starting your melodic lines from chord tones (with and without the application of neighbor tones). At this point, you may be wondering what else you can do with all of these arpeggio fingerings. One of the more interesting things you can do is to *superimpose* an arpeggio of one type over a different type of chord with a different root. To *superimpose* means "to lay one thing on top of another." When you superimpose the sound of one chord over another unrelated chord, you can imply the sound of yet another. Experimenting with this device will lead you to discover many new sounds, some of which will be uniquely yours. This will give you new ways to target altered tones as well. Check out these examples, then search for some of your own.

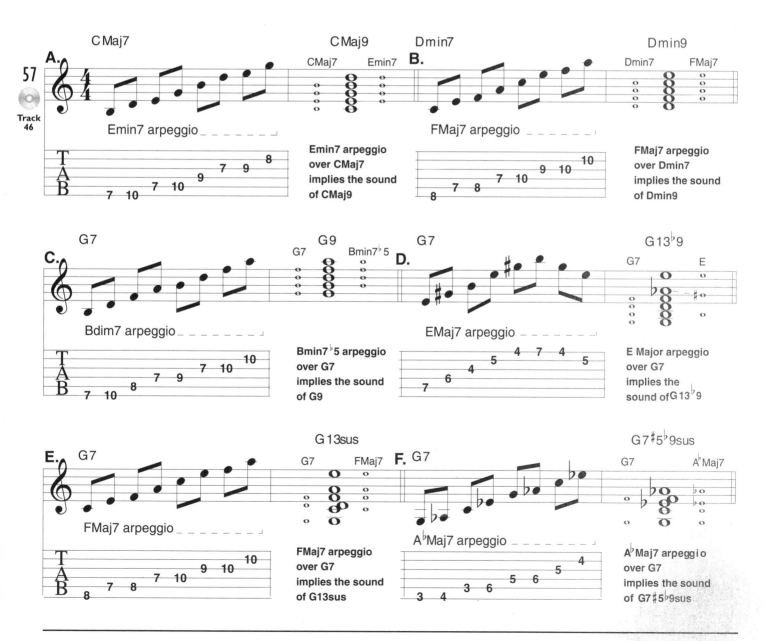

LESSON 2: MELODIC PATTERNS BASED AROUND ARPEGGIOS

PLAYING OUTSIDE AND PLAYING INSIDE

Before you are introduced to laying melodic patterns around arpeggios, it is important to discuss another concept that is important in jazz: playing *inside* and playing *outside*. Playing inside refers to a type of improvising where the melody fits perfectly within the harmonic context of the chord changes. Playing outside means that the melody actually falls beyond (or outside) the harmonies produced by the chord changes.

Why would anyone want to play outside the harmony? Won't it sound out of tune or "wrong?" When well executed, playing outside produces a feeling of excitement or tension in a solo. It keeps the listener interested and gives a solo a feeling of "forward motion." A skillful improviser can step outside and then back inside before you even know it. It takes a while to get the hang of this. Experience and listening will be your best teacher. Playing outside for the sake of weirdness is usually not very tasteful, so it is important to develop a sense of balance. Listen to players like John McLaughlin, Miles Davis, John Coltrane, Wayne Shorter and Scott Henderson for some of the most daring, yet tasteful examples of outside playing.

One device that works well for adding this element to your playing is the use of melodic patterns based around arpeggios. You simply begin a melodic pattern from each tone in an arpeggio's fingering. If you use this too often, or for too long a time, this device can give a solo a very mechanical sound, so use it sparingly. Patterns with close intervals (a 3rd or smaller) will sound more traditional, while wider intervals (4ths and larger) will sound more modern and maybe even outside. Study the following examples and then try creating some of your own.

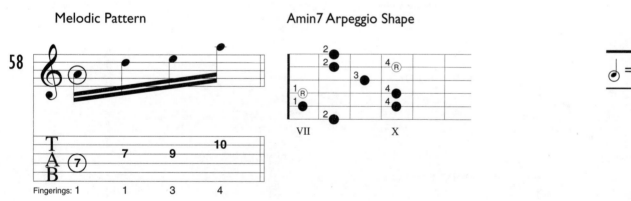

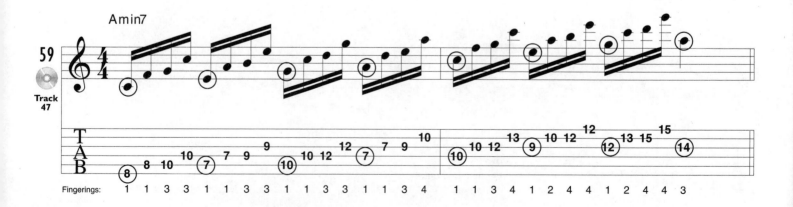

Melodic Pattern

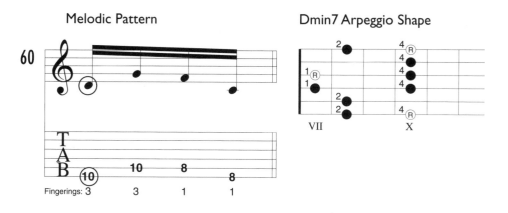

Dmin7 Arpeggio Shape

60

Fingerings: 3 3 1 1

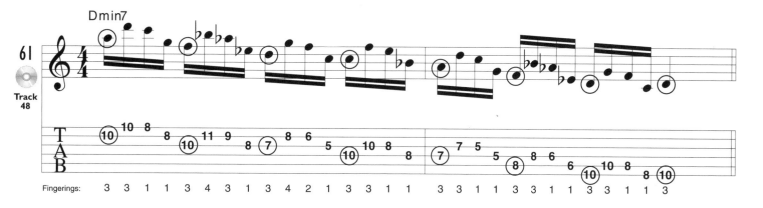

61

Track 48

Dmin7

Fingerings: 3 3 1 1 3 4 3 1 3 4 2 1 3 3 1 1   3 3 1 1 3 3 1 1 3 3 1 1 3

Melodic Pattern

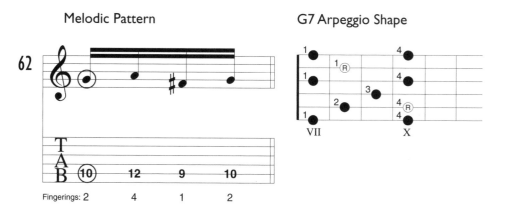

G7 Arpeggio Shape

62

Fingerings: 2 4 1 2

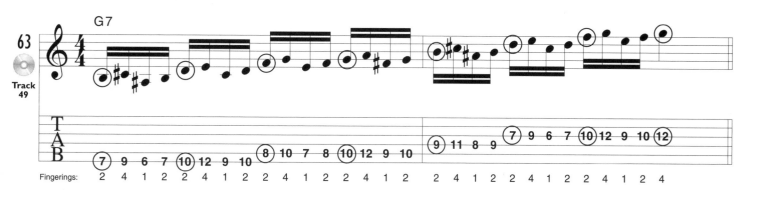

63

Track 49

G7

Fingerings: 2 4 1 2 2 4 1 2 2 4 1 2 2 4 1 2   2 4 1 2 2 4 1 2 2 4 1 2 2 4 1 2 4

LESSON 3: MELODIC PATTERNS BASED AROUND CHORD SHAPES

This is just like the previous concept, except you play the patterns around the physical shape of a chord on the fingerboard instead of an entire arpeggio. Sometimes this will be easier to visualize than an entire arpeggio shape. Experiment with many different chord shapes. Its really hard to run out of ideas with this. It is usually important to resolve on chord tones as it will bring your line back inside.

Chord Shape

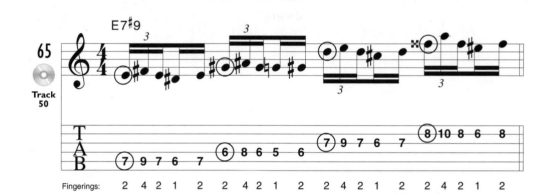

ˣ = Double sharp. Raise the note
    two half steps (one whole step).

Examples 66 and 67 illustrate that the melodic pattern doesn't have to <u>start</u> on a chord tone.

Chord Shape

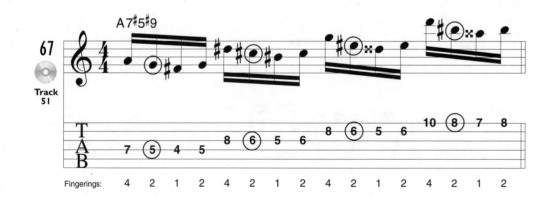

CHAPTER 4

Eight-Tone Scales

The use of eight tone scales in jazz became popular in the '40s and have since become a familiar sound. They are made by adding an additional tone to a major scale. There are many more eight-tone scales than there is room for in this book, but you should get a lot of mileage out of the two shown below.

THE EIGHT-TONE ii-V7 SCALE

This scale works very well over both the ii and the V7 chord in a ii-V7-I progression. It also sounds great over dominant 7th chord vamps. It is a major scale that includes both the natural 7 and the ♭7. Here it is in C.

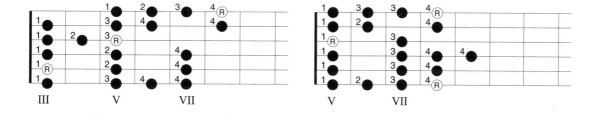

THE EIGHT-TONE I SCALE

This scale works well over major chords. It is a major scale that includes both the 5 and ♯5. It has a very smooth sound.

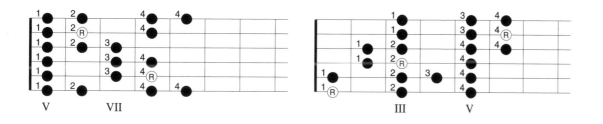

Here are some phrases illustrating the use of these eight tone scales.

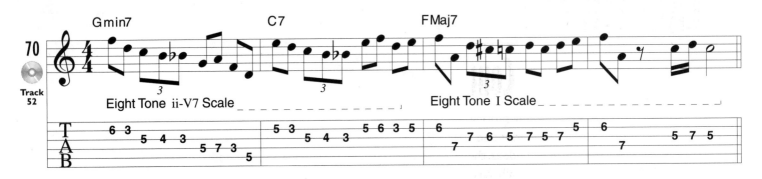

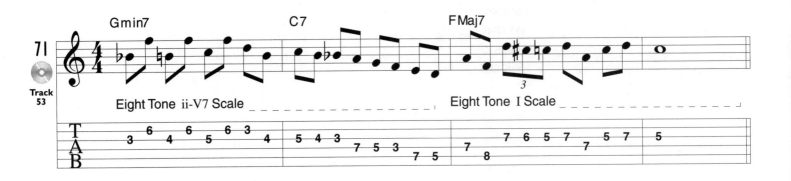

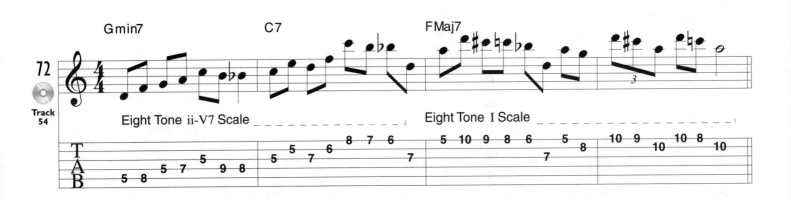

CHAPTER 5

Connecting Your Ideas

At this point you have many improvisational devices at your command and even have some pretty good flashes of inspiration now and then. If you feel you are starting to sound like a mass of devices and short unrelated ideas, then it is time that you start to consider each of your solos as a whole. A good solo generally has three parts: an opening, a body and a conclusion. Master improvisers may include several cycles of all three parts in a longer solo. This concept is explored in the CODA section of *Beginning Jazz Guitar*. Long smooth lines that connect the parts of your solo are a sign of musical maturity. Have patience; this is a lifetime study and being 100% satisfied with every part of your solo is a rare occurrence. That's OK. This sometimes frustrating factor is part of the process that helps us improve. Remember to enjoy your own progress and to pat yourself on the back once in a while. Here are some ideas that should help you create longer lines and more logical solos.

LESSON 1: THE CHROMATIC CONNECTION

This is exactly what it sounds like. You take two or more short ideas and connect them chromatically with half step, scalewise movement. It is usually a good idea to start and end on chord tones. This will cause your line to start from the inside, step outside for a while and then resolve smoothly back inside.

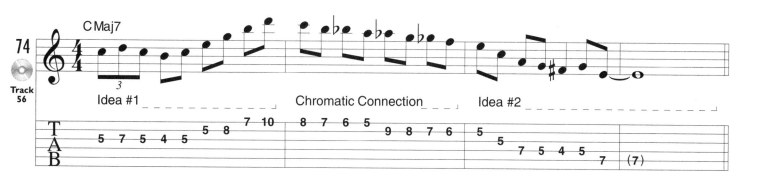

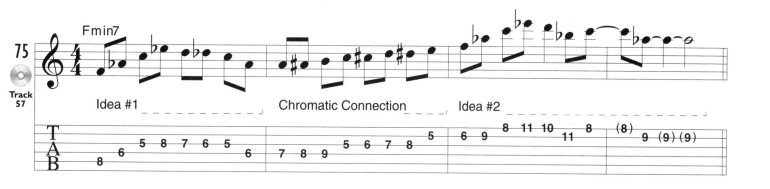

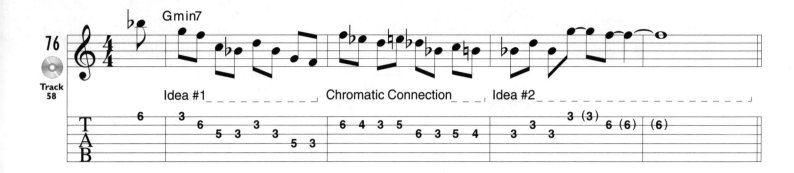

Track 58

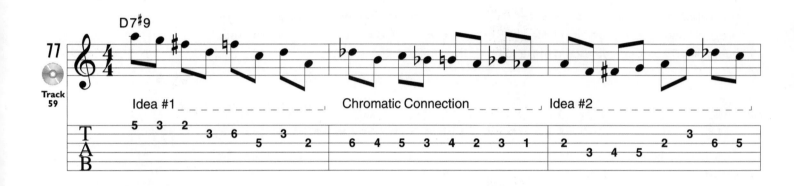

Track 59

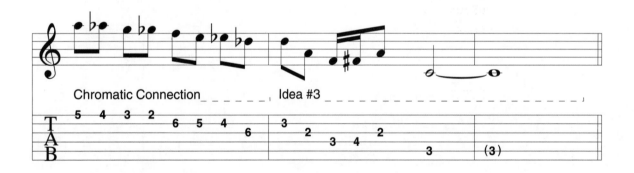

When first learning to improvise, many players tend to stop and wait when the key center changes, then begin playing again when the new key is established. This can be a very good stylistic technique, however, when beginners do it, it can reflect a limitation in their ability to travel from key to key smoothly. This lesson will introduce a technique that will help to overcome this shortcoming.

Consider the following chord progression in Example 76. It travels between two key centers. The first two measures establish the key of F while the third and fourth measures establish the key of G. The last four measures are back in the key of F again.

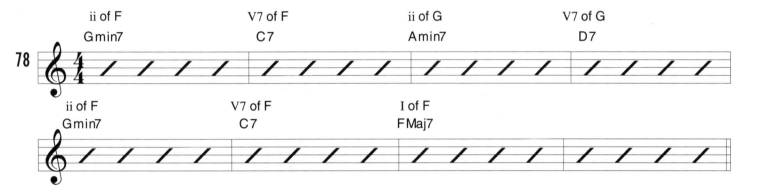

Now look at each scale.

The obvious differences between scales are the F♮ in the F scale as compared to the F♯ in the G scale, and the B♭ in the F scale as compared to the B♮ in the G scale.

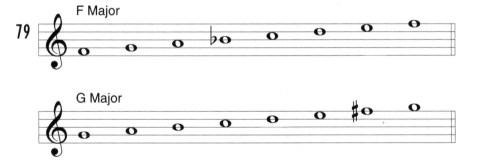

The effectiveness of this technique is based on the idea that the movement of a half step is a very powerful sound. So, while playing the F scale in the first two measures, we make sure that our last note in measure two is either a B♭ or an F. The first note in measure three should either be a B or an F♯, thereby creating a smooth half-step transition from the key of F to the key of G: F to F♯, or B♭ to B. The transition back to the key of F from measure four to measure five would work the same way, but in reverse: F♯ to F or B to B♭. It won't take long to learn this technique and the investment of time and energy will pay dividends in the form of much more musical lines.

Use the audio that is available with this book, or a recording of yourself playing the chord progression, to try this technique by playing along with Example 80.

Here are two examples demonstrating ways to accentuate the difference between keys using movement in half steps. The notes involved are highlighted.

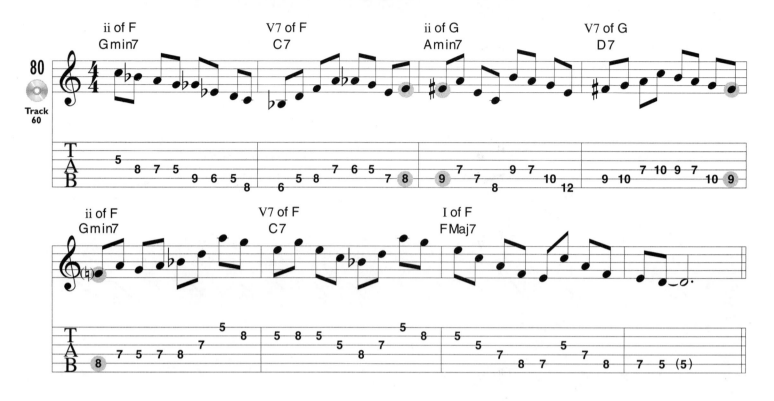

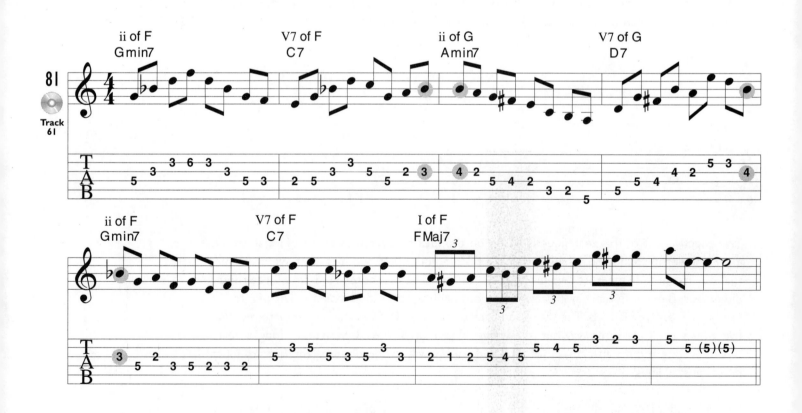

LESSON 3: REPEATING AN IDEA
IN DIFFERENT OCTAVES

This idea is easy to execute and quite effective. Repeating an idea in different octaves creates the illusion of one very long line.

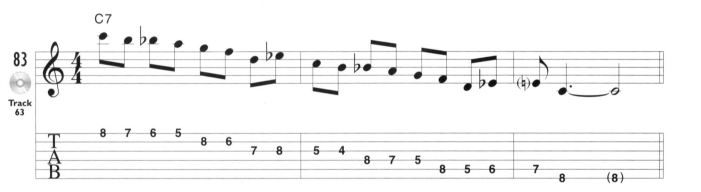

Joe Pass (1929–1994) was known for his extensive use of walking basslines, melodic counterpoint during improvisation, use of a chord/melody style of play and outstanding knowledge of chord progressions. He opened up new possibilities for jazz guitar and had a profound influence on future guitarists.

LESSON 4: RHYTHMIC MOTIVES

The element of rhythm can connect ideas very well. You can play several different melodic ideas with exactly the same rhythm. The rhythm then becomes a motive in itself, and the different ideas it is applied to will seem connected.

LESSON 5: MELODIC CONNECTION

The idea here is to find one melodic idea that will work over a series of different chords. You need to have a strong knowledge of chord formulas to accomplish this.

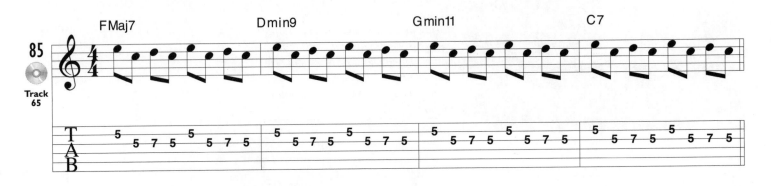

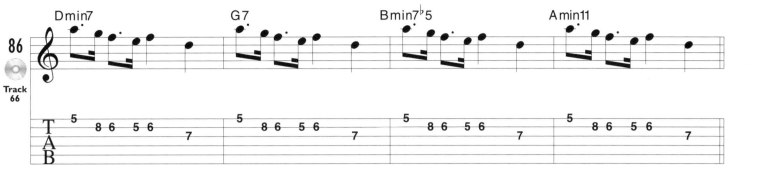

LESSON 6: DIATONIC CONNECTION

The *diatonic connection* is a technique that works well over diatonic chord progressions (progressions that include only chords found in the key). It enables you to turn one lick into as many as seven—one for each of the diatonic chords in a key.

Start with a lick that sounds good over the I chord, then raise each note in the lick one scale tone. You now have a lick for the ii chord. Repeat the process from this chord and a iii chord licks appears. While playing over a diatonic progression, these licks would provide a nice clean, connected sound. This is also a good way to compose licks.

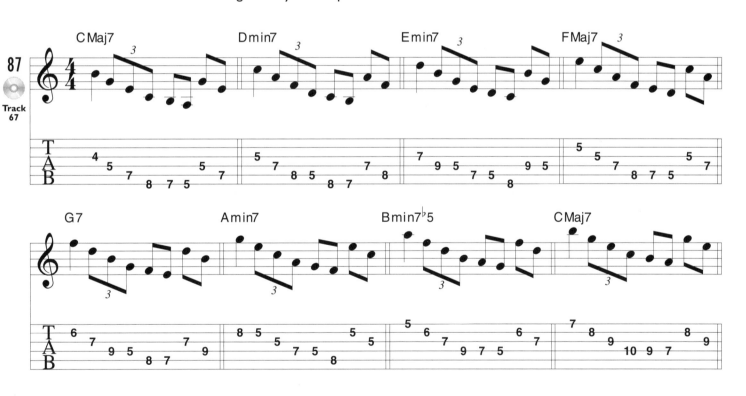

CODA

A Medley of Suggestions and Musical Concepts

There is no way a single book can discuss every improvisational device that musicians use. This series has presented the major concepts of the study of improvisation. Here are some more ideas that you should explore on your own.

PLAYING ON THE EXTENSIONS USING ADVANCED PENTATONICS

Most players use major and minor pentatonic scales in the most common way: starting on the root of major, minor and dominant chords. Some dramatic new sounds can be discovered by starting your familiar pentatonic fingerings on chord tones other than the root. This will allow you to play on the upper extensions of the chord, producing more interesting and modern sounds. Check out *Pentatonic Improvisation* by Erik Halbig, available at your local music store, for a really complete picture of this subject. Here are some ideas to get you started.

> For major chords......................major pentatonic starting on the root, 5th or 9th of the chord.
> For minor chords......................minor pentatonic starting on the root, 5th or 9th of the chord.
> For dominant sus 4 chords......major pentatonic starting on the root or ♭7 of the chord.
> For dominant 7th chords........major pentatonic starting a ♭5 above the root with altered 5ths and 9ths of the chord.

PLAYING ON THE EXTENSIONS USING TONES FROM 13 CHORDS

You can look at a 13 chord as a 7 chord with a major or minor triad a whole step above it.

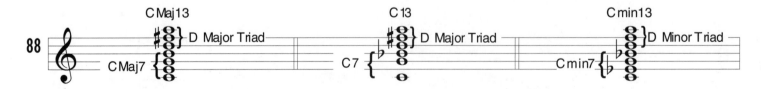

It is interesting to play ideas over a chord that are normally used for the triad formed by the upper extensions of the 13 chord with the same root. In other words, you can play D Major triad ideas over a CMaj7, because the upper extensions of CMaj13 (which is, as you know, a good substitution for CMaj7) form a D Major triad. Experiment. Many modern players such as Robben Ford think this way.

PLAYING WITH WIDER INTERVALS

Some players like the sound of very wide interval leaps in their playing. This style of playing really helps to build strong technique, though at first you may find the fingerings difficult.

One way to practice this is to learn to play major scales in consecutive 4ths, 5ths, 6ths and 7ths. This will get you used to the sound and the physical demands. Playing this way will add interest to your solos, but overuse leads to tedium for most listeners. For more interesting effects, create licks that mix consecutive 4ths, 5ths, 6ths and 7ths. Listen to Joe Diorio's playing. He is a master of this style.

OCTAVE DISPLACEMENT

This technique creates ultra-modern sounds by taking a line and raising or lowering a few of the notes to other octaves. It produces a rather startling and unpredictable effect. Sometimes the fingering is difficult but it is usually worth the effort.

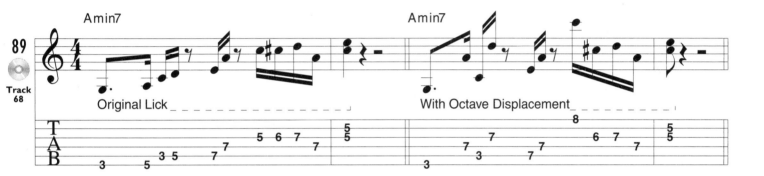

SYMMETRICAL MOTIVES

A great way to play outside is to take a lick and move it around the fingerboard. The only catch is that you need to move it around in a symmetrical pattern, like half steps, whole steps, minor 3rds or whatever you can dream up. The ear will accept these sounds even though you are leaving the key center because of their symmetry. The listener will "track" the symmetry more than the relationship between melody and harmony. Be sure to resolve to a chord tone!

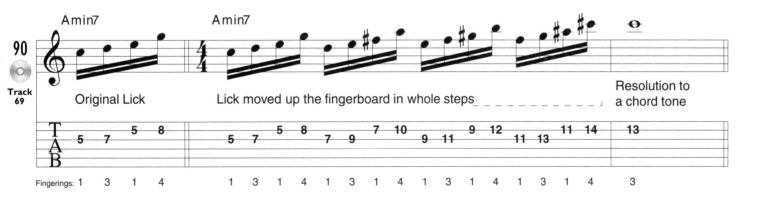